PREPUBLICATION REVIEWERS COMMENTS

"NO FOXHOLES IN THE SKY *is a wonderful book. Using large sections of the letters he sent home from England so long ago, Harry Conley combines vivid descriptions of his Eighth Air Force bombing missions with a sober look back at the young men who risked, and often gave, their lives to ensure that we all live in a free world. Here is a classic account of that war. I have never read a finer or more gripping memoir than this one. My thanks go to all concerned including Harry's proud parents who kept the letters safe.*"
—Len Deighton, Author of "Bomber," "The Ipcress File," "Funeral in Berlin,"
"Blitzkrieg" and many more published works.
Great Britain

"*Whether Harry Conley is relating the events of a great air battle or just describing the members of his crew and their adventures together, he does it with the perception, warmth and humor of a consummate storyteller. The reader of these stories will discover him to be a man of great character and courage.*"
Maynard D. Stewart, B-17 Waist Gunner
"Belligerent Beauty," 95th Bomb Group, 8th Air Force

"*Being a member of the Congressional Legion of Valor, I have known many stalwart American patriots, but the records of none of those fine men exceed the war effort of Harry M. Conley, U.S. Army Air Forces, in my opinion. The actual deeds, and to a greater import, the influence Col. Conley had in bringing victory to the Allies in World War II, can be but a debt we, all Americans, owe him.* NO FOXHOLES IN THE SKY *is vivid book of drama, of joy, of sadness and of record of the individual self-sacrifice and bravery of one of America's finest soldiers.*"
—James B. Morehead, DSC, Col. USAFR
Pacific Theater P-40 Ace; Mediterranean Theater P-38 Pilot
Author of *In My Sights, The Memoir of a P-40 Ace*

"NO FOXHOLES IN THE SKY *is a very fine book. As Historian for the 95th Bomb Group (H) Association, I have read and heard many stories and a great deal of factual information and statistics about the 95th Group's men and missions. Col. Conley's book certainly coincided well with all that information I received. The unique blending of his present recollections with his letters home during the war adds substantial credibility to the whole story. Anyone interested in knowing just the way it was should definitely read this book. It covers the glorious story of the way it was from start to finish.*"
—William "Ed" Charles, Lt. Col. USAF (RET.)
Past Historian, 95th Bomb Group (H) Association

"*Having a special interest, from boyhood associations, in Horham and the 95th Bomb Group I found* NO FOXHOLES IN THE SKY *a fascinating book. Harry Conley is undoubtedly a very talented and lucky man. He has to be lucky when he is only one of three airmen from the original one hundred squadron complement who completed a combat tour. For me, the most fascinating parts of his accounts are the letters to his parents. These give an understandable gung-ho, 'don't-worry-about-me' picture of combat service, while the true picture at Horham was very different. What an eventful and interesting career! This book finds a welcome place in my library.*"
—Roger Freeman
Military Aviation Historian and Author
Author of the "The Mighty Eighth, A History of the
Units, Men and Machines of the US 8th Air Force"

"*Pilot Harry Conley's* NO FOXHOLES IN THE SKY *is a very interesting and informative book about the men and their participation in the air war over Germany. I believe it is a MUST for all WW II history buffs. I know; I was there as a Navigator in B-26s after participating in the Doolittle Raid on Japan on 18 April 1942.*"

—Frank A. Kappeler, Lt. Col. USAF (RET)
Navigator, Doolittle Raid on Japan
Staff Navigator, 323rd Bomb Group, ETO, B-26s
Santa Rosa, California

"*Harry Conley is a great story-teller. With all my own hours in the air, I was drawn to each of his missions and, in my imagination, flew them all along with him. He made me know him and his friends, their fears during their training and their pride in their accomplishments in war. His included heartwarming stories of British people made this book more than just another collection of war stories. History buffs will love it. From the moment Harry Conley worried about whether he would be accepted into pilot training until his return home, victorious in a terrible war, I felt I was with him every step. From his storytelling I knew his friends, flew with him on his missions, shared his fears and, especially, shared the tender moments of his letters to home. This is a thoroughly enjoyable reading experience.*"

—Grant S. Pyle III
Brigadier General, USAF(Ret)
Citrus Heights, California

"*Colonel Conley in* NO FOXHOLES IN THE SKY *gives a vivid narrative of a Flying Fortress pilot and combat leader with the Eighth Air Force. Entering combat in the challenging days of 1943, Conley paints not only a picture of his own career but of the leaders with whom he was associated and of their failures and brilliant accomplishments. His own meteoric rise from flight leader to chief of staff of a combat wing illustrates his courage, determination and leadership ability. This book is a MUST for any Eighth Air Force aficionado.*"

William N. Hess
Noted Aviation Historian and Author

"*This book is a vivid and splendid description of what it was like to fly in aerial combat in World War II.* NO FOXHOLES IN THE SKY *should be required reading for anyone who wants to know what it was like to engage in air battle against the German Luftwaffe. In addition, the book is full of colorful anecdotes about life in England for bomber crews during World War II.*"

—Ramsay D. Potts, Major General USAF (Ret)
McLean, Virginia

"*A remarkable true story of the air war over Europe in World War II that rises to the sublime from the ordinary by the diary-like letters from the author to his family. Colonel Conley has succeeded in painting an accurate and vivid word picture of the terrors, courage and sometimes humor in being a warrior of the air. Memories flooded my mind. It is a great read and a historical treasure.*"

—C.W. "Bill" Getz, PhD, Former Lt. Col., USAAF
Pilot, ETO, B-24 and P-51
Burlingame, California

"*One of the legends of 'The Mighty Eighth' — A truly remarkable story of great courage and high endeavour.*"

—Ian Hawkins
Author and World War II Historian

Copyright © 2002 by

Harry M. Conley

All rights reserved. No part of this publication may be reproduced, stored in a retrieval system or transmitted in any form or by any means: electronic, electrostatic, magnetic tape, mechanical, photocopying, recording or otherwise, without permission in writing from the publisher.

Library of Congress Catalog Card Number: 2002110907
ISBN: 0-917678-55-9

Cover design was done by Ray Bowden

Front Cover: A B-17 under attack by a German fighter

Printed in the United States of America

NO FOXHOLES IN THE SKY

by

HARRY M. CONLEY*

*DECEASED

Edited by
Mark H. Miller
and
Stuart G. Whittelsey, Jr.

FNP MILITARY DIVISION
6527 MAIN STREET
TRUMBULL, CONNECTICUT 06611

CONTENTS

REVIEWERS' COMMENTS i
FOREWORD vii
ACKNOWLEDGMENTS ix
INTRODUCTION xi

CHAPTER   **PAGE**

1. The Winds of War 1
2. Metamorphosis from Cowboy to Pilot 13
3. Honing Our Skills in B-17s 35
4. The 95th Goes to War 49
5. The Battle of Kiel 85
6. The Regensburg Shuttle 109
7. Mission to Munster 129
8. A Tragic Day at Horham 145
9. A California Horse in England 155
10. Learning SOPs the Hard Way 163
11. Bombardiers 175
12. Bill Pratt, Navigator 187
13. Leadership, Our Greatest Asset 195
14. "Big B" 207
15. D-Day, June 6, 1944 235
16. "Jiggs" Donohue, Intelligence Officer 245
17. The 93rd Combat Wing 255
18 Poltava 271
19. General de Gaulle's Kiss 285
20. Ending the War at the Pentagon, or From Colonel to Cowboy 295
21. Reflections on the War 309

BIBLIOGRAPHY 319
INDEX 321

FOREWORD

"Harry, these stories are too good not to be written down!" I had just heard about three hours of stories by my long-term friend and horse-riding *compadre*, Harry Conley, from a period in his life that I hadn't heard very much about, his time in the Army Air Forces during World War II. We were riding in my truck, pulling an empty horse trailer, traveling south from Woodside, a horsy suburb of San Francisco, to Arroyo Grande, south of San Luis Obispo, where he was keeping his two gorgeous quarter horses. I had wanted to own a horse bred and trained by Harry Conley for years, and NOW it was going to happen! Harry had finally agreed to sell me "Marcy's Fancy", a beautiful 11-year-old chestnut mare, about 16 hands high. So we were driving down there to load her in my trailer and take her home to Woodside, where we live and where I keep my horses. Little did I know I would hear some exciting stories of Harry's experiences as a B-17 bomber pilot as we drove to Arroyo Grande.

Well, that was a few years ago, when Harry boarded his other beautiful and well-trained palomino mare, "Bunny" at my place; so we frequently went riding together. We talked about his writing a book about his experiences as a bomber pilot in World War II. He had thought about it for several years, but just hadn't put more than a few pages on paper. Harry had tried talking into a tape recorder and having a professional stenographer type up the copy, but the results were less than acceptable. We finally settled on a program that worked, although it involved much more of my time than I had originally anticipated. We fell into a routine of riding our horses together to a small riding clubhouse a few miles away with his tape recorder in his saddlebag. The clubhouse is always well-supplied with uncooked ground round, buns, condiments, and drinks. After arriving and tying up our horses, we cooked up a couple of hamburgers, made ourselves a scotch and soda and sat down at a table under the California live oak trees. When we finished our lunch, I turned on the recorder and Harry told one of his stories. As we left the clubhouse I put the recorder in my saddlebag, and we rode home. Then later on I went to my computer and transcribed these conversations into a written story. And I have had a ball doing it, reliving Harry's exciting experiences as I listened to these tapes and transformed these conversational stories into written narratives. Much more fun than doing financial spreadsheets, which is what I do to put food on the table.

We were fortunate to have Mark Miller, a professional writer and book author in his own right, giving us editorial advice and assistance by reviewing my drafts, making many improvements in wording, adding valuable background material, and generally making all these stories much more readable. Harry and I have greatly appreciated his help and direction in this project.

Our thanks also go to our informal "review board" of 95th Bomb Group veterans, in particular, Bob Cozens, Grif Mumford, Dick Stewart and Bill Lindley, who kept us out of trouble by their accurate memories of dates and events almost 60 years past. They, too, provided us valuable editorial assistance and suggestions.

As Harry and I are not professional writers, we value highly the editing assistance, especially in punctuation, grammar and syntax provided by John Meeker. For those same editing skills, as well as her computer knowledge and capabilities, we are also indebted to Ms. Kimberly Marsh.

I hope all readers enjoy these stories as much as I have, listening to them and putting them into writing.

STUART G. WHITTELSEY, JR.
Woodside, California

ACKNOWLEDGMENTS

First and absolutely foremost, I acknowledge the contributions of my wife, Marcy, who first found the letters I had written during the war, and after reading many of them, kept after me to write these memoirs, using those letters. That was quite a few years ago, probably fifteen or more. Getting this book written has been a long and arduous path to tread, but here we are. My dear mother, who, fortunately, didn't take my advice and throw those letters in the trash, certainly deserves my most sincere acknowledgement. The job of writing this book, with the details we have included, would not have been possible, some sixty years after these events took place, without those letters.

Inspired by Marcy's enthusiasm I tried handwriting some of my stories, I tried using a stenographer, and I tried talking into a dictating machine, but I was not at all pleased with the results that came from any of these approaches. I've always been a pretty good storyteller, but that was when I was face-to-face with someone else. Then I had a stroke in 1996 that impaired my skills in the three Rs: reading, writing and 'rithmetic. So my next acknowledgments go to my horse, "Fancy" and to my friend, Stu Whittelsey, who bought Fancy and drove with me four hours each way to pick her up. We talked along the way and I told him some of my war stories. That led to our getting together for a series of horseback rides carrying a handy little tape recorder in a saddlebag. We'd stop and have lunch; I'd tell a story and he'd record it; then back home he'd write it from the tape recording. Later he'd read it to me; I'd correct and change it, and eventually we had a pretty good version of my story.

Another friend, Mark Miller, a professional writer, had also been encouraging me for some time to write my stories, so we sent our first few of these written stories to him for editing. He did a magnificent job, which I acknowledge with great appreciation. He started mixing excerpts from my old letters into these stories, and essentially gave us the pattern to follow for the rest of the book. Mark also has been a big help in our efforts to get our book published.

Where would I be without friends? I am so fortunate to have so many good friends that have helped me in many ways to get this book published. Friends from the 95th Bomb Group, Grif Mumford, Dick Stewart, Bob Cozens, Bill Lindley, and Al Keeler have all contributed greatly from their records of events, their photo albums, and their memories. They have proofread my story drafts and made corrections, provided names that had slipped through the cracks in my memory, and even added some stories that I had forgotten over the years. A gentleman from Britain, Ian Hawkins, who has written at least two books about the 95th Bomb Group's wartime activities, has provided a great deal of inspiration and support, as well as hours and hours of "grunt work" reviewing my text and checking out the facts against his extensive records and memory. My acknowledgment of Ian and his efforts would be incomplete if I didn't credit him with leading me to John O'Neil, a gunner on Bill Owen's Pathfinder B-17, and now the publisher of *No Foxholes in the Sky*. John had previously published Ian's book, *The Munster Raid, Before and After*. Now I acknowledge John O'Neil for taking on one more military history book.

Other friends should also be acknowledged. Bill Lane, a long-term friend and a fellow horseman, as well as the former Ambassador to Australia and New Zealand, who is also now a Director of Hoover Library at Stanford University, engaged the services and archives of that famous repository of documents related to Russia in the 20th century to find some valuable information that added to the credibility of my recollections about my Poltava mission.

And only last year when my 95th Group buddies took a tour of the restored B-17 that visited San Jose International Airport, we met Phil Schasker and Chuck Holley, active members of the Confederate Air Force (recently renamed the Commemorative Air Force) who restore and fly WW II military aircraft. These fellows have helped us meet several former and retired military pilots and aircrew members, several of whom have reviewed our manuscript for us.

And lastly, I want to acknowledge my four lovely daughters, Karen, Vian, Sue and Robin, who served me by listening to me tell these stories as they were growing up, thus allowing me to refine my presentations of them, and who have for years been giving me encouragement to proceed with writing a book of my experiences during the war.

HARRY M. CONLEY
Redwood City, California

INTRODUCTION

Harry Conley and I first met in the fall of 1942 at Geiger Field in Spokane, Washington as newly assigned members of the 95th Bomb Group (H) cadre, he from Northern California, and I from West Texas. The 95th was but one of many Bomber and Fighter Groups established in 1942 and '43 as augmentation to an undermanned and ill-equipped peacetime Army Air Corps. For the next four months we underwent unit and combat training in preparation for duty in what became known as the European Theater of Operations (ETO). Both of us, like all the other combat crew members, were in our early twenties and eager to do battle for the honor of the United States and the protection of our way of life.

Harry and I soon established a friendship which was to endure throughout the war and our post-war years as we settled in California. Harry's destiny was to return to California immediately after the war to reestablish himself in the livestock business, buying and selling cattle all across the United States and Mexico. Mine was to continue my career in the Air Force, finally retiring from Hamilton Air Force Base and settling in the San Francisco Bay Area. Due to the proximity of our respective homes, we were able to continue our close relationship that commenced some fifty-seven years ago.

Long after Harry's mother died, his wife, Marcy, discovered among his old things a treasure, a box containing all of Harry's wartime letters to his mother. In these letters he wrote about his experiences as a flying cadet, as commander of a combat crew, as a Squadron Commander, and later as Chief of Staff of a Combat Wing. It was this discovery that set the stage for Harry's eventual writing of *No Foxholes in the Sky*.

In *No Foxholes in the Sky* you will discover a book in which the writer intersperses excerpts from those letters written to his mother during his service in World War II with his present day remembrances of air combat missions and individuals with whom he was associated. The result is a fresh and unique way to tell about his war experiences both in the language and style of a young man in his early twenties and in the language and writing style of an older mature man. It makes for interesting reading.

World War II brought together a highly diverse group who, for the most part, were young men and women either attending high school, college, or just starting their civilian careers. They were individuals of integrity, courage, and honor who, because of their love of America and our way of life, put their country above all else and gave us the world we live in today.

And so it was with the 95th Bomb Group — formed with personnel from all walks of life and from all parts of America. They soon assimilated strange names and learned the language of this great nation by listening to the idioms, dialects and accents of others. Lasting friendships were soon established among them that were essential to the individual and team accomplishment of the new and strange tasks before them. Appreciation and respect of the abilities of others were imperative in developing a coordinated team.

Flying high altitude bombing missions was the training objective to be accomplished in the United States; however, this objective could not be accomplished in full due to adverse weather conditions at the bases to which the 95th was assigned. As a result, in March of 1943 the air crews departed Rapid City, South Dakota, in a less than desired state of readiness. After outfitting stops in Kearney, Nebraska, and Gulfport, Mississippi, these flight crews flew in stages through Palm Beach, Florida, via South America and Africa en route to England. Meanwhile, the ground support personnel were sailing the North Atlantic, dodging German U-boats all the way.

By the end of April 1943, all flight crews and ground support personnel had arrived in England. In the next three months, the 95th Bomb Group was stationed at Alconbury (near Peterborough), Framlingham (near Ipswich), and finally at Horham (halfway between Ipswich and Norwich in East Anglia). Horham Air Base, like most air bases occupied by units of the Eighth Air Force, was carved out of what had been, before the war, productive farmlands. As a result young children and some adults were frequent visitors to the air base, much to the delight of the Yanks. Many friendships with our English hosts survived long after the war; in fact several of these friendly "Brits" still attend the reunions of the 95th Bomb Group Association.

One such person is Roger Freeman, a well-known English author who has written *The Mighty Eighth; A History of the U.S. Eighth Air Force* and several other books about the American fliers that helped defend the British Isles and put an end to the Nazi war machine. He had occasion, in 1989, to address a reunion of the 95th Bomb Group in England, and he expressed his feelings as follows:

INTRODUCTION

As a young schoolboy in 1943, I visited the airfield at Horham on several occasions and saw the Square B Fortresses of the 95th Bomb Group. You were young men in a strange land, complaining that the beer in the pubs was always weak and too warm. And you wondered if, and when, it was ever going to stop raining.

All that was a very long time ago. The world has taken several whirls since then, but here we are — our youth is gone, we are all getting a bit snowy on top, and our old buddies aren't what they were. They stick in where they should stick out, and they stick out where they should stick in. But don't worry because I might have been just a kid then, but I'm also sliding past middle age just like you gentlemen. And as I said, it was a long time ago, and since then there have been many, many changes.

You have all been down the road to see some other changes in your old airfield. It's not the Horham base that you remember some 50 years ago. You say to yourselves, "Is this really the place where there were 150,000 takeoffs and landings? Is this the place where we sent nearly 20,000 tons of bombs to Adolf Hitler and his cronies? Is this the place where the B-17s of the old Square B took off at dawn from that runway which was the highway to battlefields far away? Is this the place where we sweated in a machine shop, or where we froze on a cold winter day out on the airfield as we tried to change spark plugs on a Wright Cyclone engine? Is this the place where we spent long and sleepless nights in those tin can Nissen Huts while hearing the mechanics out in the field winding up our B-17 engines in preparation for tomorrow's mission? Is this the place from where the Fortresses of the 95th set off for the first American daylight raid over Berlin? Is this the place where the gunners of the 95th were credited with more enemy aircraft destroyed than any other outfit in the Eighth Air Force Bomber Command? Is this really the place where we spent our youth — perhaps two days — perhaps two years?"

Horham is the same place, and like everything else, it changes. But there is one thing that hasn't changed, and that is the feeling of the people at Horham and Suffolk County for what you Americans did and what you were. That has not changed.

It may surprise you that after half a century that you are even remembered. But you are and you can see that you are. Why are you remembered? You have faith in what you did and you have faith in what you are. You have faith in the many who left this airfield and never returned home. You have faith in the old "Square B."

We are an old nation, and we appreciate people who have faith in the past, who do not forget — because we do not forget either.

The 95th was only one of many Bomber and Fighter Groups to move to and operate out of that wonderful "aircraft carrier and military marshalling area" called England. And when we arrived there amid all the disruption of the local life and confusion of our frequent reorganizations and redirections, little did anyone then think that the 95th was destined to become one of the premier Bomb Groups of the Eighth Air Force in England flying combat missions over Europe, or that it would be awarded three Presidential Unit Citations before the end of the war. During the two years in England the 95th flew 321 combat missions, seven low-level, food drop missions to the starving Dutch, numerous secret relief missions for the Free French, the Polish Freedom Fighters and various Allied Forces, plus four repatriation missions returning prisoners of war from the Continent. A total of 359 B-17s were assigned to the 95th Bomb Group during this period, of which 165 were lost in combat action, 61 were forced to land on the Continent due to extensive battle damage, and 42 landed back at home base with battle damage beyond repair. Total personnel casualties suffered by the 95th were 1,751. Of this number, 553 were killed and 188 were wounded in combat action, 825 were held as prisoners of war, 61 were evaders, 61 were internees, and 36 were killed in non-combat accidents.

Behind these statistics lie many stories of human interest, of the effects of our nation's wartime activities on the lives of many individuals. In *No Foxholes in the Sky,* Conley writes fervidly and affectionately about members of his flight crews and others with whom he was closely associated. His remarks present a few particulars concerning various personnel of the 95th Bomb Group who contributed much to the success of this illustrious Group and to his own personal growth as well. Conley lets his readers relive his experiences with his unique way of telling his stories, sharpened with his keen sense of humor. This book provides a grass roots understanding of what it took to achieve and maintain the high level of operational effectiveness that the Eighth Air Force demonstrated through its successful destruction of the German Luftwaffe, giving the Allies absolute air supremacy over all of Europe and paving the way to an Allied victory.

GRIF MUMFORD, COLONEL USAF (RET.)
Tiburon, California

NOTE FROM THE PUBLISHER

We are sad to say that Harry Conley passed away suddenly on July 9, 2002 after battling a series of illnesses in 2002.

He worked on the proofing of his book up to the very end.

Harry was a beacon pointing the way to all who came to know him, and so it was for those of us who worked with him on *No Foxholes in the Sky*.

JOHN J. O'NEIL

CHAPTER 1

THE WINDS OF WAR

It was a cool morning in 1941, 18 days before Christmas. I was on my horse at a Manteca, California cattle feed lot sorting fat cattle for slaughter for the Monday morning shipment to San Francisco, when a Southern Pacific Railroad gate guard, a rotund little man, came running toward me, breathlessly shouting "The Japs have bombed Pearl Harbor!"

Those words changed my life dramatically. And they changed the lives of millions of people all over the world, as they woke up the sleeping populace of America and coalesced the nation into a mighty force singularly determined to defeat the Japanese and German war machines.

That I was on a horse sorting cattle in the rural agricultural center of California, after having graduated from Stanford University as an aeronautical engineer, was also an interesting story about the strange twists and turns in a man's life path. So I'll start at the beginning.

Born on November 7, 1916, I was raised in San Francisco. My family's home was on Seventh Avenue, near the Presidio, an active army base originally established by the Spanish in the 1770s.

My mother was a brilliant, determined and dynamic woman, active with the PTA in San Francisco, and eventually appointed to the Board of Education. A second generation American from New York, her ancestors had originally come to this country from the British Isles. She was the quintessential mover and shaker, someone who took the notion of good citizenship to heart and put it into action. One example of her activism is the Galileo High School gym and athletic field, which is located across a busy street from the school's classrooms. She considered the street a hazard because it enticed kids to jaywalk, a risky undertaking because of its speedy traffic. Before long, an underpass linked the school with the playing field, the direct result of her "button-holing" and getting commitments from the people in city government who could cut checks for it. The underpass is still there. To raise money for charity, she organized an intra-city high school football championship game to be played at the end of the season. The San Francisco City Championship Game tradition carries on to this day. She had verve and determination — she got what she went after, including my father, whom she met and married in San Francisco, where they lived for the rest of their lives.

My father was a second generation Californian, born and raised in the foothills of the Sierra Nevada Mountains like his mother, a Grass Valley native who grew up during the Gold Rush era. Their ancestry had stemmed from Northern and Central Europe. As a young man, Dad used to sell liquor to the bars in the mining camps along the foothills of the Sierras from a horse-drawn wagon. Later on he moved to San Francisco where he continued his lifelong career in the liquor distribution business. "Whiskey was made for selling, not for drinking!" was one of his favorite sayings. When the 19th Amendment ended the legal sale of spirits in America and the Prohibition era began, he was given a franchise license by the Federal Government to distribute liquor for medicinal purposes, and was thus able to maintain his business.

We were living in the Richmond District, only three doors away from the Presidio, headquarters of the Sixth Army. Established in 1776 as a Spanish colonial military outpost, the base sprawled along the south shore of San Francisco Bay, from Fort Point at the Golden Gate headlands to the Marina District and the Cow Hollow neighborhood, where cows had once grazed in dairy pastures. The entire southern reach of the Presidio was bordered by a great stone wall with large iron-gated entrances that, when unlocked, were guarded by sentries.

The Army Air Corps based several squadrons there, mostly biplanes assigned to coastal watches and launched from the grass strip of Crissy Field. Also on the base was a holdover from early-century warfare, a sizeable cadre of horses maintained for Field Artillery Officers. I used to climb over the Presidio wall to visit the stables where they were kept, struck up acquaintances with their handlers, and was occasionally invited to ride some of them. They were splendid horses, which some of the officers rode in polo matches held on the Presidio's broad grassy fields.

Neighborhood kids were welcomed by the servicemen posted there who, in the spirit of camaraderie, occasionally invited us to join them for meals in the Mess Hall. This being peacetime, and my being a kid, nobody objected to my wanderings among the aircraft maintenance buildings, where I watched mechanics work on the airplane engines and mechanical controls. I was fascinated — in that pre-electronic age these machines represented state-of-the-art technology. Flying was still something of a novelty in the late 1920s, and the public attitude toward our military was generally one of unequivocal admiration. Airplanes, pilots, horses, polo-playing artillery officers among handsome red-brick Federal-style buildings facing one of the most beautiful harbors in the world — the Presidio was an inspiring place for a kid to spend his free time. I began to build airplane models, fitted with tiny gasoline engines, and flew them from the open hills of the base.

In the early 1930s the country was mired in the Great Depression, and good jobs were hard to come by. There was no relief for the jobless and no unemployment insurance or compensation, such as we have today. There were no public assistance programs or social agencies or job training programs. Many bank and financial institutions, then virtually free of government oversight, had invested their money unwisely, betting that the stock market boom of the Roaring Twenties — at least insofar as Wall Street was concerned — would roll on into the Thirties. When the stock market crashed in 1929, the domino-like closing of banks had left the nation without cash in circulation, and one company after another shut down. Meanwhile, tens of thousands of bread-winners were suddenly out of work. The spectacle of idle, discouraged men wearing suits, ties, and fine topcoats, lining up outside soup kitchens or applying for a menial job, was a discouraging sight. Things were so bad in some places that many men, even those with journeyman skills or college educations, had no alternative to the most menial work. In a feeble attempt to feed the hungry, the government distributed free apples, which the unemployed were to sell on the streets for five cents each. Socially-conscious photographers like Walker Evans and Margaret Bourke-White made the sidewalk apple seller an enduring and pathetic symbol of those traumatic and discouraging times of financial desperation.

My family was fortunate. My father's job survived both Prohibition, which had ended, and the general downturn in commerce, and we had the luxury of an automobile. Nevertheless, cash was short, and for a while all my father's resources went to help his older brother, who was struggling to keep a failing grain elevator business going in northern California.

We got by, however, and I was able to stay in school. In my junior year at San Francisco's Galileo High, I was lucky enough to get a 6 p.m. to midnight job as a Special Delivery messenger for the U.S. Post Office, for which I used our family car. My good fortune was brought home to me daily, for the Special Delivery post office was located near the Ferry Building on the Embarcadero at the foot of Market Street, the entrance to the city's crippled Financial District. The broad boulevards and tall office buildings bespoke the prosperity that San Francisco had enjoyed, more or less uninterrupted, since Gold Rush days, but on the streets the reality was dismaying. As I came and went from the post office at night, I would pass hundreds of jobless and homeless men using a cavernous Planters' Peanut warehouse across the street as a place to sleep. The warehouse shipped raw peanuts by ship and train in huge bags measuring some 10 by 15 feet. The men used stacks of empty bags for bedding and slept atop them.

Among my friends at Galileo High was a fellow whose family also had a summer home in Atherton. Land there was relatively cheap then — today those estates are among the most expensive in America — and it was not uncommon for residents to keep horses. My friend's place was right next to the Menlo Circus Club, an equestrian center where he and I, along with some other friends, practiced "cowboying" — roping goats in a ring at the club to start with and, later, working cattle in nearby fields where they grazed.

In those days much of the Peninsula's rolling oak and savanna hill country was ranchland, supporting big livestock operations. What was most remarkable about this industry, then entering its twilight, was that most of the ranchers and cowboys were genuine *vaqueros* steeped in *Californio* traditions of training horses and managing cattle — methods refined during the so-called Mission Era that commenced with Spanish-Mexican settlement in the 1770s and ended with the Gold Rush of 1849. During their brief high period, barely four decades in the early 19th century, when California's European population was a mere 3,000 — most of them in Los Angeles and Monterey — the *Californios* gained world-wide fame as the finest equestrians ever known. Living ghosts from the past, they completed my riding education, teaching me the finer points of handling livestock from horseback and instilling in me a life-long respect for the myriad skills and pastoral gentility of Old California's Spanish-Mexican rural society.

After high school, I entered Stanford University in Palo Alto. My parents gave me $50.00 and I was on my own, the family fortunes having suffered considerably from my father's additional financial responsibility for his brother's family. I worked my way through four years at Stanford, plus another year away from school to earn enough money to allow me to finish and graduate.

I waited tables at the Stanford Union dining room serving many of the professors and their wives on a regular basis. One such customer, Dr. Cubberley, the Dean of Education, dined there every evening and always sat at my table. Over the years we became well-acquainted and I benefited from his kind generosity. Every Christmas he would tip me a crisp $100.00 bill. I also taught wood carving through the Palo Alto school system under the WPA government program and did odd jobs in the Law Library.

At this same time, President Herbert Hoover was once again in residence on the Stanford Campus following his term of office in Washington, D.C. President Hoover was to be the honored guest and speaker at a luncheon for the annual convention of the National Chamber of Commerce which was to be held at the Stanford Union dining room where I was working. It was a very big deal on campus and all of us who were scheduled to wait on table that day were excited! I must have been nervous as well. While serving the head table their salads, I managed to distinguish myself by pouring salad dressing down the big celluloid collar of the former President of the United States!

Still as enthralled with aviation as I was with cowboying, I majored in aeronautical engineering. It was a time of intense national interest in aviation, when the globe-circling "Clippers" of Juan Trippe's flamboyant and pioneering Pan American Airways were hailed as heroic symbols of what *TIME* magazine founder, Henry Luce, had recently proclaimed "The American Century." When I graduated in 1939, however, the country's economic malaise was still persisting. If there were openings for aeronautical engineers, I was unable to find one.

Like most young men full of purpose and untested confidence, I was utterly unaware that the machinations of destiny, or fate, were quietly at work. As an undergraduate at Stanford, I had worked summers and Christmas holidays at the Emporium, a San Francisco department store where I gained the confidence of the store's managers. When it became apparent that I was not going to work in aeronautical engineering anytime soon, I went back to the Emporium seeking work as a full-time employee, and in a stroke of extraordinarily good fortune, got hired as a salesperson. I took to selling and was eventually promoted to buyer, albeit for women's sportswear and corsets. It didn't strike me as a particularly manly line of work, but it was a job. Considering the misery the Depression was still visiting on so many people, it was a particularly rewarding one, and certainly one to be grateful for.

Once a month, I boarded the Southern Pacific Railroad's *Lark* in San Francisco and traveled south overnight to Los Angeles's garment districts to purchase stock. Every six months, I journeyed five days across the country by train to New York on buying trips. Travel aboard the railroads of that day was luxurious, and to have a steady salary at my age in those bleak times was extraordinary, but I was getting restless. I worked six days a week, from eight in the morning until well after the Emporium closed at seven or eight at night. I lived on the San Francisco Peninsula in the village of Atherton. I rose long before dawn to catch the morning train to the city, and often looked out at darkened households as I commuted home late at night. The routine might have comforted a man with family responsibilities, but I missed the outdoor life that I had grown to love as a boy. The generosity and support of the store's Merchandising Manager, ironically, only worsened my dilemma, for every time I complained, he responded with a promotion. By the end of 1939 I was making $200 a month, a comfortable salary in those days. But money and position were not the issues that troubled me. I foresaw a life spent indoors under fluorescent lights amid chiming bells, and it was not appealing, not for any sum of money. I yearned for a more vigorous endeavor, outdoors and in a bigger arena. What exactly that might be, I wasn't sure. Meanwhile, I had finished buying the inventory required for the upcoming season, and I had hired a capable assistant. In one of those "ready-fire-aim" moments that tend to characterize a young person's choices, I went to the Merchandising Manager with a pounding heart and told him that I was resigning.

The exhilaration of having made a decision quickly evaporated in the face of reality: I did not have a job offer, let alone a prospect, and despite nearly seven years of unprecedented federal efforts to revive the economy, unemployment was still widespread in early 1940. But there is a saying that life does not begin to take you seriously until you learn to say "no" — at least at important crossroads — and in saying "no" — albeit with gratitude — to the Emporium, the world began to open up for me.

While riding the train to and from San Francisco, I had noticed cowboys herding cattle up the cobblestones of Third Street from stockyards south of Market Street to the H. Moffatt Company, in what was then a rough district with 29 slaughterhouses, known as Butchertown. (It's now the site of upscale renovated red brick office buildings, townhouse condominiums, parks and sculpture gardens, multi-media and design firms, internet companies, shops, markets, and restaurants. Its early 20th century name has all but been forgotten.)

Pushing cattle along city streets did not square with the heroic depictions of the American cowboy flickering in movie theaters then, but it was commerce, about which I now knew a little, and it definitely was outdoors, about which I knew quite a bit. Because the H. Moffatt Company was known to be the leading livestock operation in the city, I went to their offices to ask for work. William Moffatt, the company's founder, happened to be there, and I was ushered into his office. A tall, spare man wearing an open vest and western boots, he sat at a massive roll-top desk, with a large brass cuspidor on the floor next to it, and appraised me while thoughtfully chewing a wad of tobacco. He asked me what I wanted. I told him I wanted a job.

The H. Moffatt Company was then the largest sheep and cattle producer west of Denver. Its operations sprawled across California's San Joaquin Valley, eastern Oregon, and most of Nevada. The vast scope of his operations enabled Bill Moffatt to essentially make the market for cattle and sheep in the western states. I wasn't really a cowboy, although I had been riding horses for many years at the Circus Club in Atherton — the San Francisco Peninsula was mostly rural then, a rolling, hilly Central California landscape of tawny yellow grassland spotted with the dark green of live oak trees behind a range of low coastal mountains, all wrapped in evergreen. There were dairy farms and cattle ranches here and there, and on them I had learned to rope and brand cattle. Moffatt listened as I recounted my experience, then picked up the phone and called George Devaney, the superintendent of his San Joaquin Valley Division, headquartered in Stockton, an inland deep-water port on the Sacramento River about a two-hour drive east of San Francisco Bay.

"George," he said, "I'm going to send you a man." This was about three in the afternoon. Moffatt asked me to report to the superintendent in Stockton at seven that evening. We shook hands and I trotted back to my old Model A Ford sedan — bought when I had my good paying job at the Emporium — and sped east into the San Joaquin Valley. When I arrived at Stockton, George, Moffatt's manager, offered me a job starting immediately as a night cowboy — doubling as the bookkeeper — at the company's feed lot in nearby Manteca. The pay was $75 a month, barely a third of what I had been earning. Another handshake and I was off to Manteca.

The job involved keeping records of the feed consumption of all the cattle in the Moffatt lots. As the night cowboy, I patrolled the feed pens to see that the cattle were in their proper places and hadn't gotten their heads trapped somehow between the narrow openings. The cows, I discovered, also had a penchant for eating the feed in their neighbors' troughs, and it was my job to wrestle the gluttonous ones back into their own pens.

I loved working with cattle and associating with the people who made up that industry — the cowboys, buyers, brokers, feed lot workers, railroaders, truckers and merchants. The days were long and the work was never-ending, but after the confines of the department store, and the hours spent on clattering commuter trains, it seemed a kind of dusty, raucous, smelly paradise. I was in the company of men and women I felt most comfortable with, and it wasn't long before I was the Assistant Manager of the Manteca feed lot, which corralled over 15,000 head of cattle and was the largest feeding operation in California.

The lot adjoined a Southern Pacific Railway yard where livestock arrived from various points. It was my responsibility to select those ready for slaughter and load them onto trucks for shipment to Butchertown in San Francisco. It seemed to me that I had found a congenial world that, with a little bit of luck, offered more opportunities than one could ask for in a life. But the wheels of fate were turning again, and nothing — not my life, not the lives of hundreds of millions of people, not the world itself — would ever be the same again.

But that cool, crisp December morning I heard those unforgettable words from the railway gate guard, running toward me shouting, "The Japs have bombed Pearl Harbor!" Between gasps, he told me what he had heard on his radio in the guard house.

I finished sorting the cattle and, like most everybody else in America on Sunday, December 7, I was soon bent over a radio, listening to the first reports from far-off Hawaii. The war in the Pacific had been brewing for several years, as Japan flexed military muscle in Asia and its anti-American position hardened. To prepare for the possibility of the country being drawn into the war raging in Europe since the autumn of 1939, the government had instituted the Draft. As an agricultural worker, I held a deferment similar to that offered to full-time students during the Vietnam era.

The implications of the Japanese attack on Pearl Harbor, however, coming just over two years after the Germans had invaded Poland and set Europe aflame, carried a threat greater than any war before or since. The goal of the Axis Powers was nothing less than control of the world. Their plans included the conquest of Western Europe and the British Isles, the Soviet Union and all of Asia, and infiltration of South America and the Caribbean, where Axis agents were active and many despotic regimes saw advantage in allying with the Fascists. The endgame would be the isolation and blockade of North America, turning Canada and the United States into a beleaguered fortress in a world of defeated nations under the boot heels of Nazi and Shinto warlords. We were gradually becoming aware of the fact that the entire world beyond our coasts and southern border was up for grabs. As a nation, we didn't want to become embroiled in another war; in fact, in the 1940 presidential election, Franklin Roosevelt was elected on the rallying cry, "He kept us out of war!"

However, during the afternoon and evening of December 7 in San Francisco, hundreds of people gathered on the beaches and bluffs to gaze out at the Pacific, not to watch for invaders but simply to try to fathom what had happened beyond the far horizon, and what it boded for the future. No one knew.

The night of December 7th, I telephoned Bill Moffatt, who was in Reno at the time, and told him I felt obliged to enlist in the military. Although he would have preferred that I use my deferment and stay on, he was understanding and supportive of my decision, and during the course of the war, he and I maintained our friendship through correspondence.

By 8 a.m. the next morning, instead of loading cattle in Manteca, I was standing in line with a handful of other volunteers at the Army's recruiting office at Hamilton Field, an Army Air Corps base some 20 miles north of San Francisco. A hastily-summoned physician gave us a perfunctory once-over. (When the induction process geared up, and more thorough physical examinations were given, 40 percent of draftees and volunteers were disqualified, mainly because of ailments and disabilities attributed to the deprivations of the Depression: malnutrition, tuberculosis, and injuries untreated for lack of money to pay medical bills.) By noon I was judged to be in good health. I raised my hand, proclaimed allegiance to America, and was sworn into the Army.

War had not yet been formally declared. However, President Roosevelt had delivered his stirring "Day of Infamy" radio address. Congress was still about three hours from its vote. So I had actually joined the pre-war Army.

Meanwhile, the awareness of a colossal threat was sinking into the American consciousness, adding urgency to everything, imbuing even the most mundane activity with a greater significance. The war was already accelerating the pace of American life. Great social changes were afoot. Millions of women would soon assume vitally important roles in the industrial workplace that they had never played before. By the time the war would end some three years and ten months later, 11 million Americans — nearly one in 12 — would have been in uniform, and over 550,000 — about one in 20 — would be killed in the war. In many ways, during those 46 months, the last vestiges of the 19th century would disappear from American life.

None of this was apparent to anyone the day after Pearl Harbor, of course. All I knew was that the pace of my own life had already sped up to beyond anything I had ever experienced. We were told that pilot training would commence the following morning at Minter Field near Bakersfield, a rural San Joaquin Valley town some 320 miles distant. I was told to report to the base by 6 p.m. that evening, given money for gasoline, and sent out the door. I jumped into my old Ford and headed south. There was no time to stop in San Francisco to say goodbye to my mother and father.

But I promised them I'd write. And I did. Lots. Almost every week for most of my four years in the Service. And much later after my mother died, I found among her things a box containing a large bundle of letters — my letters from when I was in the Army Air Corps. I wasn't aware that she had kept them all those years. Well, I left them in that box, and I never opened it or read any of those old letters. My wife, Marcy, found the box among my things and started to read my mother's collection of my letters. After reading some of them, she came to me and enthusiastically encouraged me to write about my wartime experiences. She persisted, and I'm finally getting around to doing just that. However, I found that those letters, while biased with optimism about my prospects for survival to keep my parents from being more than normally concerned, contained a lot of details that I had forgotten over the years, as well as the viewpoints of a young man engaged in warfare. Therefore, I am including excerpts from these letters (as indented paragraphs) in my stories for this book.

CHAPTER 2

METAMORPHOSIS FROM COWBOY TO PILOT

There were 21 of us standing stiffly at attention on the tarmac of Minter Field, just north of Bakersfield, California. Unschooled in drill, we were doing our best to affect a military bearing. We were, after all, in the Army now.

"This is a tough training program," warned one of the officers, walking around us as he spoke. "Only twenty percent of you will make it through to become pilots. The rest of you will wash out." The prediction that only four from this group would measure up was alarming. Without moving my head, I sneaked sideways glances at some of the others. They all looked healthy, fit, and intelligent.

Washing out. The expression was not a consoling one, even though washing out usually meant a transfer to navigator or bombardier school, or to an infantry officer training program, all honorable paths of service. Indeed the first two were essential to the survival and success of a bomber crew, and within a few months I would owe my life to the skill of a freshman navigator. Still, the term seemed to imply more than a susceptibility to vertigo or a defective inner ear, or a weakness in mathematics; it hinted at something else, something shameful — a deficiency in character, a personal flaw of some kind that in the eyes of the Army rendered you unfit to fly, let alone to lead others into battle.

Whatever apprehension I felt, however, I kept to myself as I commenced a correspondence with my mother and father that would span my four years in the Army Air Corps.[1] Like most

---

[1] The name, "Army Air Corps," had been officially changed to "Army Air Forces" in the summer of 1941 before I joined, but it apparently takes a lot of time for some governmental organizational changes to permeate down into the working troops. What

young men in similar circumstances, in my letters I strove for an air of confident amusement — for the most part genuine. Behind the words I wrote was my determination to spare them needless worry and maintain a positive outlook in the face of enormous uncertainties.

January 9, 1942

Dear Mom and Dad,

    Well, I'm in the Army now! And they don't let you forget it either! Boy, you really have to toe the mark. I have lost my personal identity and am now officially #19024277, otherwise "Hey, Mister!" All cadets are known as "Mister".

    They have started "washing them out" already and in the first two days washed out 15% of the class. They will be sent to other schools and made into ground officers.

    Every ten minutes they give you another physical examination. If I thought the first one at Hamilton Field was tough, I was mistaken. They take all sorts of X-rays of your heart, lungs, etc. Also electrocardiograph of your heart in action. Also a complete check again of eyes and ears. You practically have to be a Superman to get near an Army airplane.

    At present we are living in tents, but are very comfortable. The food is excellent and all you can eat. We get up at 5:30, breakfast at 5:45. Classes start at 7:00 and continue till 5:00 with an hour for lunch. We will be here up to five weeks and then sent to flying school. Here we are merely concerned with becoming Army Officers and learning discipline (and how!). We are not allowed off the post for the entire time we are here. It is all work seven days a week.

We were cadets, a quaint military term for untested hopefuls. I had the self-confidence of several winning seasons of varsity football at Stanford and the fortunate beginning of a career, and at

---

I was told I joined was the Army Air Corps, and that was what we all called it until I was in the Eighth Air Force. My orders were signed by officers whose signature blocks clearly identified them as members of the U.S. Army Air Corps. My Instrument Rating card was printed as an official document of the "Army Air Corps." Our dramatic, morale-inflating song, as many of you will remember, ended with "Nothing will stop the Army Air Corps!"

6' 2" and 230 pounds I was the biggest in my group. None of this, however, meant a thing to the officers in charge, whose objective was to instill in us a sense of military discipline.

January 13, 1942

> We've been vaccinated and shot full of typhoid and tetanus serum and then — the crowning indignity — had all our hair cut off, leaving only one-half inch on top, but that is all. As long as I'm in the Army you'll have no further haircut worries with me! It took ten barbers 15 minutes to cut 21 heads of hair, so you can see the careful job they did! No scissors used; just up and over with the clippers!

We marched, scrubbed floors, and learned to make up our bunks to perfection. We marched, ran, jumped, and then ran some more. The drilling was tedious to some, defeating to others, but I had the advantage of being used to strenuous outdoor work. My classmates, however, generally impressed me with their determination. Perhaps it was the era; perhaps it was the fact that, for the first time, the world faced the possibility of domination by a single malevolent power. Whatever it was, my cohorts were giving it everything they had.

> ...It would be hard to find a finer bunch of boys anywhere. They are truly the pick of the country physically, mentally and socially. There really isn't a heel in the lot.

In those days, the Army Air Corps' introductory flight training was divided into three stages — Primary (an orientation to military life and protocol combined with aviation ground school), followed by Basic and Advanced, the latter two in aircraft that today mostly hang by cables from the ceilings of museums. In the classroom, where the fundamentals of aerodynamics were confounding some, my training in aeronautical engineering and math finally found an application. Even my boyhood passion for building model airplanes helped bring it all into focus.

January 16, 1942

> Curiously enough, the war seems very remote here. No one ever mentions it. While we have radios, newspapers, etc., the subject is never brought up. I gather it is bad taste from an Army etiquette point of view.

When our orientation to Army life was finished, we were sent along with the other remaining members of our group to Primary Flying School at Sequoia Field in Visalia, California, another rural San Joaquin Valley hamlet. There we were joined by scores of other cadets arriving from other places. The country's expanding mobilization was becoming apparent, as was the fact that the war was already claiming American lives in faraway places whose names were unfamiliar save to readers of National Geographic. Meanwhile the pace of our training was accelerating.

It was pretty easily seen by us cadets that our training program was being developed as we worked our way through it. The celebrated response of American industry to the challenges of the Second World War eclipses the fact that, at the time of Pearl Harbor, the country was largely unprepared. A shortage of military firearms had forced us to drill in Bakersfield with wooden rifle silhouettes, and although a .45 caliber Colt pistol was standard issue to pilots, I never received one.

Meanwhile the capabilities of our air forces were generally overestimated by the American public, in part because of a beguiling romanticism engendered by World War I recruiting posters[2] followed by the stories about flying heroes in the books we read and the movies we saw in the twenties and thirties.

---

[2] Those recruiting posters for the Army Air Corps in World War I really worked; when we entered the war in 1917, some 38,000 volunteers swarmed the Air Service. But in the 19 months of American participation in the conflict, our airplane factories were able to deliver only about two hundred "Liberty" fighters to the front. Worse yet, the heavy wood-and-canvas airplanes proved so slow, so difficult to maneuver and so vulnerable to gunfire and in-flight fires that pilots dubbed them "flaming coffins." By the war's end in late 1918, some 1,200 American aviators had served at the front, yet despite their daring and bravery and the impressive aerial combat records of a half-dozen aces, the American Air Service was, after objective analysis, the least effective aspect of the nation's war effort.

Soon we were made to feel that we were really a part of the highly esteemed Army Air Corps, when in Primary Training we were introduced to the Stearman, a biplane (meaning an aircraft with an upper and lower wing like the familiar fighters of World War I) and the Ryan PT-19, a monoplane with a single low wing. Both had open-air, in-line cockpits with the student seated in front, and both required a ground crewman to manually wind up their props to start them. The Stearman, recently depicted on a Postal Service stamp honoring pioneering American aircraft, proved such a durable and airworthy plane that its career as a primary trainer lasted for many years. Occasionally, even today, you'll glimpse one swooping low across farmland, in service as a crop-duster. My Primary Training, however, was exclusively in the Ryan PT-19. I can still remember the sound of it — like a Maytag™ washing machine.

February 11, 1942

>The flying is getting tougher every day. Forty more boys have been washed out this week including two of my roommates. Another of my roommates received news this week that his brother was shot down over in Burma. It is a terrible thing, but it certainly improved his flying. So far I have managed to stick. Keep your fingers crossed for me!

The fact was, however, that I was having a wonderful time.

February 20, 1942

>Had quite a thrill Tuesday. Three of us got permission to go to the Bomber Base about 10 miles from here. They fly Lockheed "Hudson" bombers — twin motor and twin tail jobs. One of the ships was going to Burbank so we went along. Boy, they really move and handle just like a little ship (plane). The pilot did Figure 8's and flew upside down. I rode in the rear gunner's turret and had a swell time. We flew to Burbank and refueled and flew back in 2 hours and 23 minutes! They land at 120 mph, and, boy, that is really fast! It was quite a trip and we really had fun.

The real fun, however, was to be at the controls yourself. Even more satisfying was the gradual sense of acquiring flying skills — gaining confidence in the air and acquiring a sense of competence.

...Gee, it is bumpy today! It is hot and most of the fields are alternately green and plowed earth, so it is like being in an elevator. There are down drafts over the green fields and updrafts over the plowed fields. You drop or shoot up 100 to 200 feet at a time. It is a real job to keep control of the ship. You get in a steep turn and hit a down draft and end up in a spin! But it all comes under the heading of "Experience".

They are really piling the hours on us now. They won't let a ship sit on the line ten minutes. You have to keep flying and flying.

Another of my roommates washed out yesterday, so we are down to six now. Keep your fingers crossed for me! I really hung my instructor by his seat belt today when we came down, but he said "Nice ride". So I guess it was OK. We have been flying one hour dual and two hours solo each day. Have been lucky this week — not a crack-up of any sort. I guess the boys are getting better!

February 26, 1942

Well, at last we get a little peace around here! Now that we are Upper Classmen we don't have to pop into a brace every time someone comes into the room. So I will be able to sit here and write without interruption.

We fly about 3 to 4 hours every day now and are really piling up the hours. Also we are getting pretty good with the little devils! We had an examination on landings today. They put a 20 foot circle in the middle of the field and we had to land in it 4 times out of 6. It wasn't as easy as it sounds. You have to make a three-point landing and touch all three wheels in the circle.

Got our Meteorology finals back and I had the highest paper in the class. Now we have only two classes: Navigation for three hours each day and Motors for two hours. Boy, they sure throw it at you!

All the new "Dodos" are here now. It is certainly great to be an Upper Classman and be able to walk freely in the area and sit back and look around the Mess Hall. Also, to brace the Dodos is lots of fun. Last night we had twelve of them reciting their General Orders with their gas masks on. It was certainly a humorous sight.

March 22, 1942

    We are finishing up here this week and are scheduled to leave Saturday for Bakersfield. I have finished all my flying except the Final Check which comes tomorrow. Also a six hour exam on Navigation and two four hour exams in Engines and Meteorology.
    The weather has been hot and sunny. Fortunately we are flying in the morning because as soon as it warms up the air gets terribly bumpy. And it is no fun doing aerobatics between bumps.

At Basic Training, despite its name, the second level of pilot instruction after Primary, we worked on cross-country and formation flying skills in the Vultee BT-13, a single-wing aircraft built mainly of plywood. It had two in-line cockpits under a canopy, and a small Lycoming rotary engine that required manual starting. Though they were considered worthy of training pilots, I found them underpowered and dangerously unforgiving of the kinds of errors that learners tend to make. You had to fly the BT-13 every foot of the way. In particular, we had to think ahead to avoid stalls, which were made more likely by the plane's lean power-to-weight ratio. Maybe it was just a desire to put a bright face on things, or perhaps it was to avoid causing my mother more anxiety than she probably already had, but I continued to minimize the Vultee's shortcomings and extol its few virtues in letters home.

April 3, 1942

    These BT-13A's are really neat airplanes. They handle just as smooth as silk. A real pleasure to fly!
    We don't have to wear helmets and goggles any more as these planes are enclosed. We sit in what's known as the "greenhouse" — a glass cockpit cover with air conditioning — hot and cold. That cockpit is the most amazing thing I have ever seen. Three sides are covered with instruments and the radio is over your shoulder. Every time you want to climb or let down you have to change the pitch of the propeller — just like shifting gears — and let down the flaps, like air brakes. In starting you use both hands and both feet all going in different directions at the same time. Boy, I really can't get over it.

> We are well under way with our routine now. If I ever told you that Primary was tough, I was sadly mistaken! Boy, it was a country club compared to this. In our little rivet popper up there in Visalia we only had 8 instruments. Here in the BT-13A's there are dozens of instruments and switches without counting the radio controls. You have to be practically a one-man band to fly the damn things.

Smooth as silk. A pleasure to fly. Well, what I had meant to express was that it felt good to fly what I considered, in my naivete, to be a "real airplane" instead of a trainer. But the BT-13 was a treacherous airplane to fly, being underpowered and having a dangerous tendency to stall.

In Basic Training I shared a room with a fellow named Errol Crowe, a nice kid from San Jose. One afternoon Errol stalled his trainer, and a few days later I was en route to San Jose by train, accompanying his body home to his family. His death was a real jolt! It was too close! He was the first of my acquaintances to become a casualty. It could have happened to me. Perhaps the hardest part for me was confronting his grieving parents. I did my best to give them solace, even though I couldn't change anything for them. I attended the funeral with them, and then returned to Bakersfield. It certainly woke me up to the reality that mistakes in these airplanes could have deadly consequences. It also made us realize how devastating the death of any one of us would be to the parents of the deceased. So we dropped our facades of casual cockiness and applied ourselves to our lessons in earnest.

> ...The first day they took us down to the flight line and explained the starting procedure, instruments, etc., to us. Then they gave us a technical manual on the ship containing instructions for use of all instruments and for procedures for starting, take-off, climb, let down, landing, etc. The next morning when we flew we were expected to know completely the entire routine. Every mistake we made the instructor would just bawl the Hell out of us. That seems to be a favorite pastime around here. The discipline is terrific.

Much of that discipline was dished out by a First Lieutenant who seemed to have taken an instant dislike to me on the very first

Aviation Cadet Harry Conley, age 25, in Primary Training early in 1942.

All photos not otherwise credited are from the Conley Collection

Wayne R. "Big Fitz" Fitzgerald as an Aviation Cadet in 1942.
Peggy Fitzgerald

Basic Trainer, BT-13, known affectionately by aviation cadets as the Vultee "Vibrator."
Grif Mumford

AT-6 Advanced Trainers in flight formation. These were good airplanes, and many are still flying today.
Grif Mumford

The original 334th Bomb Squadron as formed at Geiger Field, Washington, standing in the snow in December, 1942. Top row, Big Fitz is third from left, Harry Conley is fourth from left; next row down, Bob Cozens is second from left; fourth row down, Little Joe Noyes is fourth from left.

Harry Conley's combat copilot, Warrant Officer Joseph Noyes, with the 334th Bomb Squadron, blown-up from the Squadron photo. Joe Noyes in second row from bottom, second from left.

Harry Conley's instrument rating card, issued by the Army Air Corps in 1942.

The nose repair job we had to rig up with sheet metal and sealing tape after another B-17 knocked our nose out when we were parked alone at Great Falls, Montana.

day we lined up on the tarmac. Unfortunately, he was the officer in charge of us. At my size, I was the biggest and most conspicuous of the group, while the Lieutenant was a foot shorter than me. He looked at me as if my very existence was an insult to everything he believed in or stood for, and throughout Basic Training he gave me hell every chance he got. I wondered if perhaps he'd been abused by older, bigger kids when he was small and was determined to exact revenge. Who knows? In any case, whenever I made a mistake, he seemed to be there and take notice. Mistakes inspired his punitive creativity. Once, after I forgot to lower my flaps during a landing approach in a Vultee — an error that increased the possibility of a stall — he ordered me to trot around the airfield perimeter carrying a parachute. It did not matter that I had made a decent landing without lowered flaps. A point had to be made; an example had to be set. Minter was a huge area of land, and by the time I staggered back, consumed by a special loathing for my pint-sized tormentor, the humiliating punishment had meanwhile created a place in my brain forever devoted to reminding me to lower my flaps on approach. I never forgot again — not once throughout the war — so I suppose I owe him.

What goes around, of course, comes around, particularly in relations between officer candidates and their instructors. Some three and a half years later, near the war's end when I had been promoted to lieutenant colonel and reassigned to the Pentagon, I had occasion to fly a P-51 Mustang fighter from Washington to an USAAF Base in Orlando, Florida. It was a beautiful day, the Mustang was a superb and powerful airplane, and the flight, which was especially enjoyable, left me feeling good about things. In an expansive mood I decided to treat myself to a drink at the Officers' Club, which was deserted save for another officer sitting at the far end of the bar, some distance away. In the dim light I couldn't see him well, but I told the bartender that I would buy the man a drink if he'd care to join me for conversation. He accepted, and when he came over I saw that he was the diminutive flight instructor who had been my tormentor in flight school. Surprisingly to me, he was still wearing the silver bars of a First Lieutenant. All had apparently been forgotten, or perhaps it was that he was aware that I was now a senior officer, able to do things like order first lieutenants to jog along the perimeter of air bases. In any case we had an enjoyable chat, shook hands amiably and parted company forever.

April 3, 1942

We are scheduled for eight weeks here, but from the way they talk they are going to try to put us through in six or seven at the most. We will get only 24 hours leave every other week instead of the weekly leaves we had at Visalia. We never realized how easy it was up there. Here we drill every day and have a Battalion Parade every week. That is really work in all the heat and dust!

It looks very much like they are going to make bomber pilots out of our whole class. They have doubled the night flying time in the curriculum and tripled the instrument flying time, as well as doubling the time we spend in the Link trainer. Also we are to get lots of formation flying. So it looks as though it is bombers for us. Our ground school classes are Meteorology, Navigation and Radio. And they really pour it on! When you complete this course you aren't only a pilot, but an expert at several sciences as well. It surely is valuable training. It would be worth thousands of dollars if you had to go out and buy it.

Our training was beginning to address the requirements of combat. We practiced flying in tight V formation, even during take-off and landing, in groups of three planes spaced about 30 feet apart.

April 7, 1942

Boy, it really takes precision flying in this bumpy air. You only can make one mistake up there!

They have a happy little scheme to make us do our ground school work accurately. The other day we had to lay out a course to fly to Palm Springs for Navigation and Meteorology combined. The next day they handed our flight plans back to us and told us to fly them! So we went down to Palm Springs and refueled and flew back. It was really fun! But with a training system like that you really have to understand what you are doing! I have never known such requirements of precision as they demand here in our flying. I got my head chewed off today during my dual ride because I leveled off ten feet too high at 4,010 feet instead of 4,000 feet. That's sure cutting it pretty fine!

I obviously didn't realize at this early stage of my military flying career that ten feet of error in altitude could, later on when we would be flying four-engine bombers in very tight formations over enemy territory, mean the lives of myself and my nine crewmates as well as the lives of the ten airmen on the nearest bomber. The instructor was doing his job to get me to understand what "precision flying" was all about.

We learned to fly cross-country, alone, taking off five minutes apart so that once in the air we were alone and forced to navigate on our own. I found it a peculiarly lonesome experience, especially when I was crossing over mountains.

>...The rest of our course seems to be designed to give us bomber training. In fact, we just got some twin motored ships in yesterday for us to fly in a few weeks to get some time in them.

We were being prepared for war, of course, but for now the experience of flying was still filled with pure wonder and the simple joy of acquiring skills you never imagined you might have.

April 22, 1942

>The weather has been overcast all week, but here we have to fly anyway where we were grounded at Primary. We just go through the clouds on instruments and it is always clear above. Sometimes we have to go up as high as 11,000 or 20,000 feet to reach clear flying. The instrument flying is a terrific nervous strain. You can't see a thing, not even your wing tips. It is impossible to trust your senses, though it's an awful temptation. When you turn to the left, you would swear that you were turning to the right, for example. So you just sit and watch the instruments, listen to the radio and sweat. Somehow you always come out in the right place!
>
>We have flown every night this week. That's lots of fun, but you certainly have to be able to concentrate and keep alert! You take off and fly until they radio you to come in and land. Then you let down on

> instruments and when they tell you the field is beneath you, you start to land. No lights at all now, so you come in at 130 mph and feel for the ground. If you trust your radio and instruments again, you always seem to hit the runway. It is certainly precision work of the closest type. You can't afford to make a mistake!
>
> Flying above the clouds is a sight beyond description. It is beautiful to say the least. Just like a layer of cotton batting with the sun shining on it. Some day I'll take you up there so you can see it for yourself.

It was now mid-May. I had been in the Army scarcely four months, but in those 16 weeks I had been transformed from a rural Central California feed lot manager to a military pilot. Where I was headed was entirely up to the Air Corps, which had not yet decided on a future for me. All we knew was that our class was to be split up and sent to specialized schools. As near as I could deduce, I was destined to be a Basic Training flight instructor, or sent on to a multi-motor class, a bomber school. In a few days I would take my final check ride, the last test I had to pass in order to advance. I considered that I had mastered flying, but still felt uncertain when navigating solely on instruments.

> ...But my instrument flying is showing improvement every day. Had to use it last night. Ran into some clouds north of Sacramento and had to go on instruments for almost 15 minutes, and came out exactly on my course and at the correct altitude. It is tedious disagreeable work, but as they say around here, "Next to your parachute, it is your best insurance policy". Boy, it was rough in those clouds! Hit one bump that turned me over on my back. But got her righted and only lost 500 feet. It is hard enough to fly instruments in smooth air, but in rough air when you are pitching like a cork in a stream (as it always is when in actual instrument conditions) it practically drives you crazy trying to keep all the needles in their proper places. I was in such a sweat when I hit clear air again that my clothes were soaked through.
>
> All I have left to finish is about 15 hours of instrument time and 10 hours of formation work.

I passed, and was sent immediately to Advanced Flying School at Stockton Field, California. The change was dramatic; we flew new North American AT-6s, burly all-metal fighters still known as

Texans. Their cockpits were in-line under a tall sliding Plexiglas canopy, and their huge radial engines generated considerable power and an awesome roar. These AT-6s proved phenomenally durable; today, nearly 60 years later, many T-6s are still flown privately. Besides, they are sharp looking planes even by today's standards, prized by "warbird" collectors who frequently show them off at antique aircraft shows.

May 31, 1942

> Boy, this is really the place. Quite a change from the previous schools. Here they treat you like an officer and a gentleman. It is, "Gentlemen, please do this"; etc. The quarters are the same as in Bakersfield, but the food is much better. In fact, it couldn't be better. Also the physical layout of the post is much nicer — grass and trees instead of sagebrush and jackrabbits. Our class is small, only 120 boys, all supposedly the hottest pilots of the West Coast Training Command. We have already filled out the necessary papers for our commissions and Wednesday we order our uniforms, so it won't be long now! The only way you can wash out is by breaking the rules.

Here in Stockton we met many new cadets who had completed their Basic Training elsewhere. As we arrived we lined up alphabetically, and I found myself standing next to Robert Cozens. Army logic held that the proximity of our surnames on the roster meant that we should be roommates, and roommates we became. Fortunately, we hit it off and became friends. Our alphabetical proximity also decreed that if we survived flight school we would receive our commissions together. It might have had something to do with the curious way our service careers seemed to parallel each other; some two and a half years later, we would be awarded our promotion to Lieutenant Colonel on the same set of orders. Then, however, we were just two crewcut kids with an uncertain future in a darkening world.

As I proceeded in my flight training to more advanced and faster airplanes, my parents, remembering my recklessness as a boy, expressed concern about my safety in the air.

June 18, 1942

> Don't worry! I'm much more careful with these airplanes than I am with horses because I don't trust them for a second! If one of these tosses you, it is for keeps; there is no getting up and walking away! And as I realize it, I'll never give them the chance!

August came, and with it graduation from Advanced Flight Training in Stockton, the awarding of our wings, and our commissions as Second Lieutenants. On that same day, Bob Cozens and his long-time sweetheart Patty exchanged wedding vows. There was no time for a traditional honeymoon — we had been ordered to Salt Lake City to report for our assignments — and the newlyweds had no car. I did, however, so we packed up everything in my Model A Ford, a four-door sedan. Then we invited our other roommate, a fellow named Dick Cordell, to ride with us. The cross-country jaunt had to be an exotic adventure for Patty, who doubtless had not envisioned a honeymoon in the company of two other men besides her husband. There was also the matter of Dick Cordell's nickname, "The Raunch," reflecting the general run of his humor.

Entertained by The Raunch's considerable wit, our unlikely quartet rolled up the piney western slope of California's Sierra Nevada Mountains and down the Nevada side's sagebrush flank to Elko, where we stayed but one night — at last giving Coz and Patty the benefit of some time alone. Early the next morning we pressed on to Salt Lake City. The military, which often works in ways inexplicable and unfathomable, allowed us but one night in Salt Lake City before ordering us back out West, this time to Geiger Field near Spokane, Washington, for four-engine flight training with the Second Air Force. We got back into my dusty car and headed northwest, bride and groom in the back, The Raunch and I alternating at the wheel.

Our luck on the ground followed the same fortunate vein as it had so far in the air. Somewhere out on the alkali flats that stretch from Utah into Idaho, we punctured a tire. We had driven barely 50 miles further on a spare when a loud bang followed by the dismal flopping of a blown tire brought us to a stop. Our second flat! It was a Sunday; there was probably never much traffic out there, and now that gasoline was rationed, we figured that the chances of a motorist coming along were slim. And even if we could get to a service station, in those days they were mostly closed on Sundays.

Eventually an automobile appeared on the horizon, and when it reached us the driver stopped. We were of course complete strangers to him, but that was a different time in America, so when he understood our predicament, he insisted on loaning us the spare wheel and tire from his Ford. He was en route to Burley, Idaho — a town on our route — and asked only that when we got there, to drop it off at a designated place.

We made it to Burley where Dick telephoned his father, who owned an auto dealership in Boise. Though tires were also rationed, the senior Cordell arranged for us to purchase two new ones for my car. Riding confidently on new rubber, we dropped off the stranger's spare at the address he had left with us, and headed west again. Even though our military credentials helped vouch for us, his trust and generosity seem extraordinary from the perspective of today. But his generous acts were simply aspects of the wartime spirit in this country then.

In Boise we said farewell to Dick, who had orders to report to a different air base and wanted to see his family before departing. We assumed we would cross paths again — so far, after all, Coz and I had walked a virtually parallel path — but that would be the last time either of us would see The Raunch again. I have no idea whether or not he survived the war. That was how it worked in those days.

As we rolled west across the Rocky Mountains bound for Four Engine Flying Training, America was entering its eighth month at war. The news from the Pacific had not been heartening. In January 1942, the Japanese had battered American and Filipino forces and marched into Manila. In February they invaded Singapore, taking control of the primary sea route between Europe and Asia. A month later they occupied most of the Philippines, and by May, after four months of savage fighting, they had taken 36,000 American prisoners on the Bataan Peninsula.

The situation was not much brighter in Europe, although Britain's Royal Air Force was beginning to strike back at the Nazis, pounding U-boat bases on the French coast and starting heavy raids on German cities. Bolstered by dozens of captured American, British and French tanks, the Afrika Korps, German Field Marshall Erwin Rommel's fearsome armored phalanx, had blasted out of Libya and pushed deep into Egypt, forcing the British Army into retreat. Although the Allies were beginning to fight back and land punches, the Axis armies were still marching toward their objectives with frightening success. In Russia, Sevastopol fell to the Wehrmacht after a ferocious month-long Blitzkrieg killed 12,000 Soviet troops and left nearly 30,000 Soviet soldiers wounded or missing. The assault on Stalingrad was next.

August 1, 1942

> Well, Coz and Pat and I got to Spokane, where we stayed at the Davenport Hotel. It was a gorgeous old hotel with marble floors and all of the old luxuries. Coz and Pat finally got into a room to themselves for a time there.

We were assigned to the 34th Bomb Group at Geiger Field, near the headquarters of the Second Air Force in Spokane. The Second Air Force was the Training Air Force whose mission at that time was to supply copilots for four-engine aircraft. Most of the group were destined to go to the South Pacific as replacement copilots for B-24's, the huge four-engine bomber known as the Liberator.

> ...I'm attached to the 391st Bombardment Squadron and we are flying Consolidated B-24D's, the newest, biggest thing the Army has in service at present. They are like the St. Francis Hotel with wings. I'm First Pilot and have a crew of eight — co-pilot, navigator, bombardier, radioman, flight engineer, and three gunners. We also have more guns than a battleship — all 50 caliber, but the number is a secret. Everybody but me handles them in case of attack. This ship is really tremendous. It lands at 120 mph and is unbelievably fast in the air. If I ever thought

that there were many instruments to contend with in an AT-6A, I was sadly mistaken. Here there isn't room enough for them all on the panel, so they are on both side walls, the floor and the ceiling as well.

Incidentally, before we could take the ship off the ground we had to be able to sit in the cockpit blindfolded and touch every instrument and switch as they were called out to us. Some achievement!

There were no off-hours anymore; we were considered to be on duty 24 hours a day, six days per week. We flew day and night, no flight less than three hours, and many often much longer. Patty Cozens and the other junior officers' wives had gone into nearby Spokane and rented rooms, so they at least had each other to talk with while Bob and the rest of us were busy with our training. None of them complained; they knew, just as we did, that the training we were receiving would be crucial for us when we got into the war. And the more training, the better would be our chances of coming back alive.

...Last night I flew from 12:30 midnight to 6:00 a.m. This afternoon I'm going out at 4:00 p.m. and will fly until 11:00 p.m. It is quite a job pushing one of these elephants for that long at a stretch. It is honest to God work to move them. The pressure on the controls is terrific.

Our training flights were now taking up to 100 hours a month. Ahead was a month of bombing and gunnery training, and extended cross-country flying. We were told that by the first of November we would be abroad, perhaps in England, possibly in Africa or Australia.

August 9, 1942

I flew this morning from 3:00 a.m. until 11:00 a.m. and am scheduled to fly from 12:30 a.m. until 6:00 a.m. tomorrow. So you see they keep us in the air practically all the time. We also have to sandwich in two hours of Link trainer time in between flights every day.

My seat-of-the-pants flying days were behind me now. The emphasis was on instrument training. Unlike the single-engine trainers, these B-24 bombers were so large you could not rely on your senses to fly them. You could not determine by sight or sense of balance if you were flying level, if a wing was low, or if you were slipping into a descent or a climb. The only reliable technique was to fly by instruments at all times. The Link Trainers, an early generation of the flight simulators that pilots train and re-qualify in today, allowed us to improve our technique and occasionally experiment in ways that would have been unsafe aloft.

> ...We are flying 12 to 18 hours out of every 24. However, none of us mind it because it will stand us in good stead in the future. Experience is what we need and also what we are rapidly getting. We have a great advantage in having several men attached to the group who have recently returned from the battlefront and their information on our and the enemies' tactics is invaluable.

One of those veterans was the Operations Officer of our squadron, a captain named Wheeliss who was a decorated hero of the Philippine campaign, praised by Franklin Roosevelt during one of the president's weekly "Fireside Chat" radio addresses. His prowess at the pool table only hinted of the steel behind the man's affable manner.

> ...It's all a great experience and I'm really enjoying it. I still gaze in awe at these damned things and can't really believe they actually fly. They weigh over twenty tons empty and better than fifty tons loaded. They land at 120 mph, which is really moving. If you drop them in from over a foot above the ground the wheels will flatten out and you come in on your belly. A couple of the boys here have already had that experience in the last week. Nobody hurt, but airplane scattered all over the field!

Accidents did not slow the pace of flying. We sensed the urgency behind the crowded training schedules posted on the barrack walls.

August 12, 1942

> I flew seven hours last night and four hours today. Tonight I have four hours of Link trainer work and tomorrow, eight hours of flying. It is a tough schedule, but the more time we can get in the air over here, the better off we'll be when we get into the actual fighting. They absolutely require that we know every detail of this airplane inside and out so that no matter what arises we will be equal to the situation. That means hours and hours of study, both the technical manuals furnished by the manufacturer and actual going over of the airplane inch by inch. It's a slow process, but it gives you a comfortable feeling when you're in the air to know that you are thoroughly familiar with your airplane.

Like any parent with a child in the military during wartime, my mother worried about me and what lay ahead, and also about my morale. I tried to reassure her, but was perhaps too candid for her comfort about the fatalism that was beginning to characterize our group.

> ...After a person has been engaged in military flying for almost a year he becomes of necessity a hardened realist. You have to develop that philosophy because in this game you live from day to day. I've seen too many crack-ups and then had to go right up myself to prevent it having any effect on me anymore. We all realize what we are up against. It takes a peculiar psychology to face it, but we who are in this game have developed it. So don't worry about my reactions to all this.
>
> There was a bad accident here today. One of the boys blew a tire on landing. Thirty tons of airplane at 120 mph is pretty tough to handle at a time like that. As a result, the airplane is a complete washout and five men are hurt. No one killed, fortunately. Everyone discusses the cause of the accident, but accepts the thing as just part of the game. That's the way it goes; you live for today and let tomorrow take care of itself.

One thing we were clear about was that our job was to learn all we could about flying multi-engine heavy bombers, so that we could go either to Europe or the Pacific to help put down the enemies that were threatening our way of life here in America. We left the decisions about how, when and where to those in higher positions of command. Europe? The South Pacific, or somewhere else? It was routine in those days not to know where you were going to end up. Part of the reason was wartime secrecy, and part of it was because the war was an ever-changing puzzle, forcing the military to constantly reassess and innovate. One result was that rumors were sometimes more reliable than official predictions. Originally, Coz and I were part of a group of replacement copilots destined for the South Pacific. Half way through our 30-day checkout in four-engine B-24 bombers, however, we were both ordered to report to the Athletic Officer at Headquarters of the Second Air Force in downtown Spokane. It seemed like a curious request, but it was in any case an order, so we showed up as we were told.

Despite the emergencies of the time, the military occasionally focused its energies on projects that seemed utterly unrelated to the fact that the world was at war. This was one of those times. The Athletic Officer had been given the job of forming a football team for the Second Air Force. Somehow he had learned that Coz had been an All League Football Player at San Diego State, and that I had played at Stanford. He asked us if we would like to be on the team. He'd already recruited the legendary Tom Harmon. He informed us that we were indeed scheduled to check out as co-pilots and ship out to the South Pacific, but that if we agreed to play football for the Second Air Force, he could arrange for us to be kept on at Geiger as instructors. We couldn't refuse.

Whether it was because of the urgencies of wartime or the Second Air Force's enthusiasm for football I can't say, but on my last day as a student pilot, immediately after I had checked out on four-engine aircraft, the Operations Officer pulled me aside, informed me that I was officially an instructor, and ordered me to report to the flight line at eight that evening to meet my first student. He was a captain, older than I, an experienced fighter pilot named Al Wilder. By the time we strapped ourselves into the cockpit of a B-24 for a familiarization flight, it was dark. As a P-40 pilot, Al was used to the relatively simple instrumentation of a single-engine fighter plane. He had never seen the inside of a bomber and was overwhelmed by the array of glowing instruments surrounding the pilot and copilot's seat on all sides and overhead.

We flew around the Spokane area for about an hour and a half, with Al repeatedly looking at the clutter of instruments, switches, knobs and levers and shaking his head in wonder. After the flight was over, he invited me to the Officer's Club for a drink. He needed one. Over Scotch and sodas he said, "God, this is a complicated airplane. I don't know about this." I assured him that it would all begin to make perfect sense in no time. He asked me how long I had been flying. I held my breath, but you don't lie to a superior officer. "Well," I admitted, "I graduated three weeks ago — and I just checked out in four-engine aircraft this afternoon." He dropped his glass on the bar and exclaimed, "Well, I'll be a son-of-a-bitch!" About that time, Coz entered the Club and ambled over. I introduced him to Al and we all quickly became fast friends. Al never questioned the official wisdom behind my four-hour transition from student to instructor.

As August moved toward September, we began to practice bombing. Our flights were designed to resemble as closely as possible the physical conditions we would encounter overseas. Because of the altitude we would have to maintain for a measure of safety from anti-aircraft fire and enemy fighters, we wore fur suits and oxygen masks, sweating on the ground (in eastern Washington's rolling wheat country) where daytime temperatures sometimes topped 100 degrees. At 28,000 feet, however, the mercury dropped to about 12 degrees below zero.

I felt the change in the way the airplane flew when it had a load of bombs, and later when these bombs were released. With a full crew of nine, the fuel tanks topped off, and a one-ton load of practice bombs in the racks just aft of the cockpit, the margin of safety was narrowed. It occurred to me that if we were to blow a tire on the plane or had any kind of mishap and piled up, we might not walk away from it.

It was my first experience with live bombs, albeit in this case 100-pounders painted blue and holding only five pounds of black powder — but enough to make an impressive detonation when they struck. From seven miles up the bombardier had to release them about nine miles short of the target. That was because the bombs, when released, continued in the forward motion of the plane until gravity overcame their forward momentum.

August 22, 1942

>It is 12:30 AM and I just got back from a bombing mission that lasted eight hours. We flew down to the range near Pendleton, Oregon, and dropped our load of twenty bombs singly, which meant twenty runs over the target. We bombed from 28,000 feet and at 320 mph so it was pretty hot stuff. We did OK as long as it was daylight; we'll have to wait until tomorrow to find out how we did after dark.
>
>On our way back that night I made the kind of simple, sudden, inadvertent error that airmen dread: I reached for one switch but flipped another by mistake. Fortunately, it was the bail-out alarm bell. One long ring meant "get into your chute and open the exits"; two meant "Jump". I sent the copilot scrambling back to tell the crew that it was a false alarm. He found them in their chutes, poised at the escape hatches. My mistake, however, precipitated a useful if hair-raising drill: afterward, the crewmen observed that they had not known that they could move as quickly as they did when the alarm sounded. Most claimed they were disappointed that they couldn't try out their chutes.
>
>I've often heard it said that military airmen were crazy; I'm beginning to think it's true.

In its scramble to prepare for war, the Air Corps was improvising as it went. With about ten days and 90 hours logged in four-motored aircraft, we thought we were well along toward being certified as "first pilots" — meaning the flyer in command of the aircraft, the occupant of the left seat in the cockpit. Somewhere up the chain of command it was decided that we had to log 300 hours in the big ones before we could qualify as first pilot.

>...Starting tomorrow we are going to have to ride as copilots until we build up more time. If we leave at the end of the month as scheduled, it will be as copilots, but from the talk around here today we'll probably stay another month and leave as first pilots at that time. But who knows? It doesn't even make us curious anymore. If we go, we go, and that is all there is to it. We spend so little time on the ground now that it doesn't make much difference where it may be.

CHAPTER 3

HONING OUR SKILLS IN B-17s

In the first week of September 1942, our training took a new and fortunate twist. We were introduced to the airplane that we would fly into battle, the new B-17E Boeing "Flying Fortress." On paper it fell somewhat short of the range, speed, rate of climb, bomb load, and ceiling of the B-24 Liberator we were getting to know and love; however, its qualities were immediately evident, starting with the fact that it was a pleasure to fly, being more stable than the B-24 and requiring less pressure on the controls. For me, as a pilot, our new B-17 was an extremely welcome change.

It bristled with .50 caliber machine-guns like a porcupine and the fuselage surrounding the cockpit was fitted with sheets of armor plate and window glass said to be bullet-proof. I described these last two safety features in a letter to my mother, believing them to be true. (Later on in combat I found that the description "bullet-proof" should be stricken from the English language.) Whatever the Boeing lacked in speed and muscle it would make up for in durability, acquiring a legendary reputation for its ability to sustain damage and keep flying.

Officially deemed a heavy bomber, the Flying Fortress was an impressive thing to behold. Its slender fuselage stretched nearly 75 feet; the vertical stabilizer stood 19 feet tall, and its thick wings spanned 103 feet, each supporting two 1,200 horsepower Wright R-1820 Cyclone engines. The Boeing's cruising speed was 170 mph; at full throttle, unloaded, it could reach a little over 300. It was designed to carry a crew of ten: pilot, co-pilot, navigator, flight engineer, bombardier, radioman, and four gunners. It could lift up to 5,000 pounds of bombs, over two tons, to an altitude of 36,000 feet, about seven miles. Fully loaded with fuel and bombs, the airplane weighed in at 47,000 pounds, over 23 tons. Stood next to some of the massive bombers that followed it, of course, it now seems runty and even a bit quaint. Its first prototype flew in a test demonstration in 1935. But in 1942 it was a state-of-the-art airplane, awesome in aspect. Its 3,000-mile range — greater than the distance from Los Angeles to New York — meant we could fly it from London to Berlin and return with fuel to spare.

> ...Getting these new ships means having to read 1,500 to 2,000 pages of technical data about them which will give me something to do in my spare (?) time. The reading is required and we have to sign a statement saying that we have read every order. It is all very technical stuff but in order to go into combat with these ships, or any other for that matter, you really want to know everything there is to know about them in general and in detail.

As autumn approached and the days grew shorter we began to concentrate on flying at night, logging as much as ten hours in the air between sundown and sunrise.

> September 28, 1942
>
> I finish flying about 6:00 a.m. and go right to bed and don't get up until around 4:30 in the afternoon. Just in time to clean up and eat before going on duty at 6:00 p.m. Last night I went down below Pendleton, Oregon, to bomb and on the way back I thought I'd see how fast the ship would go as I had never let one out before. I was flying at 15,000 feet and gave her everything she had. The air speed indicator read 280 mph but the navigator calculated our true ground speed and it was 438 mph. The difference is due to the temperature and pressure effect on the air speed indicator at altitude. We made the 175 miles from the range to here in 23 minutes!

At the end of September our co-pilots shipped out. Pilot training went on, however, with all of us doing double duty, flying in the right seat while half of us practiced in the left, then switching places. The flight schedule took on the fatiguing regimen of a war zone. In the first five days of October I logged 70 hours in the air.

> ...Last night as I was waiting for a plane to land so I could take off, a poor guy spread it all over the runway, so they called off flying for the night as they had to clear the wreckage away.

It was a crash landing following a stunningly close call. They had taken off into a pitch-black night and were flying on instruments. About three miles off the end of the runway there was a pointed hill about 250 feet high. If you climbed at a normal rate you would clear it, but for some reason they were slow in gaining altitude and grazed its summit — bounced off it, really — shearing the propellers and cowlings from the inboard motors, and ripping the bomb bay doors and gun turret from the belly of the fuselage. The impact would have crumpled most airplanes, but the B-17 kept flying, now on only two motors. The pilot circled around for an emergency landing — his wheels had been torn away as well — and put it down on bare metal in a shower of sparks. He and his crew crawled out of the aircraft uninjured to find a barbed wire fence, ripped from the hilltop, wrapped around the bomber's nose like a crown of thorns. With a foot less altitude, they would not have made it off that hill.

We were beginning to appreciate the phenomenal strength and durability of the Flying Fortress, which could stay in the air and even land with but one engine running. In anticipation of losing engines in combat, we practiced flying with three of our four power plants shut down. This practice gave us a greater sense of security about our home in the air.

> ...The B-17s have had a remarkable record in Europe to date. In four months of operations with about 200 planes taking part, they have only lost six airplanes and two crews.

Those 1942 missions, however, were mostly coastal raids that did not venture far into eastern France, let alone Germany. It would get much worse over there before it would be that good again.

As October progressed the 391st Bomb Squadron was reorganized into a new combat outfit, designated the 304th

Bombardment Group, and ordered 100 miles west to Ephrata in the eastern corner of Washington's "high desert" country.

> ...We'll also have a new squadron number, but I don't know that as yet. We'll be at Ephrata for about a month, then to either El Paso, Texas, or Great Falls, Montana, for another month, and then ON TO ENGLAND! The sooner the better! Our squadron is to be made up entirely of boys from the present 391st Bomb Group; we really got all the best ones, including Bob Cozens, my roommate from Stockton. We have been very fortunate by being able to remain together.

Following the move to Ephrata would come the assignment of a specific airplane, the bomber we were told we would fly across the Atlantic to England and into battle. In anticipation of these long journeys, we were ordered to commence cross-country trips lasting up to ten days.

> ...The bad weather is really setting in up here. Almost every flight we run into rain, snow, sleet, ice, etc., upstairs. That means real instrument flying, not just practice under a hood or in a Link trainer. It gives you a funny feeling to get into that stuff at night several hundred miles from home over these mountains and not ever be able to see your wingtips. Then to have to fly through it for several hours and get over Spokane only to find that the ceiling is only 500 feet and about a dozen peaks near here are over 3,000 feet high.
>
> This experience is not exceptional, but is the usual run of things; it happens six nights out of every seven around here now. It leaves no margin for error. There is no second chance. You stay on the instruments and radio and the combination brings you out of the overcast at 500 feet about a quarter of a mile from the end of the runway. I just can't describe to you what a welcome sight it is to see the field right there, and then to feel your wheels hit the ground. It is really the most wonderful feeling in the world.

We transferred to Ephrata at the end of October. The airfield was not an inspiring place, set as it was in a dusty tan void of sagebrush running in all directions to the horizon. The field, in fact, was not even in Ephrata, but six miles from its approximately 900 citizens. There were no trees, and we lived beside our airplanes in canvas tents.

> ...It is supposed to harden us for the rigors of combat, if it doesn't kill us first!

My crew was coming together, with everyone performing well. We got along, all nine of us, and I had confidence in each.

> ...They are a swell bunch and I couldn't have done better if I'd picked them out myself. I have the privilege of disposing of any of them if I want, but I couldn't do better.

Bob Cozens and I were now the only two left from our original class of trainees. Our crews had been assigned to other pilots. We were still in Ephrata, training new pilots in instrument flying, bombing techniques, and the handling of the B-17.

> ...It is amazing to me that I am qualified to instruct and examine these other pilots, many of whom have been in the Air Corps for several years, but flying other types of aircraft. But when I stop to consider that I now have more than 500 hours experience in the B-17 airplane and under all imaginable weather conditions, it loses its wonderment.

Teachers, of course, keep learning right along with their students. There is an old saying in aviation which, although exaggerated, has a core of truth, that flying is composed of long hours of boredom punctuated every now and then by moments of sheer terror. Commercial pilots point out that they earn their pay not so much in those uneventful hours but in the rare moments, emergencies in the making, when every bit of their experience must be called upon to avert disaster. I gained an appreciation of that one night during a training flight.

November 2, 1942

> We took off at midnight last night into a beautiful moonlit night for a routine cross country flight to Ellensberg, Portland, Bend, and

Pendleton, then back over Walla Walla, and home. I had a new pilot along and I was just showing him the country. All went well until we hit Pendleton. There we ran into a dense overcast with sleet and snow, and ice began to form on the wings. We were at 10,000 feet, so I didn't dare to let down for fear of hitting the mountains. I tried to climb above it, but after reaching 25,000 feet and getting no better, I dropped back to 10,000 feet and came home on instruments. I have never seen ice form on the wings so determinedly. Had the de-icers working and the ice was flying off in great chunks. We could hear it hit the sides of the plane. Sounded like someone beating a big metal drum. When we got back to Spokane, it was a regular blizzard. Besides all the rest of the soup there was a 40 mile wind blowing across the runway in gusts.

I made the calculations for flying to Spokane, starting at 10,000 feet on the radio beam and gradually letting down through the storm on instruments. As we approached the vicinity of Spokane my altimeter slowly turned counter-clockwise down to 1,000 feet, but I was still in blinding fog. At 500 feet we were still in the soup. Then, at 400 feet, the clouds suddenly lifted and we were in clear air with the lights of Geiger Field twinkling below — a vision of Heaven. But now the problem was wind — 40 mile-per-hour gusts blowing erratically across the runway, jerking the big bomber around like a kite. As soon as I would get the airplane aligned for the proper drift correction on approach, the wind would change and we would slide off to the side. I'd correct for that and then the wind would change direction and my landing would be ruined. The pilot beside me had just graduated from flying school. He had never flown in overcast, had no idea how I'd managed to find the field, and admitted that he was scared to death. I finally lined up with the runway, which was hardly visible because of the driving snow and sleet, and just as I was about 15 feet off the ground, a great gust blew me clean off the runway. I shoved the outboard throttle full on, on the proper side, and got back onto the concrete strip just as my wheels hit the ground. I had never been bounced around so much in my life. Rolling along the concrete airstrip in the blizzard, I recalled the difficulty of learning instrument flying in cadet school, the most challenging aspect of my training. But once again it had saved my skin, and the lives of the nine men flying with me. I said a prayer of thanks each night for every hour of instrument training that I had behind me.

By the second week of November, the gray overcast of Pacific Northwestern winters lay over most of northeastern Washington. In Europe the war was raging; in Ephrata, we often sat on the ground, socked in by chilly fogs so dense we could not see across the runway.

Meanwhile, Al Wilder was checked out as a four-engine pilot. His "student" status notwithstanding, as a Captain he was my superior, and he had been assigned to be the commander of a new B-17 Bomber Squadron, the 334th, part of the new 95th Bomb Group. His first order of business was to assemble the squadron. He needed officers, and he invited us to join him. "If you fellows would like to go to Europe with me," he said, "we'll go fight some Nazis! I have some slots to fill in my organization, and I think you two would be good guys to have on my combat team. If you'll go with me, I can make you Flight Commanders, with an immediate promotion to First Lieutenant." We had been Second Lieutenants for barely a month. A round of handshakes delivered our fates to the 334th Bomb Squadron. We never did play football for the Second Air Force. That was how things worked then.

November 12, 1942

> Bob and I have been made Flight Commanders in the new combat outfit now being organized. We are certainly riding the crest of the wave. Here we get the promotions and get transferred to this new outfit, which will stay here next month while the 391st will move on to Ephrata. That ain't hard to take! Things here are much more comfortable than at Ephrata. This is the break we have been waiting for. We've jumped all the First and Second Lieutenants on the promotion list. We'll each have command of three airplanes and thirty men. Also the new squadron C.O. is a very good friend of ours and that never does any harm. He is now a Captain and being promoted to Major.

November tilted toward December, with us in the air much of the time, building up our flight time, refining our skills, mastering the B-17 and dealing with the occasional happenstance.

...I was flying along at 6,000 feet and had a mid-air collision with a duck. The damned bird flew into my #2 engine and got jammed between the cylinders so that it disturbed the flow of air over the engine and made it heat up. So I had to cut off that engine and land with three engines instead of four.

The occasional duck was one thing, but the Northwest's weather was another.

...I had a hair-raising experience the last time I flew. It was at night and we had taken off with a load of bombs to drop down in Oregon. We ran into a snow storm about half way down to the bombing range. I was flying at 7,000 feet and dropped down to get under the overcast but couldn't do it; so I climbed to 15,000 feet and still couldn't get out of it. But, as we were considerably higher than any of the country for hundreds of miles in any direction, I leveled off and continued on my course. Well, finally we reached our destination according to the instruments; so I let down through the soup. We finally broke out at about 800 feet above the ground. That was much too low to drop bombs; so I started to climb up again to return to Geiger Field. I had just reached 15,000 feet and leveled off when I looked back at one of my gunners and noticed his face was covered with oil. Looking out the right window next to my copilot I saw this great spray of oil coming from #3 engine. Then a quick glance at the oil pressure gauge showed me that we had broken an oil line. We had no oil pressure on #3 engine. I immediately cut off that engine and gave the other three all the throttle they would take as I turned the plane and headed for home.

It was bad. We were at 15,000 feet over a desolate wilderness, in overcast so dense that we couldn't see the navigation lights on the wing tips. Oil was spewing over the dead engine, still so hot that it began to smoke. The broken line would have to drain all 35 gallons of lubricant before the danger of a fire would abate. If one broke out, there was no guarantee we would be able to suppress it. I ordered the crew to stand by to abandon ship as we barreled back toward Spokane on three engines through an immense blackness, guided only by our instruments.

Fortunately, the ceiling over Geiger Field was at a relatively high 3,000 feet. Emergency crews cleared the runways for an emergency landing and a possible fire, but the B-17 came through again. When we touched down and rolled to a stop, I noticed that the fatigues under my flight suit were soaked with perspiration.

I learned a lot about the airplane that night. You learn more in ten minutes at a time like that than you do in ten days of routine flying when everything goes perfectly.

As we progressed in our flight training to take us eventually into combat, the war went on. It had been exactly one year since the Japanese attack on Pearl Harbor. On December 1st, gasoline rationing went into effect on a national scale, limiting America's 27 million passenger cars to a maximum weekly consumption of four gallons apiece; in those days that was just about enough to travel 60-70 miles. Coffee was declared a rationed luxury, creating a market for "ersatz" brews like Sanka. In the Pacific, the battle to wrest control of Guadalcanal in the Solomon Islands from the Japanese was in its fourth month. On December 4th, US planes made the first air raids on Italy, striking Naples and other targets. In North Africa the British were gaining advantage over Rommel's Afrika Korps, forcing it into retreat. In Hollywood, Fred Astaire and Bing Crosby were about to introduce Irving Berlin's classic ballad *White Christmas* in the movie *Holiday Inn*, and at USO shows, singers were belting out the morale-building tune *Praise the Lord and Pass the Ammunition.*

I was still polishing my flying skills, hopping around the Pacific Northwest and the Rocky Mountain states.

December 8, 1942

> I realize that by this time you have no doubt lost track of me, but here I am in Missoula, Montana. We didn't get out of Sacramento until yesterday afternoon at 2:00. According to the weather reports it was cloudy on the way up north, but Ephrata was open. So we took off, and the last we saw of the ground was over Oroville, until we hit an opening in the overcast right over Missoula. We had gone to Ephrata, but by the time we arrived the field was closed to landing; so we went on to Walla Walla, Pendleton, and Spokane and all were closed. By radio we were told that all fields along the coast were also closed. So we headed for Great Falls, Montana, or Rapid City, South Dakota, when all of a sudden this hole appeared in the clouds and there was Missoula! It was pitch dark and never had lights seemed so good to me! We had dumped our bombs, all 4,000 pounds, in the mountains west of here to lighten our

load as our gas was running low. Also we were struck by lightning near Walla Walla and that put all but one of our radios out of commission. The snow affected our remaining set so that our reception was very poor.

We flew into a thunderstorm with updrafts and downdrafts so violent that they lifted the airplane as much as 2,000 feet one moment, then dropped it just as far the next. By the time we reached Montana, we were down to about an hour's worth of fuel. I knew that if it was not clear over Great Falls, I would have to give the order to abandon ship. The prospects of ordering my crewmen to jump into a thunderstorm above snowy Montana wilderness were grim. But once again a combination of superb navigation, this time by crewman Johnny Clark, and extraordinarily good luck spared us. His guidance led us directly over Missoula, which we would not have known had the overcast not miraculously parted. I aimed for the runway and in a few minutes we were on the ground, exhausted. The improbability of our luck became apparent when the airport manager told us that Missoula had been socked in all day, save for roughly 15 minutes that came just as we flew overhead. Within minutes of our landing, the airport was shrouded in fog.

Right now it is snowing heavily and we received a wire from Colonel Rendle telling us to stay here until he wires us otherwise.

What we didn't realize until we had been in Missoula a while was that this storm was a colossal weather system, covering nearly half of the country from the Pacific Northwest coast to the Great Lakes. In Missoula the snow just kept falling. We got telegrams from Geiger Field ordering us home, but the runways were buried under four feet of snow, with drifts piled up much higher. The airport manager kept apologizing for not being able to get snow plows to clear the runway, explaining that they were all needed to clear the streets and highways. There was no way we could take off. All we could do was to sweep and shovel snow off the airplane's wings, and start the engines several times a day to keep them from freezing up. We ended up snowbound for four otherwise pleasant days.

...I guess we are the first B-17 to ever land here. The whole town turned out this morning to view the ship. Also, the AWVS (American Women's

Volunteer Service) has taken us in hand and put cars, etc., at our disposal.

The outbreak of war had engendered a friendly, supportive community spirit across the country, and the citizens of Missoula were especially gracious. We never got a bill for our hotel rooms, nor could we get anyone to accept payment for our meals.

> ...This evening Bruce and I went to dinner at the home of the President of the University of Montana. They had several friends in and we were quite the social lions. We had roast elk for dinner, and it was really quite good. This is really a most hospitable town, and we are real curiosities to the townsfolk.

Aware that our commanders wanted us home as soon as possible, the airport manager somehow arranged for two snow plows to take a break from road work and clear a stretch of runway long enough for us to take off. While we prepared the plane, the plows wallowed out over the drifts and split up, one mushing out to the far end of the runway and the other beginning beside us at the take-off point. The plan was to plow toward each other until they met. After a few hours they were nearing a rendezvous at about the midpoint of the runway when the airport manager noticed that one was clearing the left side of the strip, and the other was clearing the right side. We couldn't use just one of the runs; each was only half the take-off distance we needed. Meanwhile more snow was imminent, and Spokane wanted us back to base, *pronto*. Necessity being the mother of invention, I had the snowplows push away the snowbank separating the two cleared paths where they paralleled each other at the midpoint of the runway. The plan was to use the first half of the run to pick up speed, then wrestle the airplane over to the parallel runway and keep going. It was not a take-off technique discussed in the flight manual. When the plows had made a big cut between the two cleared paths, we revved up the engines, crossed our fingers, and released the brakes. The airplane commenced its roll. Just before I got to the midpoint, I lifted the tail off the ground, then used the two outboard engines to swerve the plane sideways through the cut, gunning one side to turn the airplane's nose left, and then the other to straighten it out again. It was essentially like jumping the median strip on a divided highway. It worked, and we had the distance we needed. I pushed the throttles ahead to full and we were airborne over a vast world of white, headed home to Spokane.

During the course of our training the cadre of the 334th Bomb Squadron continued to build its B-17 crews up to fighting strength. Coz and I, as Flight Commanders, were not only the pilots of our own bombers, but we were also responsible for the pilots and crews of two other B-17s. We were struck by the quality of the men who reported for duty, filling the vacant slots on our crew rosters. They seemed to be the cream of the crop of available pilots, navigators and bombardiers. Many of them were experienced senior Sergeants as well. We needed ten men for each crew, which was organized under the leadership of a pilot whose responsibilities reflected the traditional role of a military ship's captain.

New bombardiers arriving for duty brought with them the top-secret Norden Bombsight, one of the most valuable technological advances of the war. Its design enabled American aircraft to drop bombs with near-pinpoint accuracy in clear weather; neither British nor German bombsights were capable of actually "aiming" bombs. In essence a mechanical computer, the device permitted the bombardier to enter data including airspeed, wind drift, altitude, and outside air temperature, and then fix optical cross hairs on the target. During this time on the bombing approach the bombardier was actually in control of the airplane's heading. The Norden computed the effects of all these variables and indicated precisely when the bombardier should issue the command "Bombs away!" At that moment the pilot resumed control of the airplane. If evasive action was unnecessary and the airplane continued on same flight path, the bombs would strike the target at the moment that the plane flew directly above it, dramatic evidence of a direct hit. Outfitted with the Norden, our bombers (we were told by our instructors) were able to conduct devastating daylight raids, while the British and Germans relied on nighttime "area bombing," a tactic that offered somewhere more safety from fighters and antiaircraft fire, but was far less accurate and considerably less effective. The device was so coveted by enemy agents that the bombardiers to which they were issued were held personally responsible for their security.

In mid-December, 1942, we were still at Geiger Field, far from the war in the frozen grip of a Northwest winter. We had progressed as far as training could take us; the next level of skill to be acquired was combat. As the snow fell and the streets iced over, we awaited orders, speculating endlessly about where they might take us. When the papers arrived, they instructed us to move the 95th to Rapid City, South Dakota. It was to be the first leg of our journey across the world to join the war.

Bob Cozens and I packed up our gear and began to lug it from the Bachelor Officers' Quarters to my old Model A, which was parked just outside the airfield's front gate. A freshly minted Army Private was on guard duty. Every time we staggered by with a load, according to protocol he shot us a snappy salute. As every salute requires one in return, each time we shuffled past him, slipping on the icy pavement, we had to put down all our gear in order to salute him. On our fourth and final transit, I was carrying two large and heavy military cloth suitcases known as "B-4 bags." As he had been taught to, the private saluted once again. I commenced to unsling my B-4s and salute him, but instead my feet shot forward. I hit the ground like a gaffed tuna and slid slowly downhill through the gate, dragging my bags with me. I sledded on my back nearly all the way to the car, not so much injured as embarrassed, my military bearing in a shambles. I looked back and saw the guard still at attention, a startled look in his eyes, his right arm frozen in salute. It was my farewell from Geiger.

CHAPTER 4

THE 95TH GOES TO WAR

We waved goodbye to Bob Cozen's wife, Pat, and she went on south to the San Francisco Bay Area to stay with her folks while we would be gone overseas. Our CO had made it clear that he thought it best that wives not go on to Rapid City with us because of the heavy training schedule planned for the Group. Before we left Geiger Field, we found out that our B-17Es that we had spent so much time in these past few months were to be left at Geiger for use in training the next batch of air crews, and all of us in the 95th Bomb Group, both the air and ground crews, would be taking the train to Rapid City, where we were to be issued new airplanes. These would be B-17Fs that we would take overseas with us.

The B-17E that we had been using for training was a formidable "Flying Fortress" with a great deal of heavy armament. However, Boeing had made over 400 changes in their Flying Fortresses to create the redesigned "F" model. Most of these were internal, but they all added up to making it a more potent fighting machine. For the latest model 1,200 horsepower Wright Cyclone engines, the propeller blades were widened to get a bigger "bite" of air; and the results were higher top speed of 325 miles per hour, a higher ceiling of 38,500 feet, a longer range of 4,400 miles and an increased maximum bomb load of 6,000 pounds. We would be getting these new B-17Fs when we arrived at the Rapid City Army Air Base in South Dakota. And, of course, we would have to do a lot of training in them before we would be ready to take them into combat.

December 21, 1942

    We arrived here at Rapid City Army Air Base by train yesterday morning from Spokane. We got on the train Friday morning and had a rather interesting trip. The scenery was lovely and I enjoyed just sitting and looking out the window.

We spent most of yesterday getting settled here on the post. From now until we leave the country we will be confined to the post except for twenty-four hours each week. We have lots to accomplish; we'll be working twelve to eighteen hours per day between flying and ground duties.

Despite the confinement, this isn't such a bad post. It has the best mess and club of any post I have hit in my travels. We are beautifully situated, scenically speaking. Rapid City Air Base is located at the eastern edge of the Black Hills, and the prairies roll away to the north, south and east.

Sightseeing by air in a B-17 became a way of life, as well as part of building flying hours and experience in these new model aircraft.

...Mount Rushmore with its great stone faces is only a few miles from here. In fact, we can see it from the post, but we are not able to distinguish the faces at this distance. However, yesterday afternoon Bob and I took a ship and looked over the immediate countryside, because we were scheduled to fly last night and we wanted to get an idea of the local flying hazards. On the course of our tour, we circled the faces very low. They are certainly impressive, to say the least. Washington and Lincoln are by far the best of the four.

Last night was a beautiful moonlit night so we took a long navigation trip: Rapid City to St. Paul to St. Louis to Omaha to Rapid City. We didn't land at any of those places, but it was quite an interesting trip. Uneventful, just a routine navigational flight.

I've been able to see a lot of new country since joining the Air Corps, and, as you said in your last letter, it is certainly not a dull life. I enjoy it very much and feel that I have profited by my many experiences. I'm looking forward to the future of going "across." It's what I joined up for and as we get into the final stages in this country it makes me itch to be in the middle of things. I have a top-notch crew and combined with our superb equipment we are more than a match for anything we shall be called upon to face.

Training, training, training and practice, practice, practice, practice. But we were all eager to learn everything we could that would benefit us when we would get into actual combat.

December 27, 1942

    We fly nine hours each day and spend another four hours in a sort of informal school learning about enemy equipment and tactics, etc. The enemy information is exclusively German and Italian, so it is pretty certain which way we will go. It's all very interesting and extremely important. We are also developing some new flying tactics for use in the Spring drive against the Continent for which we are now preparing. Besides using the B-17's for high altitude bombing, we are experimenting with really low level (like 50 feet off the ground) bombing and even dive-bombing. Both techniques seem to be quite successful. It is a terrifying thing to see a dozen of these big ships dive down from ten thousand feet and level off fifty feet off the ground, roaring at the target at 400 mph with all seventeen machine guns firing tracer bullets, and then dropping 1,000 and 2,000 pound bombs. Boy, you can't miss with that system! It is also quite an experience to ride through one of those dives, believe me!

    The more I fly this airplane, the more I marvel at its versatility. Despite its size, you can do absolutely anything with it that it is possible for any airplane to do. I'll take it anywhere through anything and never worry. The new ones we have are all equipped with all the secret British high frequency radio equipment — something more for us to learn all about.

    A pilot in one of these ships really has a job. Besides being able to fly it, he has to know all about maintenance of the airplane and be able to do it, as well as know the jobs of each and every man in the crew, be familiar with each man's special equipment and be able to use that equipment and perform the man's duties. What a mass of technical equipment is in these new B-17's we now have — almost twice the amount and types of equipment that was on board the first planes we started flying at Geiger Field. They have twice the number of guns, too.

With all the navigational training flights we were making, usually flying our plane alone, we were seeing a lot of the western states. On one of these flights we had gone out over Billings, Montana, and Pierre, North Dakota, then up into Canada over the Canadian Rockies, and then suddenly I became aware that my Number 4 engine had sprung an oil leak. It was spreading a generous amount of oil over the top of the wing and into the air, and that kind of problem can get much worse very quickly. I feathered the engine and started looking around for the closest airport. We were then over Glacier National Park. I had a quick conference with my navigator, and we decided that the nearest place we could land was the Army Air Base at Great Falls, Montana. It was a large airport, which at this early stage of the war effort was not then being used. As we approached for our landing, we could see that there weren't any airplanes on the ground. We taxied up to the control tower and parked. We all got out and then the engineer and I examined the leaky engine and quickly determined what the problem was. I then called Rapid City on our radio and told them about our situation. They responded that they would round up my crew chief and fly him up to us, but first they had to order a particular part for our leaking engine, and that part would take a day to obtain. So we found some people with cars to take us all into town for dinner, after which we came back and slept in the plane.

The next day another B-17 from some other base landed there at Great Falls. As I said, this was a very large airport covering hundreds of acres of flat ground, and ours was the only other plane there. Nevertheless, this newly arrived B-17 taxied over toward the control tower and then, for reasons I never understood, the pilot ran his wing tip right into the nose of our B-17, breaking out the whole side of our plexiglas nose cone. With all the unoccupied space in this big airport, it really surprised me that this pilot would want to put his plane in the same space I was in. Anyhow, I had to cope with the fact that flying home in that condition was not a viable alternative, as that open nose would become a big air scoop.

So I made another call to Rapid City with this latest development. By then our crew chief was winging his way toward us with the necessary engine part and tools, and it would take several days to get a replacement nose cone from Boeing. We got to thinking about what we should do about this. We hitched a ride into the town of Great Falls and went to a hardware store, where we got a large sheet of galvanized metal, some tin snips, boxes of bolts and some sealing tape. We brought all this stuff back, and with the ingenuity of my engineer and the help of our crew chief, who had fixed the oil leak, we covered the whole side of our nose cone with sheet metal and bolted it down with over a hundred bolts. Then we sealed all the edges with tape to close up all the air leaks. This took us a couple of days to complete, after which we flew back to Rapid City. Once there, our B-17 got fixed up with a new nose cone from Boeing.

Even with all the flying training and practice missions, we made time around the holidays for a bit of unwinding. And, as my letters revealed, we were all, from our top officers on down, still very young men.

> ...We really spent a WET Christmas. Partly to drown our sorrows for being stuck here away from our loved ones and partly a celebration. You see, our promotions arrived on Christmas Eve. The orders were dated December 1, but they have been chasing Bob and me around the country ever since. So we now can officially wear our silver bars. With a little luck, our Captaincies should come through sometime in February. Then there will be the BIG celebration. As it was, it was quite an affair. Bob and I stood several rounds of drinks and cigars for the boys in the squadron. Then Christmas Eve the squadron gave a big beer party for all the officers and men, and, believe me, it was the real thing. Twenty kegs of beer for 300 men! Everyone was really feeling high. Then on Christmas Day we had a lovely squadron dinner to which came Colonel Kessler, the Group Commander and his staff. It was really a wonderful affair. We even had menus, and as you could see from the menu, nothing was lacking. We had the squadron Mess Hall all decorated, so it looked very nice. Christmas night most of the officers from the 334th went into town and really had a great time of it. We didn't have to fly for two days so we really made the most of it.

Colonel Kessler was a smart old bird. We found out that, just after being assigned to form the new 95th Bomb Group, he had been moving around at Geiger watching all of the crews there, making notes, and selecting the best of us to be in his new command. We were honored and proud to have been selected. We used to call him "Uncle Ugh," a nickname for "ugly" used quietly out of his earshot because he was probably the homeliest looking man you could imagine. I firmly believe that the record that the

95th Group achieved later in combat was a result of Uncle Ugh's selectivity, enhanced greatly by the rigid and extensive training program he set up for us.

> ...This is a swell outfit from the Colonel on down. We were certainly very fortunate to get in on the organization of the Group. It is a hand-picked lot, we learned after getting here. The Colonel picked every man himself, right down to the cooks. He was around Spokane there for a month, snooping around the field and riding with all the different pilots and crews. Nobody knew what he was doing. In fact, we didn't even see the connection until our Squadron C.O. happened to mention it in a conversation the other day. It made me feel pretty good to know that we were picked for the job.

Weather conditions in South Dakota in the winter were pretty tricky and very cold. But this was to be excellent experience for what we were going to face in the coming months and years of flying.

> ...I've never seen such winds as there are around here. We always have a wind of 15 to 20 mph and it is nothing to have it increase to 60 to 70 mph. We fly anyway. It is really quite a touchy trick to take off and land in such a blow. Looking back and remembering that in Cadet School we were grounded every time the wind blew 15 mph, we recognize we've come a long way.
>
> Tonight I just landed the fastest I've ever set an airplane down. The wind was blowing across the runway — a real crosswind with gusts up to 65 mph. I was afraid to land at the usual speed of 90 mph, because if I was caught by a gust I could easily lose control. So I brought her in and set her down at 125 mph. Believe me, that is mighty fast to hit the ground! Fortunately I just greased it in to a perfect three point landing.

I was by this time realizing that I was engaged in a serious and dangerous business, and I started to express some of that realization to my parents, albeit well couched with youthful optimism.

> ...This is a funny game. After you fly these things long enough, nothing bothers you. Things that once seemed to be daredevil and

hair-raising stunts are now commonplace. This is certainly anything but a dull life.

We flew whenever the weather permitted, because the most important thing we could do at this time was to fly, fly and fly some more, so that each crew and its B-17 became one in a team that was soon to go into battle with Germans who had been flying and training since the mid-1930s.

> ...The other day we flew over the Rushmore Memorial and took some pictures. As soon as I get them developed, I'll send you some. We flew level with the faces and so close that I practically parted George Washington's hair with our wing tip. We were so close that the Bombardier down in the nose thought that we were going to hit old George right on the nose.
> We also took some pictures of my flight in formation — really close with our wings overlapping. I know it sounds like foolhardy stunts, but that is the way they fly in combat; it's the secret of their success against enemy aircraft. It is nerve-wracking work, though, to keep these big ships in position, as you might well imagine.

We continued on with a run of Arctic training. It was well below zero most of the time we were there, but we learned a lot about how to warm up the engines to get them to start, how to thaw out the frozen lubricant on the moving parts — on ourselves as well as our planes — and so on. It was early in 1943, and winter had not left us. At first, our engines would freeze up between the taxi strip and the runway. Then our maintenance guys figured out how to mount heaters around the superchargers on the engines to get them warm enough to not freeze up before takeoff.

A number of the married guys, other than Bob, had their wives come to Rapid City and stay in the local hotel, the Alex Johnson. So they had some good social life while we weren't flying. The Alex Johnson became the social headquarters for the 95th Bomb Group. With the problems we had getting our planes to operate well in that freezing weather, there were quite a few times when the only thing to do was to go into town.

Unfortunately, as we were the first large Army Air Corps group coming into Rapid City, the Base Commandant had ordered that we, the visiting combat crews, should be restricted to the Base and not allowed off Base to go into town without a special identification badge. One of our enterprising Bombardiers, Basey DeWolf, managed to snaggle such a special ID badge, get it duplicated in town, and soon, for five bucks each, almost every one of us had "special" ID badges to get off the Base. For us single guys there wasn't much to do but to go to the watering holes, which of course led to some pretty wild parties.

January 3, 1943

New Years Eve Bob and I went into town just to have some dinner as we didn't feel like celebrating, but we ran into the Colonel with our Squadron Commander and another Squadron Commander. They insisted that we come up to the hotel and have a couple of drinks with them. I don't remember an awful lot, but from what I've been told by persons that saw us, we had a wonderful time. I remember that Bob disappeared and we finally found him directing traffic at the town's main intersection. Only he was convinced that the autos were airplanes and he was calling off the runway for them to land on.

We woke up the next morning, all five of us in the Colonel's room. For some odd reason we didn't use the door, which was unlocked, but all climbed in through the transom. Boy, it was a real party. A little wild, perhaps, but better, I think, than sitting around with our thoughts.

The next day we all drove up to Deadwood and several other picturesque towns in the Black Hills. They are all old mining towns and resemble the Mother Lode towns very closely.

Right now it is bright and sunny, but we are having a cold snap — it's about 15 degrees below zero today. Except when the wind blows, it doesn't seem half as cold as 40 degrees in San Francisco. We have about two feet of snow on the ground and it is so dry that you can't even make snowballs!

We flew from six until noon today and again tonight we'll fly from midnight to morning.

All the experiences we were getting, as long as we survived them, would add greatly to our skills in handling these big airplanes. Our whole crew was getting benefits from these experiences, too. Later on, we would find that the flying we had done in the winter of 1942 had given us the skills and confidence that would hold us in good stead as we faced similar or worse challenges in the future.

> ...Had a close call this morning. Just as we left the ground, when we weren't even two feet off the ground, my #1 propeller ran away, up to 3,600 RPM instead of the 2,500 RPM for which it was set. It tipped the plane up until the right wing dragged in the snow before I got the motor cut off and the prop feathered. It was the closest thing to a crash that I've ever experienced. Thank your lucky stars that I have an excellent engineer. He was right on the prop feathering button and superchargers. Without him we probably would have cracked up. But with his aid I was able to concentrate on righting the ship and counteracting this additional power of the runaway prop while he took care of the prop and engine. We got off on three engines and circled the field and landed. A REALLY tense moment!
>
> Under separate cover I am sending you a photo of our planes in a formation. It shows Bob flying in really close formation. He was about ten feet above me and his wing tip was over my rudder. That is precision flying!
>
> January 12, 1943
>
> Glad you liked the picture! The Colonel liked it so much he has one in his office.
>
> We saw a movie the other night, *Flying Fortress*, all about the English flying B-17s. It was pretty corny. They used old B-17Bs instead of the new B-17Fs and some of the procedure and drama in the ship were pretty ridiculous. It was funny to hear the hoots and hollers from the audience that really fly these ships. They are really a most critical audience when it comes to airplane movies.

Uncle Ugh kept coming up with new training situations for us to experience. Little did we know that this next one would be an essential addition to our base of experience for the bombing missions we would be doing later in Europe.

> ...We've been running some interesting missions this past week. Day before yesterday we pulled a tremendous fifty plane theoretical raid on Minneapolis. The planes took off individually from fields all over the Midwest which then rendezvoused into Flights at various designated points; then the Flights rendezvoused by Squadrons, which then met at a predetermined spot. We flew on as a Group in formation to Minneapolis and bombed Hell out of it, theoretically speaking. Boy, the sky was black with B-17s. Quite an impressive sight!
>
> The boys are pretty hot. I had my Flight out for bombing practice the other day and we dropped bombs on a battleship target. We bombed from 25,000 feet and flew over it in formation, making five runs. Each ship dropped one bomb each time. Out of fifteen bombs dropped, fourteen hit the ship and the other one missed by only about twenty feet!

The way all this flying together produced a real team in each of our crews was one of the major benefits of our constant flying training.

> ...You are correct about my having an exceptional crew. I think they are the best in the Air Corps. I realize that that takes in a lot of territory, but I've never seen their equal. I promoted all my enlisted men the other day; now we have four Staff Sergeants and two Tech Sergeants. They all really know not only their own jobs, but each other's. Never have to tell them anything twice. They are really on the ball. I wouldn't trade them for a million dollars. They are the best life insurance I have.

The major problem with having us train out of Rapid City was the weather. At least, it certainly was in the winter of 1942-43. Too often we wasted time on the ground because it was just too darn cold to fly.

> January 17, 1943
>
> Brrrr! It's COLD! In fact at the present moment it is 37 degrees below zero! It's not bad enough that it is that cold, but the wind is blowing at 52 mph to boot. The combination is terrific to say the least. The sun is out and there's not a cloud in the sky, but we can't fly because it is so cold we can neither get the ice off the planes' wings nor can we start the engines.

We are dressed warmly, however, and the only place we feel the cold is on our faces. Your breath freezes on your face, and if you step outside for ten seconds, your face is a mass of ice. Consequently, we stay here in our quarters and play cards all day and night, aside from catching up on our sleep. It's a welcome respite from the usual routine. No one ventures out unless he has to, except to go to the Mess Hall to eat. In plain language, "it's just too damned cold!"

One night about 6 p.m. our squadron was ordered to take off and go to "warmer weather" for a temporary stay in La Junta, Colorado. We were to alert our crews and get them ready to leave at Midnight. Coz and I discovered that both our bombardiers, Basey DeWolf and Big Fitz, were not on the base. So we got a car and went into town to the Alex Johnson Hotel. We walked in and asked the desk clerk if he had seen them, knowing that they were both very well-known there. He replied, "No," he hadn't seen them. Well, I knew damn well there was only one place they could be, so I grabbed the clerk by the necktie, pulled him across the table, and said sternly "Where are those guys?" So he pointed toward the elevators and meekly said "Third floor" and gave me the room number. Coz and I went up and knocked on the door. No answer. So I knocked again and we heard some scurrying around in the room. Then I said "C'mon Fitz, we know you're there, so let us in. We have to take off at Midnight." When we then mentioned going to get the key, Fitz said "Wait a minute, we're just in here asleep" and he opened the door. Fitz and Basey were both there in their shorts. As I urged them to get dressed and come back to the base with us, I opened the door to the closet, and there were two Indian girls, stark naked and giggling, in the corner. Somewhat surprised, I told them to get clothed, too, so we could get Fitz and Basey back to the base. We made the flight out just in time and stayed in La Junta, close to Pueblo, Colorado, for about a week.

But that was a pretty exciting week. It included a cross-country training flight, an easy one in clear weather, to the southwest into Arizona and New Mexico. We had a beautiful smooth ride all the way down, and part of the way back. It was the last part of the return flight that was the real challenge. A terrific storm came over the Rockies and basically cut us off from our base at La Junta. The closer we came to La Junta, the worse the storm became. It was snowing and sleeting and we were completely in clouds, flying exclusively on instruments. I wrote a lengthy and detailed letter to my parents about this adventurous training mission.

January 29, 1943

This is the first opportunity I've had to write since I spoke with you from Pueblo, Colorado, last Sunday. Quite a lot has happened since then. No doubt you read in the papers of the terrific storm we had in that section of the country, and of the four B-17s that crashed in Colorado and Kansas that night. There were six of us in the air that night. Only two of us got down safely. It was quite an experience.

Fortunately, I had my experience of my trip from Sacramento to Missoula behind me and it stood me in good stead. Poor Woody was the least experienced pilot in our outfit. He had done all his flying in the southeastern part of the country and had never to our knowledge been caught in a snowstorm before. Consequently, when his radios went out he evidently lost his head as he spun in at a terrific speed. I saw the wreckage back at Pueblo yesterday, and there wasn't a piece left over six feet square of that big ship. The wreckage was spread over more than a mile, they told me. Naturally, all ten men were lost. It was a tough break.

As I told you over the phone, I took off Sunday, just after speaking to you, for Tucson, Arizona. We had a beautiful smooth trip down and had lunch there.

We left there in mid-afternoon to head back for Pueblo. Before takeoff I checked with the weather office and they told me that there was a big low-pressure area backed up over the Rockies, but that it wouldn't spill over before the next afternoon. In other words, that Pueblo, Colorado Springs, Denver, and Cheyenne would be open all night.

Well, we got off and all went well until we got to Trinidad, Colorado, about dusk. We had noticed that the upper winds from the west had picked up in velocity to around eighty mph and didn't especially like the looks of it. Around Trinidad, about 180 miles southwest of Pueblo, we ran into overcast and had to go on instruments. So I climbed up to 18,000 feet to assure us of ample altitude to clear all peaks. The temperature dropped so I turned on all the de-icing equipment and proceeded on to Pueblo in hopes that it wouldn't extend up that far. Pretty soon the radios all went out and I knew we were in a snowstorm. We could neither receive nor send because of snow static. It was pitch dark by this time.

We continued on our course, and at the time we were supposed to be over Pueblo, we were still in the soup. As Pueblo is at an elevation of 4,700 feet and twenty-three miles to the west the mountains are 14,000 feet, I took no chances, but turned to a heading of 90 degrees (east) and flew for twenty minutes before attempting to let down through the stuff. All this time my radioman was trying to get through and finally succeeded in getting rather poor reception for me on one set. I tuned in on the Pueblo beam and located myself — about sixty-five miles due east of Pueblo. I let down on the beam until we were only about 400 feet above the ground. I continued at this altitude and passed over the field, but it was so thick and snowing so hard that I couldn't see the field lights. I still couldn't transmit, so I couldn't communicate with the field. All of a sudden that radio went out, also. That was enough for me. I immediately turned around and headed east again to get away from the mountains and climbed until I reached 18,000 feet. I knew that the storm was traveling from west to east, and if I headed east I would eventually come out of it. So we headed east and finally broke out at about 250 miles east of Pueblo.

By this time almost all our gas was gone. In fact, I had to cut off both my inboard engines in order to conserve gas. We were going just fast enough to stay in the air and make the remaining gas last as long as possible. Two tanks were bone dry and we were ready to leave the ship if we didn't get down real soon. We had been in the air over twelve hours by this time.

We continued east and the first lighted airport we saw was Dodge City, Kansas, Municipal, a little tiny field with only 3,000 foot runways, compared with the usual 8,000 foot runways at our bases. I circled once to look it over and came in. I set the wheels down at the very end of the runway and put on the brakes. We made it! We had to, as the motors were spitting and we didn't have enough gas to go around again if we had overshot.

I immediately phoned to Pueblo and told them we had landed safely. Needless to say, Major Wilder was tremendously relieved to hear my voice. They had received reports of the crashes, but hadn't been able to identify the ships as yet.

They had no 100-octane gas available at Dodge so they had to truck it in to us from 80 miles away. It arrived the next evening.

Then when we started the engines the prop governor on #1 engine acted up. Now we had no mechanics available, so Chief Cook and

Bottle Washer Conley proceeded to remove the governor and attempt to locate the trouble. It took me from 7:00 PM until 3:00 AM to do the job, but it was a successful attempt. An amusing incident — I had to completely disassemble the thing to locate the trouble, and when I put it back together there was one spring there on the workbench. So I took it all apart again. I couldn't see any place for that spring — it must have been left on the bench before I went to work; so I reassembled the governor again, without it. Fortunately, it worked.

We were in Dodge City two days and nights before we got off. It was quite a visit. As in Missoula, we were the first B-17 that they had ever seen. People came from miles around to see it. One old duck who brought his wife and seven kids told me he had come thirty miles. The mayor and all the town notables came out. They were very nice to us and gave a big party for the crew. Unfortunately I wasn't able to be present as it was the night I was exploring the insides of the prop governor. However, I was called upon to address both a luncheon meeting of the local Kiwanis Club and a dinner meeting of the Civil Air Patrol. I'm really getting to be quite an after dinner speaker. It was fun!

When we took off, there must have been six hundred people out there to bid us goodbye! So not to disappoint them I put on a little air show. After taking off, we circled the field and dove toward it, leveling off at about twenty-five off the ground and crossed the field at 310 mph. At the end of the field I pulled her straight up and climbed in a chandelle to about 3,000 feet. It was really pretty. As we passed the crowd we could see all their mouths open and their eyes wide. It was quite a sight!

We returned to Pueblo, and picked up our clothes and the Major who had stayed behind to take care of the details of the crash. The next morning we came up here to Rapid City.

My mother wrote back to me, after reading this letter about our adventures in the big storm outside of Pueblo, that I should write a book about my experiences as an Air Corps pilot. I didn't pick up on her suggestion, however, until over 50 years later, with this writing.

February 7, 1943

The weather has been beautiful here for the past week, and consequently we've spent every possible hour in the air — twelve to fourteen each day. We cleaned up almost all of our high altitude bombing for this month with missions of several hours each day at altitudes between 30,000 and 40,000 feet. At those extreme altitudes even the slightest exertion really takes the sap out of you; and as almost all our bombing is in formation, which requires a great deal of pushing and pulling on throttles and controls in order to hold your position, by the end of the day we are all dead tired. Almost every hour that we aren't flying or eating, we spend in bed. You can readily see why.

I did get a break in the routine last week, however. Bob and I went down to Sioux City, Iowa, to pick up a couple of planes and bring them back here. That is one advantage of being Flight Commanders. You get the good jobs when they come up.

We had planned to go down in the morning and come back that afternoon. It is only about 450 miles by air. But when we got there we learned that the ships couldn't be ready until the next day. So we went into town and put up in a hotel for the night. We met some classmates of ours down there and went to dinner with them. We had a big reunion. They are in the 100th Bomb Group and are scheduled to go across at the same time as we are. That makes the eighth B-17 group that I know of that will leave this country for the same destination at the same time. I feel certain that F.D.R. and Churchill discussed our future at their little tete-a-tete in Casablanca. Though I don't flatter myself by believing that my welfare was the sole topic of their historic conversation.

Something big is brewing, though, and it's going to be fun to be in on it.

Every person on each crew had to practice his role for our upcoming combat missions. One of the most critical crew members was the Navigator, who had to do a lot of complicated calculations interspersed with feeding new variables into those calculations, while working in the nose at a small desk in front of the pilot and copilot while coping with the tremendous noise and vibrations of the four large 1,200 horsepower engines mounted in the wings.

> Yesterday was a clear, sunny day and I had to take a 1,500-mile navigation trip as practice for my Navigator. This part of this work included a study of fuel consumption at various throttle and propeller settings. We coasted along and it took about six hours. We had a really glorious trip. We left here and flew across the Black Hills and

Wyoming to Cody. Then we sneaked up the river valley between the peaks into Yellowstone Park. We nosed around the Lodge, Old Faithful and other scenic spots and then followed the Yellowstone River out to the north and went up to Glacier Park and Watertown Lakes National Park in Canada. We looked them both over and then came home. It was really beautiful. The country is magnificent and it was lovely with all the snow. It is remarkable the territory you can cover in one of these ships in a short period of time. Distance means nothing anymore. It will be quite a letdown when it's all over and I'll have to spend all day traveling a few hundred miles by auto.

Coming back from Sioux City the other day I made the 450 miles in an hour and fifteen minutes from the time my wheels left the ground until they touched down here. Not bad!

But, of course, my crew and I weren't the only ones with adventures. Bob Cozens had quite a few of his own.

...Like yesterday, Bob lost two motors on takeoff and had to fly around the field and come in and land. To make it worse, they were both on the same side. But it is the same old story. Experience counts and he came through just as though nothing had happened. There is no substitute for experience and every time you come through a tight spot you are that much better prepared for the next one.

Not only were we issued the very latest in aircraft with our B-17Fs, but in every way the Air Corps was keeping us equipped with all the aids that would improve our abilities to succeed in the combat for which we were preparing.

...The Air Corps made me a present of a new wristwatch the other day. It is a very accurately timed piece for use in navigation. In five days it has only lost four seconds!

The frequent storms and bitter cold of the winter of 1943 persisted, and the Colonel began to be concerned that this weather was keeping us on the ground too much. So he arranged for the Group to move for better weather a bit further south and east to Kearney, Nebraska. The weather continued to be too bad for flying at Rapid City and as he set up our move he gave us all a week's leave to go home. He told us this would probably be our last leave before we would go overseas.

Bob and I quickly hitched a ride on an Air Corps plane going to San Francisco, and had a short visit with our families. Bob went out and bought a train ticket back to Rapid City, but I had arranged to hitch another Army plane back; and I talked him into cashing in his ticket and coming with me. Big mistake, it turned out! The flight I had us "booked" on got scrubbed, and we had to wait for another. Finally we caught one, but it only went to Reno, Nevada. There we had to wait for other flights. The weather was so bad that both military and commercial flights would over-fly Reno, so there was no air traffic for us to use to leave there. We kept getting delayed and sidetracked, and we kept calling back to the Colonel to keep him informed as to our whereabouts. Finally, from Wichita, I believe, we had to take a train to Cheyenne, Wyoming. Then the Air Corps had to send a truck to get us back to Rapid City. By the time we arrived, the 95th had already gone on to Kearney. The Colonel had to send a plane up to Rapid City to pick us up. We were two days late, and the Colonel was not pleased, to say the least. When we landed at Kearney, we had to report to his office and receive a chewing out, professionally delivered, followed by a fine of $200 each for delaying the Group. For some reason, Bob, to this day, doesn't let me forget about this low point in our military experience.

Kearney, Nebraska, was a staging area for newly manufactured B-17s to be flown overseas to England, and, as it turned out, our jobs at this point were to take delivery of brand new B-17s and fly them to the European Theater of Operations. We were all assigned these new planes there, and, under the Colonel's direction, we had to fly them to get familiar with them. The weather at Kearney didn't turn out to be any better than it was at Rapid City, so we had to get to warmer weather if we were going to get any concentrated flying. Uncle Ugh arranged for us to move to Gulfport, Mississippi. When we arrived at Gulfport, Mississippi, it was considerably warmer. We didn't stay long there, though and after a few weeks we headed for Morrison Field in West Palm

Beach, Florida. We still had not been told where we were going from there, but by that time we were pretty sure we would be headed soon for Europe.

At Morrison Field our planes were loaded with spare parts in our bomb spaces. We were called into a secret briefing and told that we would be leaving West Palm Beach. We could not then be told where we would be going, but we were told that we could only fly from West Palm Beach separately at the rate of two planes a day instead of flying together in our squadrons. The idea behind this was that our Squadron's departure should go unnoticed with all the other air traffic coming and going at Morrison Field. The pilots would be given orders just before takeoff, but these orders could not be read before each plane was in the air leaving Morrison Field. Then, as we departed, each crewman was issued the unheard-of sum of $1,500 in cash "to cover emergency expenses on the trip." In 1943 that was a great deal of money, probably worth over ten times what it is now in 2000. With ten crewmen on a B-17, each plane then had $15,000 in ready cash on board! And we were given only very broad and vague instructions about how this money was to be used. So the pilots were made "Class B Finance Officers" and assigned their copilots to keep this cash and account for it. Because we would be stopping at civilian airports, we would be paying cash for food and lodging. Anyhow, we were well supplied with "emergency funds." As the trip proceeded, we found that we were able to define the word "emergency" quite liberally.

The idea of flying separately two planes each day rather than in large formations was to try to keep the Germans from figuring out where we were going. As we concluded later, the Germans already knew where we were headed as they had their U-boats tracking us. After we were airborne, we opened our orders and found that we were indeed going to England, that we were to maintain radio silence while airborne, and that our route was to be south to Borinquen Field, Puerto Rico; then to Atkinson Field, British Guiana; then south of the Equator to Belem, Brazil; and from there to Natal, Brazil. We would cross the Atlantic at its narrowest point, from Natal, Brazil, to Dakar, Senegal, in North

Africa. The trip there went on to Marrakech, Morocco, and from Marrakech over the sea to avoid Spain, a neutral but Fascist "Axis" country, to finally arrive in England. These bases we went to in Central and South America were civilian stopover stations for Pan American Airways. Some, but not all, of these bases were equipped to handle the refueling and minor maintenance of our aircraft. We took our time to enjoy each of these places along the way. We visited the beaches and the bars; and we had the money to go "First Class" when we wanted to. None of us was in any hurry to leave these resort-like places, either; but we did, sometimes reluctantly.

Things went pretty well for our particular crew until we approached Belem, near the Equator and the mouth of the Amazon River, when we encountered a torrential rainstorm the likes of which we'd never seen before, and I personally have never seen again. We couldn't even see the nose of the airplane, the rain was so heavy! We flew around blindly in circles for about twenty minutes, and finally the rain subsided and we landed. We stayed there overnight and left the next day. We wanted to get out of Belem before the next rainstorm hit!

From Belem we went to Natal, Brazil. Natal was quite a bustling place. It was a takeoff place from the Americas across the South Atlantic to Africa. There were a lot of different airplanes coming and going. Most of the airplanes there were flying east across North Africa to India. This was an established supply route to the Far East. Natal was chosen for our planes to use because it was thought that our two planes per day would hardly be noticed by the Germans and their agents. We were still trying very hard to keep the Germans from knowing what we were up to in moving all these Flying Fortresses to England. When we got to Natal, no matter where we had come from or how we had got there, we could see that this was a bustling community. There was even a 24-hour poker table going on continuously, with cash table stakes that took $1,000 to get in. The $15,000 that each plane had been issued covered well this "emergency." After all, there were no explicit rules about how this money was to be used. As I said earlier, this was a pretty loose arrangement. To jump ahead for the moment, when we finally got to England, nobody there would accept the return of this money from the pilots, despite our various attempts to return it. No one in the American Army establishment in England knew anything about this money or wanted to be responsible for it. No one had ever heard about this arrangement. And nobody would take the money. The last I knew, no one ever collected any money. I really don't know where it went or what happened to it. Eventually, I guess it got distributed within the crews and anyone who knew about it got shot down or shipped home later. The money just disappeared!

While we were at Natal, we got our airplane engines tuned up and our planes serviced, and we got ready to go across the South Atlantic. When we left West Palm Beach, our planes had been well-loaded in the bomb bays and every other open space with spare parts. This was how we were to replenish stocks of spare parts to service our planes in England. We were actually carrying about a plane and a half, with all these spare parts! So we were fully loaded when we took off. In leaving Natal, we also had our fuel tanks filled to the top, because we had a long and uncertain flight ahead of us. Natal, incidentally, was where the famous aviatrix, Amelia Earhart, flew from to reach Dakar only six years before us on her "round the world" flight that ended with her disappearance over the Pacific Ocean.

We took off from Natal at about ten o'clock at night. With all that weight, we staggered off the end of the runway, but we got airborne, skimming over the beach at the end of the runway and rising gradually over the ocean waves below. We rose gradually up to about 3,500 feet altitude. We were only about two miles out from Natal when we suddenly heard a big KA-BOOM! With a big flash! Just one shot, but obviously some German submarine crew had been ready for us with their deck cannon. Fortunately, we weren't hit and we got out of their range, but it scared the hell out of us! That one cannon shot brought us all into the sudden realization that we were getting into war, and that there were people out there who were going to do their best to kill us. That realization was like a splash of cold water that woke us up to reality.

Anyway, we proceeded on our flight. It was uneventful until we got to the Equator. There is a perennial strip of air roughness right around the Equator. We hit it, and it was really ROUGH air! Some of our planes, I later heard, were in this strip of violent roughness only a few minutes. We were in it for forty-five minutes. It turned out we were right in the middle of a real thunderstorm. I thought the airplane was going to tear itself apart. We had St. Elmo's fire dancing all over the airplane; it was like a ring of flame coming from the edges of the wings and propellers. Every once in a while a big ball of fire would run right up into the cockpit. It scared the daylights out of me! That was the most frightening experience I'd ever had. Besides the fireworks, there were terrific updrafts and downdrafts that jolted us about. We would move violently up for 2,500 feet, and then violently down for 2,500 feet. We went on big swings up and down and to the sides. I put the flaps fully down and then I even lowered the landing gear to stabilize the plane and hold down its movements. Then there were these great hailstorms that hit us. The hailstones sounded like gravel hitting a tin roof. Later when we had landed, we saw that the de-icing boot had been ripped off the tail, most of the paint was gone from the leading edges of the wings and really the whole surface of our plane had big dents from the hail hitting it. It looked like someone had been hitting it all over with a ball peen hammer. Big bumps all over!

We finally emerged from this big belt of instability. Our compass was operational, but due to the required radio silence we had had no radio communication since before the hailstorm. We had to determine our position, and the only way we could do it was by astral navigation, by "shooting the stars." After we had gone through this bad weather for some time it was still dark. We checked our gas, and found that the combination of fighting the turbulence and flying with the flaps and gear down had caused us to use an exceedingly large amount of our gas. My navigator, Jimmy Warner, took a shot on the stars and then announced to us that we were beyond the point of no return. And here I was looking at our gas gauges and figuring that there was NO way we could get all the way to Dakar with the gas we had left! So the first thing we did was to cut back to the minimum power setting to stretch out our usage of gas. Then we started throwing out all our spare parts to lighten our load. By the time we had unloaded all those spare parts, we were in daylight with no way to triangulate the stars for navigation. So I just pointed the plane to the east. We looked at the map and saw that about 200 miles south of Dakar was a French patrol station with a landing strip. By the time I was reading "Empty" on all my gas tanks, Big Fitz, my Bombardier, called up from his station in the nose of the airplane saying he could see the coastline of French West Africa. As we came close to the coastline we followed it in a northerly direction, and pretty soon we spotted what looked like a landing strip.

In a situation like this, when a plane needed to make an unscheduled landing at an Allied airport, there was a formal procedure to make an approach, from a certain direction with certain radio signals, called "IFF" to identify whether the plane was friend or foe. Well, I didn't have time or gas to make anything but a direct approach, and we didn't want to break radio silence with all the German U-boats in the South Atlantic. We saw the runway, and I decided I had to just go straight in. I did break radio silence to call them, but I never received any answer. As we came close, I saw that this was a new temporary airstrip made up of steel mats. I didn't make the designated approach, but went straight in and landed. We didn't see a soul around, but we did see a couple of British patrol planes parked near the landing strip. As we landed on these steel runway strips our plane rattled a lot, but that was minor compared with the rough ride we had been through. As I got to the end of the runway, I slowed the plane down and then turned it around and — suddenly — phfutt — ALL THE ENGINES STOPPED. We were totally out of gas! We had JUST made it!

Well, then we all piled out of our B-17 and walked into the flight control shack, which turned out to be the headquarters for a British RAF submarine patrol group. They were all busy having their morning tea and didn't hear us land. They were delighted to see us and were very hospitable, and they invited us to join them for tea, as we told our story of our harrowing flight. When we got to the end of the story about our plane running out of gas at the end of the runway, they graciously helped us gas up the plane so we could continue our journey to Dakar. We didn't stay long there, but after getting gassed up, we flew on to Dakar. We made the short trip to Dakar in less than two hours, and landed there a little after noon. Then, since we had been up all night with our transoceanic flight, we proceeded to go to bed for an afternoon nap. After we got up we went to the mess hall and had a bite to eat; then we decided to go to town and "see the lights." Dakar had just been "liberated" by the Free French from the Vichy French. So the town was being run by a whole new regime. All the officials governing Dakar were members of the famous French Foreign Legion, wearing their colorful uniforms — red hats with stiff brims, khaki pants and blue tunics. They looked like they had just come off the stage of a musical comedy.

Dakar was sort of a desolate town, right on the beach with palm trees, typical of an equatorial beach town. But there were some bright lights, which we proceeded to investigate. One brightly lit place with the brightest of the bright lights had a big sign that said "Madame Lilly's." It looked like it had a bar and we could hear music coming from it, so we went in. As we entered this building, we came into a large open area that was apparently a restaurant with lots of people eating and drinking at tables. Looking up, we saw that it was a two story building with balconies all around the open area, with people coming and going up and down the stairs and in and out of the various rooms off the balconies. And there were lots of good-looking women there who were obviously not native Senegalese. The natives of Senegal were generally black as ebony and quite tall; many of them, both men and women, were over seven feet tall. These gals were lighter-skinned and shorter than the native girls. Suddenly it occurred to me that, by God, this was a whorehouse! They had all these beautiful women there and they were imported from somewhere else. Probably Europe. Anyway, the ten of us sat down at a couple of the tables and ordered French champagne. We had lots of money to party. The evening wore on and the band played. Our group was having a great time, getting louder and louder.

A detail of American Army Military Police were making their rounds of the hot spots frequented by French and American servicemen, and Madame Lilly's was definitely one of the places they visited. As our crew got more into champagne and became louder, the detail of four MP's and their officer, a major, stopped by our tables and cautioned us to remember to be gentlemanly and "keep it down." They came by several times, and each time our crew became one octave louder. Finally the major came down to our group and said quite forcibly that we HAD to quiet down! Whereupon Big Fitz, who was feeling no pain, picked up a champagne bottle and hit the major over the head! It dropped him on the floor, even with his metal helmet on. All the MP's were startled and went to the aid of their major. I shot up from my chair and exclaimed, "Let's get the hell out of here!" I quickly gathered up our group and got them all outside. We were in luck, as an available two-and-a-half ton Army truck was just passing in front of Madame Lilly's, and we all piled in. We got a ride back to the base, but we were greeted by the Base Commandant, a colonel, who met us as we arrived. He ordered us all out of the truck and made us line up and stand at attention while he lectured us about what we should and should not do while visiting a foreign country. In the middle of this dissertation my copilot, little Joe Noyes, an 18-year-old Warrant Officer — a baby-faced kid who looked about 12 years old — stepped forward and said, "Excuse me, Colonel", then he turned around and stepped about three strides, and relieved himself. Then he turned around, buttoned his pants, stepped back into line at attention and said, "Carry on!" The Commandant then went on with his lecture about what we had to do and the responsibilities of presenting a proper image of the United States Army and how we musn't act in a manner that brings disgrace to the U.S. Army Air Corps. Then he stopped and asked us "Do you gentlemen have anything to say for yourselves?" Whereupon, little

Joe, smiling as proud as he could be, stepped forward and said, "Sir, I have only to say to you that we have conducted ourselves like officers (HICCUP!) and gentlemen." At that point even the Base Commandant had to laugh, and he said "You guys go to bed, get a good night's sleep, and be out of here by 12:00 noon tomorrow!"

So we did just that and departed the next morning for Marrakech. We left about noon. Our route took us over the sands of the Sahara Desert, and even from an altitude of about 10,000 feet we could see three camel caravans winding their way across the sands, generally headed northwest. As we approached Marrakech we could see snow on the Atlas Mountains, which was quite a contrast from the barrenness of the desert below us. It reminded me of flying in Southern California westward towards Palm Springs; it was generally the same type of terrain. We had to fly through a pass in these mountains to get to Marrakech, and when we did we suddenly came into a totally different and beautiful view of a verdant valley, with orange groves and cultivated fields with irrigation. This was the city of Marrakech in Morocco. It appeared to be a well-ordered and agriculturally-prosperous area. We landed there, and headed for the place where we had been told was the best hotel in Marrakech. It was the Mamounia Hotel. What an interesting place! It was a world famous resort hotel, and reminded me a great deal of hotels in Honolulu with its beautiful shaded gardens, except that the architecture was Moroccan, very much like we have in California. It had a large veranda where the main attraction was to sit and drink. After we got cleaned up we spent an hour or two on the veranda drinking iced muscatel and enjoying the scenery.

After a few drinks we decided, my crew and I, that we would investigate the Medina, the native quarter, which in some Moroccan cities would be called the Casbah. We had hired three horses and buggies to take us, but the buggies were too wide to pass through the narrow crowded streets of the Medina. We had to get out and walk to enter that area, so we asked the drivers to wait for us at the gate. The Medina was a walled city with an arched gate as an entrance. There were narrow streets but no sidewalks and those narrow streets were filled with sheep, goats and camels, as well as people. The businesses and shops were all transacting their business in the open air in literally "holes in the walls." The street was quite crowded with many people, so I had to keep counting our crew to be certain that all ten of us were still together. Suddenly I took another count, and I could count only nine of us instead of our crew of ten. We were all in khaki uniforms, so it was fairly easy to spot all of us. I counted again — only nine — we were short Big Fitz! Nobody saw him leave. So we started backtracking our route and opening doors we had passed. I kept calling for Big Fitz. Then we came upon an open door where we could hear guitar music. We proceeded on in, and found a beautiful garden with fountains and a large patio surrounded by verandas. Big Fitz was up on a veranda and responded to my calls saying "Hey, Moo! (my nickname due to my cowboy history) C'mon up here!" Fitz had done it again! He had a special talent for this! We went to find him there, sitting in a big bunch of large colorful cushions with three lovely young girls and a guitar player, looking like a sultan. He was in Heaven! How he could work his way into this intimate scene so quickly I never found out. But I didn't want us to get delayed there past dark, not in the Medina. So I put on my stern voice and ordered him to come back out with the rest of the crew. We finally exited the Medina together and got into our horse-drawn buggies. We all arrived back at our hotel by dusk.

Just as we arrived, the Sultan with all his dignitaries were parading in the street in front of the hotel on their way toward the mosque for evening Muslim prayers. The Sultan was dressed in a colorful blue tunic and tan breeches, with a white turban and a large white cape. With great formality, he rode a beautiful large gray Arabian Barb stallion accompanied by a troop of 20 to 25 Moroccan cavalry, also riding beautiful matched gray Arabian Barb horses. The cavalrymen all wore white turbans and flowing white capes over sky blue uniforms and highly polished boots, with magnificent long curved scimitars at their sides. From a minaret in the background we could hear the strong, loud voice of the Muslim calls to prayer. It was all extremely impressive and very colorful. We were fascinated. It was like something out of the movies. We just stood and watched this procession as it passed, after which we went back into the hotel for a delicious multi-course dinner elegantly served. We stayed at the Mamounia Hotel a couple of days and rested as we enjoyed the resort atmosphere. We didn't return to the Medina, however. This hotel, as I told you, was world famous, and it still is. This was Winston Churchill's favorite resort retreat, before and after the war. Fortunately we had the cash available to stay there — our emergency funds, you know. And they were pleased to have us stay there.

Despite our new found pleasures in Marrakech we had to get on with our journey. Our route was to go out over Casablanca and Gibraltar and then fly over the ocean to the west of Spain and Portugal. We took off at night, being careful of German patrol planes and U-boats, as this was their space. We flew parallel to the coast of Portugal, and then veered out to the west, finally making landfall at Penzance, in England. We looked around searching for an airfield that resembled the one on our map, but, not finding one, we went ahead and landed at an airfield just north of Penzance. We were greeted by a bunch of very angry looking English farmers with pitchforks. They thought we were Germans invading their island! These people had never seen an American airplane before and didn't recognize the markings on it. We were the first Americans they had ever seen. I had to do some good talking to get these farmers to put down their pitchforks and let us go. We were able to refuel there near Penzance, and then we flew on to Bassingbourn near Cambridge where the RAF had a depot. It was a big grass landing field, something we had not experienced before. We left that same afternoon for Alconbury, where the 95th was to assemble. There we were met and welcomed by Uncle Ugh Kessler himself. Our plane and crew were among the first two or three to arrive at Alconbury. Eventually all of the 95th aircraft and crews made it safely there.

Security requirements now restricted me from writing my parents the details of my doings as I had done in the past.

April 18, 1943

> Well, here we are, finally "somewhere in England."
> We had a wonderful trip across. Saw a tremendous amount of strange and fascinating geography as well as coming in contact with all sorts of different races of people. It was most interesting. We also hit about every type of weather possible from perfect right down to what under ordinary circumstances would be considered unflyable. But we hit the bad stuff about a thousand miles from land and had to plow right on through it. Just chalk it up to that much more experience, which it was and then some! All in all it was a grand trip and I wouldn't have missed it for the world. I thoroughly enjoyed ALMOST every moment of it.

There were some interesting things I had to say about the new — to me — country where we were now based. Housing and basing the 95th Bomb Group in England at this time was a "work in process."

> ...We're very comfortably situated here. Have a swell field to operate from. We are all quartered in these large homes a couple of miles from the field. The accommodations are really fine and the mess is excellent. Everything we could possibly want and lots of it.
> We have all been issued bicycles to get around on as everything here is disbursed to the Nth degree. So we go merrily rolling along on our bikes, and at night cycle into town to the village pub and drink ale. Quite a life!

I found that I couldn't discuss our bombing missions because of the censorship of all overseas mail; so I wrote about what we did on our off-duty time, our living conditions, people we knew and the like.

> ...Last night, being Saturday, I went in to London for the evening. It is an amazing city. Despite the blackout it is extremely busy and gay. There are practically no signs of the bombing left in the main part of town. I stood in Picadilly Circus for fifteen minutes and saw more people that I knew and hadn't seen for some time than if I had stood at Powell and Geary in San Francisco. In fact, almost every place I stopped on the way over I met someone I knew.

> A good many of my classmates and former squadron mates from Spokane are over here. The other night I ran into Keith Beirlem from San Jose who was up at Spokane with me. He was with Clark Gable who is his top turret gunner!

Clark Gable was quite a guy. He was officially an Intelligence Officer, a "ground pounder," but he wanted to get into combat and the way he did it was to volunteer to fly with several of the crews as a top turret gunner. As far as I know, he was never injured doing these hazardous missions.

> ...It is Spring here now and the countryside is really beautiful. It is a good deal like the California coastal country. The climate is the closest thing to San Francisco that I have ever seen. It's just lovely with all the blossoms and green fields and trees. Every inch of the country is cultivated; instead of fences dividing the fields there are Hawthorne hedges which are very pretty.

Uncle Ugh wasted no time in getting all of us in the air practicing the skills we would need in actual combat. He was a stickler for flying in close formations, reminding us again and again that a B-17 alone was no match for a squadron of Me-109s or FW-190s, but that a flight of three or four B-17s flying in a close formation could defend themselves by their concentrations of firepower. A squadron of three or four flights would be even more defensible. We also had to practice our timing in everything we had to do: preparing for takeoff, taking off and assembling into a group formation, changing directions in a group, preparing to bomb, and so on.

At last on May 13 we went on our first actual bombing mission.

We received the "alert" the evening before the mission. It was posted on the Bulletin Boards in front of the Officers' Mess and the Enlisted Men's Mess. The tension began to build and the crews assigned to the mission conjectured about where we would be sent to bomb. We were all eager and anxious to get going into combat, after all the training we had received to prepare ourselves for it. But there was fear in the back of it, too, because real combat was unknown to us. Many of us played poker into the early hours because we were too excited to sleep. Early the next morning — very early, at 3:00 a.m. — all members of the crews assigned to the day's mission were wakened. We got dressed quickly and got ourselves to breakfast — today we were treated with real eggs, which we found out was something saved for those men going out to do battle with the enemy. Then we got into GI trucks that took us to the preflight briefing. The briefing room was like all the other buildings we used, a Nissen hut made from corrugated sheets of metal imported from the States and assembled and erected on the base at Alconbury. We all filed in, where the folding chairs were set up like an auditorium, with a couple of tables with chairs at the far end. There the wall was covered with a large map of Europe. A long piece of red string hung down from a pin placed on Alconbury. When the room became filled by all the men in the crews participating in the mission the sound of excited, nervous voices raised the sound level pretty high.

After we were all inside the briefing room, Colonel Kessler walked in with his staff, including Captain "Jiggs" Donohue, the Group Intelligence Officer, and all the Squadron Commanders. Our Squadron Commander, Captain Al Wilder, walked in with them. The room suddenly hushed as we all came to attention. Then the Colonel spoke, first saying, "At ease, gentlemen." We sat down and he told us that today we were going to use the training he had insisted we get, only this time in real combat. Today we would meet the Luftwaffe. Live ammunition would be fired at us! Today we must remember all those vitally important lessons we had been taught. Then he turned the meeting over to our Group Intelligence Officer, Jiggs Donohue, a tall, dignified middle-aged gentleman who stood and approached the map with a dramatic air. He announced, in the stentorian tones of a Shakespearean actor, that our target today would be, as a part of the Eighth Air Force's overall mission of putting the German submarine fleet out of action, a necessary preliminary to shipping millions of tons of supplies, arms, and men from America to England, the submarine pens at St. Omer on the French coast. With that he went to the big map and pulled the colored cord across the map, pinning it at various points to illustrate the route we were to follow toward our target. Then he proceeded to brief us on the details of the route and the proper headings to be used by our navigators. He told us the assembly procedure and the ultimate cruising altitude to the IP, the Initial Point where the approach to the target begins. He gave us the specific description of the aiming point for our bombs. He told us the types of bombs we would be taking to drop on the target, and why they were chosen for this particular job. The latest weather forecasts for the route of flight and over the target area were then shared with us in detail. Next he gave us as much information as he could from British Intelligence about what kinds of enemy resistance we could expect — the types and numbers of German fighters near the target area, the types and numbers of anti-aircraft guns that would be trying to shoot us down, and the like. Questions? We had none, being already saturated with data that we hoped we would remember at the proper time. Watches were synchronized to ensure that we could assemble the Group with to-the-second precision. With that, the pre-mission briefing was concluded.

Given a final admonition to keep our formations tight, protect each other from fighter attacks, and fly straight and level between the IP and the point of bomb release, we were asked to leave and board GI trucks that were waiting outside to take us out to our individual B-17s at their hardstands. The ground crews were already there loading the bombs. The gunners were given their machine guns; and we were all given our parachutes. We boarded our planes and went through our pre-flight procedures, including last-minute bladder relief. All in the proper order, we gunned our engines and moved our planes into takeoff position. It was just about dawn and we could see that the skies were going to be clear as we took off. We proceeded through our proper ascending procedures, climbing up to the assembly point at a rate of 500 feet per minute. At an altitude of 20,000 feet we assembled the squadron, and the squadron assembled itself into the group formation. As we crossed the English coastline I checked my watch and, yes, we were right on schedule. The 95th Bomb Group continued on, as briefed, to our target area of St. Omer.

We assembled 19 bombers over East Anglia, but four dropped out with various mechanical problems. The remaining 15 of us went on over the French coast. We spotted the target, the submarine pens, and then kept on going, as briefed, 25 miles further east where, at the designated spot, we turned around 180 degrees and headed west toward the IP. About 20 to 25 enemy fighters, probably a couple of squadrons, came up from their fields in the French countryside to attempt to drive us off, but they seemed unable, or perhaps unmotivated, to penetrate our formations. This was our first meeting with the Luftwaffe, and it certainly was a thrilling experience. As we neared the submarine pens on the coast, German 88 millimeter flak guns started shooting at us, but their bursts of shell explosions missed all of us.

The submarine pens were covered docks excavated into the coastline of the Atlantic Ocean and fronted by heavy locks. The subs would float through the locks into these pens under their concrete roofs, the locks would close and the sea water pumped out, and there the maintenance crews would work on the subs, readying them to head back out to sea. We dropped bombs on the tops of those pens hoping to put them and the subs inside them out of commission. After we dropped our bombs we headed back over the sea to England. All of us returned safely from that first mission of the 95th Bomb Group, with only a few holes from bullets or flak. After the horror stories we had been told by some of the "old hands," we felt pretty lucky. That first mission was really a very gentle initiation to aerial combat in Europe; none of us were really tested yet for what was to happen only a month later at Kiel. Aerial reconnaissance photos taken after that raid told us we hadn't done much damage to the sub pens, even though we thought we had hit them squarely.

We kept after those sub pens in future missions. The next day we went a little further north on the coast and hit sub pens at Antwerp, followed by Emden, even further north, on May 15. Then our Allied Intelligence reports told us what was really happening.

The reinforced concrete roofs over the sub pens were 30 feet thick and impervious to our bombs! Our bombs weren't making a dent in them! So we changed our aiming point and started aiming at the locks in the sea outside in front of the pens. That worked much better. The German Navy couldn't use those pens when their locks were disabled, so their subs weren't able to enter and be maintained for return to sea duty. In subsequent missions we continued to strike against the German submarine pens, wrecking the locks at the pens at Lorient, Flensburg, Emden again, Rennes, and then Wilhelmshaven.

German fighter resistance was stiffening noticeably, and on the second mission, to Antwerp, we lost our first plane with its crew. Ten of our crewmen didn't come back. Ten empty bunks that night, ten men we knew, we had stood at the bar with, we had trained with, were gone forever — the reality of what war meant was suddenly made clear to us. From then on we were losing planes and crews on each mission. We had become the targets for a group of experienced fighter pilots we called the "Abbeville Kids" because they were based near the French coastal town of Abbeville. We learned we could always recognize them by the distinctive yellow and black checkerboard designs painted on the noses of their fighter planes. Very quickly the Abbeville Kids became old and respected acquaintances. They were good fliers, having the benefit of experience in Germany's air battles since the attacks on Czechoslovakia and Poland; some of them had even experienced flying fighter planes in the 1936 Spanish civil war. They were one of the Luftwaffe's elite units.

In retrospect, these first missions were "warm-ups" for us. Later, when we had to take our bombs deep into Germany, we would run into much more dangerous resistance from very large groups of experienced fighter pilots. Here on these coastal missions, we sharpened our skills and discipline in formation flying and timing. And our strict and conscientious commander, Colonel "Uncle Ugh" Kessler, kept us practicing every day whenever we were not on a bombing mission. Unfortunately, the 94th, 96th and 100th Bomb Groups were not as conscientious about training and practice and perfecting these vital skills; later on they paid a heavy price in combat casualties.

I guess that I, like a lot of my fellow Americans overseas for the first time, facing the possibility that they might, just might, become a casualty of this war we were engaged in almost daily, started to think about our mothers when Mothers' Day approached. In case — the remote case — that I might never see her again, I thought it wise to tell my mother a few heartfelt sentiments.

May 9, 1943

> It will be close to next Mothers' Day by the time that you receive this, but, at any rate, I want you to know that I am thinking of you today. Not that I don't think of you every day, but today has special significance. I've spent quite a bit of time since I've been over here thinking of the past from childhood forward. Not because I'm homesick because I'm certainly not that. But I guess the particular situation we find ourselves in lends itself to such retrospective thinking.
>
> You know, Mom, I don't think that I ever fully appreciated you until after I had flown from under your protective wing, and then spent these last twelve months or more in musing over the past. When I lived at home and was dependent upon you, everything was taken for granted. I never fully realized what great sacrifices you and Dad made in order that Bill and I might get all the wonderful advantages that we received. I didn't notice how you kindly and gently molded, or attempted to mold, me into a decent sort of man, or how your really great Motherly wisdom was all the time preparing me to face the world. Honestly, as I look back on it now I'm ashamed that I didn't recognize it at the time and show proper appreciation and better results. Honestly, Mom, it just appalls me what a brat I must have been. However, I realize all these things now, and while late, it isn't too late. When this war is over, I shall most certainly repay you, and with fullest interest!

And, of course, I went on to tell her about the life outside of combat that I was experiencing here in England.

> ...There isn't much I can tell you about our doings over here. You read the newspapers and they do a pretty good job of keeping

everyone informed on the Eighth Air Force activities. In fact, on most of these airdromes there are as many newspaper correspondents as pilots. We practice an awful lot. Lots of formation work and bombing. Also, trying to improve our techniques and develop new ideas. Bob Cozens, Harry Stirwalt and I and our Bombardiers just returned from a week's stay with another outfit a few miles from here where we worked on some new techniques.

Outside of flying, life is swell. As I had previously written, we live very well. When off duty, our time is our own. We get down to London every weekend and into Cambridge several times each week.

Cambridge is a beautiful town. The colleges are magnificent and there is quite a bit of life in the town. It is so funny to me having been at such an informal college as Stanford; all the students here wear black gowns and the seniors wear mortar board hats. They wear them all the time, on the streets and even out at night.

Noel Coward has three plays going in London. So far I've seen two, both very good: *Blythe Spirit* and *Present Laughter*, in which Mr. Coward appears. We try to go to the theater every time we get to the City, but the ticket situation is very difficult.

Things are very expensive over here. You spend Pound Notes, worth about four dollars in American money, like dollar bills, especially in London. Liquor is awfully hard to get, so we drink our beer like real "limeys." It isn't bad stuff after you get used to it.

We play a lot of poker and my luck has been good. So far I've sent about $300 home to the bank. I hope my luck holds up.

In reading of the great Allied air successes in Africa I've come across the names of a good many classmates, several of whom I saw when I was down there. Those boys certainly had a picnic, with no fighters or flak to speak of. Wait until they come up here, if they do; they'll find things quite a bit different. No getting away from it, though, they really did a job in Africa. It won't be long now, I imagine, before the fireworks will really start. Then, oh boy!

This is without a doubt the worst country in the world to fly in. First off, the weather is terrible. Secondly, you never know where you are. There are no landmarks to rely upon. Every town is exactly like another. Each has a railroad, highway and stream and all are laid out in the same pattern. So you get a radio bearing from the field you wish to land at and fly the course they give you. You can go right past the place because it is camouflaged or there about six airdromes within a radius of five miles; so you invariably land on the wrong one. Boy, I can't tell you what a pleasure it will be to fly in the United States again! That will be the day!

Alconbury was the takeoff site for our first seven bombing missions. Then, late in May 1943, the 95th Bomb Group was moved to Framlingham, Suffolk County. This was another temporary base, where we stayed for about three weeks while new facilities were being constructed for us at Horham, also in Suffolk County. Horham was to become our permanent base in June 1943.

CHAPTER 5

THE BATTLE OF KIEL

In May of 1943 the 95th Bomb Group was participating in almost daily missions over Europe, mostly over France and western Germany. My crew had been experiencing a pretty good run of luck in dodging the bullets and flak that might have been etched with our names. Between missions, I wrote in my breezy, upbeat style, which was the way I kept my parents informed that I was still alive and well.

May 16, 1943

It's been a week since I last wrote, but we have been so terribly busy in the interim that I haven't had much time. When I did have the time I was so tired I just went to bed instead.

We have had over a week of really beautiful weather and, as you no doubt know from the newspapers by now, we have been active every day. That means getting up at 3:00 every morning we go "out," and at least three hours on oxygen during the trip. That alone is enough to exhaust you without the excitement that accompanies the preparations and, later, the actual fighting.

Really, though, it's lots of fun, and the boys in my crew all fight and beg to go on every raid. They are all eager and spend their time on the ground cleaning their guns and equipment, and making certain that all is in perfect working order. One trip across the Channel is enough to impress the necessity for the above on their minds.

Boy, Mom, no air battle manufactured in Hollywood can approach the thrills and sights of the real thing. They rarely last over a half-hour but the thrills of a lifetime are contained in that short space of time. It's a funny reaction. I sit there flying my airplane and I can hear and feel all my boys' guns going off. The only enemy planes I can see are those coming from the front or side, and I can see whatever flak appears in those regions. Yet you sit there quite calmly and watch the flak explode around you in little puffs of black smoke and you see the fighters dive on you from the front — sometimes as close as fifty feet — with all their guns firing. But you sit there watching it all as if it were a movie. Then a couple of hours after you are back on the ground it begins to dawn on you, and it is then that you get properly scared.

The German boys are marvelous pilots and really have guts. Of course, some are better than others. But the best ones will dive on our formations and attempt to break them up by flying right between our planes! It must take great nerve and skill with all our guns firing at them. Yesterday I had a fellow come right at my nose with all guns firing. He turned off at about forty feet from me and as he pulled away he waved. It is a funny sort of game.

Toward the end of May it was apparent to our commanders that we needed a break from the game, and they granted us all a three-day leave. Bob Cozens and I hustled off to London, racing around to take in that great city's trademark tourist sights, including, of course, the changing of the guard at Buckingham Palace. We couldn't get hotel reservations, so we stayed at a hotel then being run by the Red Cross, an organization I had never appreciated until I arrived in England and saw how hard they worked to accommodate those of us far from home. In London they had taken over at least a dozen large hotels and set them up as residences for transient servicemen.

...Two or three at the most to a room and usually a bath for every two rooms, all for sixty cents per night. Also they serve the best meals in town at forty cents per. Besides, they have large recreation bureaus set up for the men. The same is carried out in every major town in England on a corresponding scale.

The Red Cross also have traveling "clubmobiles" — coffee and donut cars — that visit every camp several times each day and night, driving among the boys who are working "on the line" and distributing free coffee, donuts, cigarettes, candy, gum, etc. It is all certainly worth the contributions that you at home are asked to give. And believe me, it is all well spent.

My Captaincy came through in March 1943, but the paperwork had been mailed to Rapid City and I was already at Palm Beach. The documents never caught up with me, so I was a captain without portfolio. Without my order number, I couldn't claim my pay.

So in the interim I just have to wait until the order catches up to me or I can get another copy from Washington. I'll have quite a bit of back pay piled up when I finally get hold of it.

As May turned to June, the 95th Bomb Group was temporarily stationed at Framlingham, in Suffolk, awaiting the completion of a permanent base under construction some 12 miles west at Horham. From Framlingham we continued to go out on bombing missions as often as the weather and operating conditions permitted. In May we made six raids in an eight-day period. In the following two weeks, we went out only a couple of times. My crew was remarkable in that they never seemed to get infected with the "fear of aerial combat" bug, and for this I was very thankful. My crew at this time included: Joe Noyes, copilot; "Big Fitz" Fitzgerald, bombardier; Elias Bacha, navigator; Art LaJoie, radioman; Howard Medford, top turret gunner; Tom McArthur, ball turret gunner; Bill Cochrane and J.L. MacNeil, waist gunners; and Ray Provost, tail gunner. An outstanding crew, one and all!

June 2, 1943

Contrary to your belief, the strain isn't terrific at all. In fact, there just isn't any strain. The more frequently we go out, the happier the boys are. It is only when we have to sit around on the ground and have nothing to do but play cards that everyone gets bored. That is about the extent of the strain.

It was the custom for each crew to name its plane, just like all ships have names. The one we took across the Atlantic in April and flew on the first couple of missions was called *Trade Wind*. But by this time *Trade Wind* was no more. Some German fighter pilot got our range and made a strainer out of her. Besides better than a hundred holes in her, a 20 mm cannon shell exploded in the tail right where the stabilizer joins the fuselage and shot away most of the elevators and rudder. What was left was almost useless as the control cables were cut. But we got them patched in flight with some wire from the radio aerial and flew her 300 miles home. How we made it, I don't know, but we did. Poor *Trade Wind* became a salvage heap. Happily, none of us was even scratched! Our new ship, which we were given in May, we called *Blondie*, named for a cocker spaniel puppy, not Dagwood's wife. In early June, *Blondie* was still doing fine, even though she had to have a new right wing after an anti-aircraft shell went through without exploding, leaving a hole about the size of a wash basin. Outside of that, she hadn't even been scratched. It absolutely amazed me what these ships could take and still fly. I saw it with my own eyes and I still had difficulty believing it.

The 95th Bomb Group continued to be under the command of Colonel Alfred Kessler, known to us fondly but quietly as "Uncle Ugh."

> ...Colonel Kessler seems to be quite proud of his boys. We have shown up the older groups out here pretty badly in bombing accuracy, gunnery, and all related subjects. We set a record for bombing on one raid where we all dropped our bombs in an area less than 700 feet in diameter. Needless to say, that target will be out of commission for some time to come. Also, we have the lowest loss rate in the Eighth Air Force, and the highest record of enemy planes shot down. Let's hope we can continue as we have started.

What I did not tell my parents, however, was that overall the Eighth Air Force was sustaining inordinately heavy losses during our daylight raids over Germany. The chain of command, from Framlingham to the Pentagon, was alarmed and determined to reduce these losses. The question was how. Attention focused on the way we flew into battle — the positioning of our bomber groups in flight, arrangements known as formations. Curtis LeMay, then a colonel and commander of the 305th Bomb Group, had developed a formation for B-17 raids known as the "combat box," designed to reduce the bombers' vulnerability by grouping them together in a way that afforded optimal mutual protection and concentrated fire power. LeMay's method was also self-repairing; if airplanes were diverted or lost, the remaining planes repositioned themselves according to a pre-arranged plan to preserve the integrity of the "box." LeMay developed his formation flying

An aerial view of Horham Air Field. The living quarters are not shown; they were off to the right of this picture.

Eighth Air Force

This beautiful, stately mansion, containing over 200 rooms, was known as Elveden Hall. The Eighth Air Force 3rd Air Division used it as a Headquarters.

Eighth Air Force

The Ground Crew readying our B-17 for the upcoming mission.

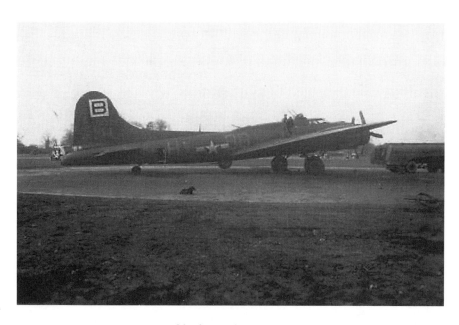

My plane and my puppy.

In combat at last, as we were "welcomed" by a German ME-109 fighter trying to knock us out of the sky.

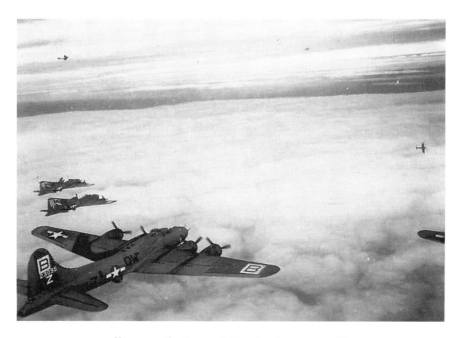

Here come the German fighters in a head-on attack!

The day after Blondie II's *narrow escape from Kiel, I returned to the barley field and took a picture of her in her final resting place.*

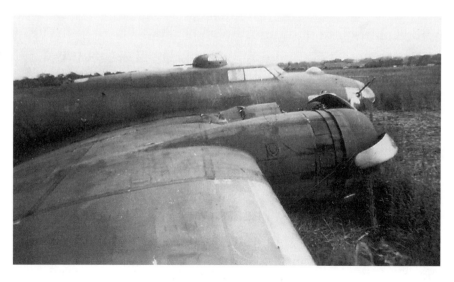

Another photo of Blondie II *after her last landing in England. Neither picture shows the crack where she broke in two behind the wing.*

techniques by personally commanding his first 25 combat missions in late 1942 and early 1943 in a process of trial and error under fire, incorporating the best ideas expressed by crew members during post-mission critiques. Though nothing could guarantee our safety, the colonel's tactics added a welcome measure of it. He valued good advice, regardless of who offered it, and made reviews a standard procedure at his air bases, when he was assigned to the 4th Bomb Wing as CO in June, 1943. In spite of his innovations, however, the loss of men and aircraft remained at a level deemed intolerable. Something more had to be done.

The Army Air Forces looked to Brigadier General Nathan Bedford Forrest III, the namesake grandson of a Confederate Cavalry officer whose dash and bravery distinguished him in the Civil War. He was known by his contemporaries for winning battles by being "the fustest with the mostest." Like his celebrated grandfather and father, General Forrest was a West Point graduate, but instead of an infantry career he chose to become an Air Corps pilot. He rose rapidly through the officer ranks and won his general's stars at age 38. Although he had never flown in battle, he had somehow acquired a reputation as an authority on air combat formation flying. The high command sent him to us directly from the States. Upon his arrival, General Forrest unveiled a new formation system that he had designed on his own and ordered us to use instead of LeMay's combat box. When its structure and procedures were described to us, I sensed immediately that the concept was flawed, a clear case of untested theory flying (literally) in the face of experience that refuted it. I was not alone in my skepticism; it was shared by virtually all the pilots and crew members of the 95th Bomb Group. This being the military, however, the general prevailed.

June 8, 1943

> Hello again. Nothing new to report as we have been inactive for quite a few days now. We just sit around and get fat. If the weather permits, we fly a short practice mission. Yes, even over here we still practice. We experiment with new methods and perfect the old ones.

You know the old proverb, "Practice makes perfect." Well, it seems to be bearing fruit. The Group has just received THREE commendations for outstanding work on three particular missions. One target in particular they had tried to hit on seven previous occasions with no success. We got it the first time. It was an exceedingly difficult target, a single building. Yet its destruction immobilized a great and highly important submarine yard. Naturally the Colonel is quite proud. He just beams at everybody these days. In fact, a good many of the silver star boys have been around to pay their respects and all seem exceptionally jovial.

I believe you can send things over here without a request. At any rate, you can send me a box of chocolate bars. Candy is really scarce over here and we never do see the American variety.

General Forrest ordered a practice mission for June 12, 1943, and we dutifully rehearsed his new system. Despite our doubts, the run-through went smoothly enough. But practice is not combat. After the exercise, we delivered our airplanes to the ground crews, who as usual worked through the night to prepare them for the next day's mission. We went off to the mess hall, still privately expressing doubt that the new formation offered the defensive and offensive advantages of LeMay's battle-tested tactics.

Every evening after dinner, if we were not scheduled to fly, I joined some of my fellow flying officers for a poker game. The regulars included Bob Cozens, my friend from flight school days, "Big Fitz" Fitzgerald, my bombardier, Coz's bombardier, Basey DeWolf, and pilots Bill Lindley and Grif Mumford. On one such occasion, General Forrest asked to join us. The game was still in progress at midnight when an alert was sounded for a mission briefing at 5:30 a.m. The word was that it would be a "maximum effort," meaning that every available aircraft and crew would participate. Speculation on where we might be headed got the adrenaline pumping, and the poker game continued through the night and through breakfast as well, breaking up when the briefing commenced in the darkness just before dawn. General Forrest proved a pleasant enough poker partner, but the egotism he displayed in forcing his untested formation theories on us worked against his playing. Fitz, a shark with cards, cleaned him out along with most everyone else at the table, and as often happened scooped up the pot. He was said to have a substantial bundle of British banknotes stashed somewhere.

The sky was still dark when the briefing began. Our Group Intelligence Officer, Major Jiggs Donohue, emphasized the strategic importance of our primary target, a submarine base at Kiel on the eastern coast of the northern German district of Schleswig-Holstein, on a narrow neck of land shared with Denmark. Although the Allied invasion of Europe was still a year away, the Allies were already laying the groundwork for it. Our role in that preparation was to cripple the German U-boat fleet by destroying its bases so that supplies and troops could be shipped across the Atlantic without falling prey to the German torpedoes that were savaging our Liberty Ship fleets. Because shipping loss rates were so high in the first months of the war, the Allied high command assigned the highest priority to the destruction of U-boat bases. This mission, said Jiggs Donohue, was vital to its achievement. He announced that we were going to put up the largest number of aircraft flown in combat to date, and that this mission would be the USAAF's deepest penetration into Germany so far. Our forces, however, would be split between a flight of 80 B-17s from the First Bomb Division that would bomb the port of Bremen and hopefully divert German defenses, while our group of 76 B-17s would fly further east to attack the sub pens at Kiel.

The 95th Group would lead the formation slated for Kiel, followed by a 95th "Composite Group," the 94th and 96th, and a Composite Group made up of elements from three other outfits and under my command. I was assigned four aircraft from the 95th and 14 bombers recruited from the 94th and 96th. These were to be crewed mostly by airmen flying together for the first time, many of them survivors of crews that had suffered combat losses. The Mission Commander was my former student in Ephrata, Major Al Wilder. Grif Mumford was assigned to command the 95th Composite Group, riding in the right-hand seat in Bill Lindley's aircraft.

Grif Mumford, whose first name was really Harry, though he never used that name, was one of Uncle Ugh's original cadre in forming the 95th Bomb Group. He was a Captain, having gone through his early Army career and flight training before the war started. His initial assignment was Commander of the 412th Bomb Squadron; in July he became Operations Officer of the 95th Bomb Group; and that was when he and I became good friends.

Bill Lindley was another appealing guy, a standout even among strong personalities, of which we had quite a few. (Grif Mumford has recalled that when Bill was in his younger, wilder days, he was Grif's "burden," much like Big Fitz was to me.) Bill was from Mississippi, and spoke with a broad Southern accent. Once, when we were ordered into an unexpected, quickly called mission briefing — we had been relaxing with drinks — Bill listened intently until the target was announced, then stood up and announced in his unique Ole' Miss drawl, "Ah just loves to kill those Nazis!" Like a true good old Southern boy, he loved to fish and was an integral part of our group who traveled north to Scotland. He could spend the whole day fishing, and would have if we had let him. We dubbed him "Catfish." He was a character. In Ian Hawkins' book, *B-17s Over Berlin*, Grif alludes to one time in England when Bill consumed more than his share of after dinner toddies and ended the evening by shooting out all the lights in his quarters with his .45. Apparently this was not officially noted — or perhaps it was and deemed a sign of nascent leadership ability. In any case, Bill survived to become a Major General in the Air Force, for a time commanding the Air Force in Viet Nam, and was eventually honorably retired.

My Composite Group would bring up the rear, a position we referred to as "tail-end Charlie." It was not a desirable place to be, for airplanes in this wave were the last to fly over the target and typically were the ones subjected to the most aggressive attacks by German fighters. The Luftwaffe's standard tactic was to dive from above, bypassing the leading Flying Fortresses to concentrate their fire on those at the rear of the formation: airplanes without the benefit of protective firepower from trailing bombers. In a departure from usual procedure, General Forrest himself would accompany us, flying as an observer at the front of the 95th in the point position aboard Harry Stirwalt's airplane. Then came the bad news: because Kiel was beyond the range of our fighters, we would have to fly into Germany and back without defensive escorts.

Takeoff was scheduled for 7:30 a.m. from Framlingham. The 95th commenced its departures first, at one-minute intervals. A dense cloud ceiling hovered at about 1,500 feet, but the low fog that sometimes slowed our take-offs was absent. I took off in my airplane with the four 95th Group bombers in my command. We climbed up into the soup, and kept climbing on instruments. At 6,000 feet we broke out of the gray void into a beautiful clear morning. We continued to climb, at 500 feet per minute, flying a prescribed route over Peterborough where we rendezvoused with the 14 additional B-17s assigned to my Composite Group.

Meanwhile the 94th had encountered trouble getting airborne — a delay on the ground while topping off fuel tanks. It was the kind of hitch we dreaded because, while usually mundane, they had the potential of triggering a domino effect, expanding exponentially into major problems that decreased our margin of safety. This one was already showing every indication of going in that direction. The 94th's tardiness in getting off the ground put it far behind the lead planes in the 95th, immediately stretching out our defensive formations which above all were to be kept compact. It was not in accord with even Forrest's theories, let alone LeMay's. My group, being the last and having no protection from behind, was now even more vulnerable due to the excessive gap between us and the groups ahead. There was another unexpected development: a 100 mph tailwind at our cruising altitude of 26,000 feet. During the time that elapsed between each successive group entering the powerful jet stream, the bombers already riding it eastward were pulling away from the others below at a rate of about one mile every 36 seconds. The formation was already being stretched out dangerously far.

We proceeded on a northeast heading, the 95th at the point position, Grif's 95th Composite Group second, followed by the 96th and 94th, with my Composite Group bringing up the rear. Our course routed us over the North Sea, directly over the island of

Helgoland about ten miles off the north German mainland. As we approached the island, I could see the lead formation some two miles ahead of us — too far. High above them I saw a dark swarm of enemy fighters approaching from the east and closing fast. There must have been about 200 FW-190s, Me-109s and Me-410 twin-engine fighter-bombers. As we closed, they took on the appearance of a huge flock of black birds. They were headed directly toward the lead formation. Suddenly the Germans split up, about half heading straight for the lead B-17s, the rest, true to form, vaulting over them and heading for those of us at the rear. I felt a sense of dread as the weakness of our position became obvious. The attenuated formation gave us the appearance of stragglers, always the Luftwaffe's first targets.

The Germans raced astern, turned around, and fell into single file parallel to us but out of the range of our .50-calibers. It was obvious that they were going to attack us systematically, according to a pre-arranged plan, sizing us up first. They abruptly accelerated en masse, pulling ahead, still in single file, leaving us far behind them — one mile, then two miles. They kept going. They were about ten miles beyond our formation when they banked into a tight arc and headed directly back at us, flying four to six abreast, closing with us at an air-speed of more than 700 mph and intending to hit us head-on. They shot through our formation, machine-guns firing, their wingtips missing ours by only a few feet. They were superbly trained. We knew that their intent was to break up our formations. As they flashed by, they immediately rolled upside down and went into a so-called "split S" maneuver to avoid being hit by our tail gunners. Simultaneously, from about 1,000 feet above, the Me-410s were dropping time-fused bombs in an attempt to blast us out of the sky.

The two waves of German fighters regrouped to concentrate on those of us farthest behind. They swarmed around us, attacking from every direction. We noticed that some had brightly colored checkered noses, the emblem of an elite group of battle-seasoned fighter pilots we called the "Abbeville Kids." They were joined in their attack by members of Hermann Goering's "Flying Circus" based on Helgoland Island. We could not have met more ferocious resistance. The first wave of fighters to attack my airplane were four Me-109s. They bore down on me from dead ahead, each firing six machine-guns, our guns firing back. It was a heart-stopping sight, watching them close on us. There are no foxholes in the sky! No amount of evasive action was possible within the formation that could prevent our catching many of their bullets. As they veered past on both sides, I heard my left outboard engine cough and saw that its two topmost cylinder heads had been shot away. Their severed necks were spraying brown plumes of oil. I feathered the prop, turning the blades edgewise to the windblast to prevent them from windmilling and continuing to pump out oil.

Looking out the other window, I saw that my right wingman was on fire, his bomber slowly drifting out of formation. At about 50 yards distance he exploded. Immediately my upper right wingman moved in to take his place. I looked left to scan my group and saw that my left wingman was hit. He dropped out of my sight, and as we were all trained to do, my upper left wingman quickly took over the position. The attacks on my group continued as the German coast slid beneath us, but we stayed on course for Kiel. We estimated we were facing about 150 fighters. They were like a swarm of small swift birds attacking large slow ones, swooping down to peck at us again and again.

Our plan was to proceed across this narrow arm of the German mainland and out over the Baltic Sea, then turn around and start our westbound bombing run at the Initial Point or "IP." We noticed, however, that the lead group, with Harry Stirwalt's plane in front, was continuing past the IP. We assumed the mission commander wanted to give the rest of us time to close ranks and get our formations into tighter defensive positions. Stirwalt flew east some ten miles beyond the IP before commencing his turn and leading the 95th around. We later realized that his idea had been for those of us strung out behind the 95th to turn sooner, so that all of us could have come together on our way back to the IP, forming a tighter defensive formation. Perhaps he tried to radio us. The intensity of the German attack, however, made complicated radio conversations impractical and on occasion impossible — we were too busy defending ourselves. So Stirwalt's plan, if it had been radioed to us, went uncommunicated. Instead of perhaps turning sooner, which might have enabled us to fall in close behind the 95th on its return, we dutifully followed them out ten miles past the IP, forfeiting our last and best opportunity to close the distance between us.

We were still flying at 26,000 feet. As each of us commenced our 180-degree turn to start back toward the IP and begin our bombing runs, we suddenly found ourselves pushing against the gale that had sped us across the North Sea. The impact of the headwind felt like a huge ocean wave slamming against the bow of a ship. Although our engines were throttled up and the speed of the airflow across our wings was unchanged, our actual ground speed was abruptly reduced by some 200 miles per hour — the loss of the 100-mph tailwind plus the 100-mph push against our nose. The visual sensation in the cockpit was as if we had slowed to a near-standstill. I looked down at the Baltic Sea; its rippled surface barely seemed to move beneath the wing. There was nothing to do but to hold our heading and commence the run on Kiel, battering against that jet stream, with our formations still strung out. The sight of us would probably have brought tears to LeMay's eyes.

Moments after the lead formation dropped its bombs, German fighters attacked its point man, the B-17 piloted by Harry Stirwalt and Mission Commander Al Wilder and carrying General Forrest in the jump seat. I couldn't see what was happening — they were too far ahead of me — but others later told me that they thought they had seen some crewmen bail out. One of them was the navigator, Willard "Bill" Brown, only a few years out of Yale where he had been a captain of the University's swimming team. They saw Bill jump from the crippled bomber and fall away out of sight, his parachute unopened. Although watching them was not my most urgent duty at the time, I thought I saw their plane dive down and level off as if they had regained control. I heard later, though, that moments later Harry's airplane exploded into flames and fell from the sky, taking him with it along with Al and General Forrest, whose first day in combat, it turned out, was his last.

Meanwhile, we were engaged in a furious battle to avoid the same fate. Our radios crackled with shouting voices, warnings, questions, reports of damage and casualties, and occasionally the frantic announcement of an aircraft being abandoned. About a mile ahead of us, Coz, as Deputy Commander of the 95th, had moved his plane into the lead position, replacing Harry Stirwalt and assuming command of the mission. Besides Harry's plane, the 95th had lost two others. I could see from Coz's movements that he was trying to regroup his remaining bombers.

Peering through the laminated glass of the cockpit window, I saw Me-109s bearing down on us in an aerial game of chicken, their 7.9 mm machine-guns emitting the telltale flashes that meant they were firing. With them came FW-190s with their 20 mm nose cannons firing slugs as thick as a thumb. High above, so far without hitting us, the Me-410s were still dropping time-fused bombs in our midst. The Germans came singly, and sometimes two to six abreast, from all directions. The noise of our guns mixed with the cacophony of voices on the radio and the explosion of the aerial bombs from above.

The Germans kept pounding us, attacking again and again. We were now in a particularly vulnerable part of the operation, on the final approach to the target, a time when the bombardier had control of the airplane. This, however, was the purpose of the mission, hitting the target, and only success could justify our losses. My copilot, "Little Joe" Noyes, and I sat in our seats as Fitz, crouched in the bombardier's area in the nose below and in front of the cockpit, guided us toward the target. There was nothing to do but wait and watch out for attacking fighters. Once our run commenced, we were instructed, by Colonel LeMay in no uncertain terms, to hold to our course no matter what. I peered out my side window to check the position of the other airplanes in our group. There weren't any. I asked Joe to check on his side. Nothing. I switched on the intercom and called Ray Provost, our tail gunner, and asked him how many of our planes he could see behind us. His reply came quickly. "None, sir."

A bullet shot through the fuselage with the awful popping sound that hits make and struck the inflation button on our escape raft. The raft, as it was designed to do, popped out of the right side gun opening and inflated, hanging there on a mooring line about 25 feet long, thrashing around like a captive kite and causing a tremendous drag that pulled the airplane to starboard. Our radioman, Arthur LaJoie, whipped out the hunting knife he always carried and cut it free. The raft blew back and wrapped around our tail, flopping wildly for a few moments before slipping away and disappearing astern.

We were still minutes from the target, unable to take evasive action and thus a sitting duck for the fighters and anti-aircraft batteries on the ground. Then suddenly, WHAM! We took a stunning cannon shell hit on the forward left side into Fitz's area that threw the airplane sideways. The Boeing's Plexiglas nose cone blew away, turning the forward crawl space between the nose and the main body of the fuselage into a wind scoop, slowing us even more. We virtually stopped; it felt like we had hit a brick wall. The 200-mph gale shot Fitz and navigator Elias Bacha back down the tunnel like BBs in a peashooter, slamming them against a bulkhead. They were on their backs, disoriented but miraculously unhurt. Fitz had lost his hat, so he grabbed his steel helmet and strapped it on. He looked at me, shook his head, and crawled back up into what was left of the nose. His Norden bombsight was still there, undamaged, so he resumed command of the airplane to complete the run on the U-boat base. The fighters kept attacking, sending slugs through the wings and fuselage. The B-17 was full of holes, but it kept flying.

As we approached the drop point, it occurred to me that, given the extensive damage to the airplane, the bomb-bay doors might not work. When I flipped the switch, however, they fell open. Fitz shouted "Bombs away!" and released our bomb load. The airplane was instantly about 5,000 pounds lighter. But when I hit the switch to retract the bomb bay doors, they didn't budge. Between the dangling doors, a green patchwork of farmland far below slid slowly by. The German fighters kept up their attacks. Fitz and Bacha crawled up to the blasted nose where a pair of .50-caliber machine-guns remained on the right side. Fitz got down on his knees and gripped the firing handles while Bacha sprawled behind him, holding Fitz's legs to keep him from falling out of the airplane. For 20 minutes he fired away at our attackers, with Bacha holding him in place.

I tried the intercom. Dead. I looked back into the communications area behind the bomb bays and saw that our radio equipment had been shot to pieces. Wires dangled like discarded spaghetti. We couldn't communicate with other aircraft. That our radioman had survived was miraculous. Art LaJoie's small space was shredded by bullets, but so far he didn't have a scratch on him. He could have been killed instantly by any one of the dozens of slugs that ripped through there — but he wasn't.

In an attempt to distance ourselves from the wasp's nest of Germans, we all pushed our yokes forward, and the entire force, what was left of it, dropped into a thin cloud layer at about 3,000 feet. As we passed over the western coast of Germany, the Luftwaffe fighters broke off their attack, probably because they were low on fuel. For some reason, our lead group, now far ahead and nearly out of my sight, deviated from their designated return flight path, which would have continued to take us out to sea, and instead flew south, skirting the shore. That change in flight path, we later learned, alerted the German coastal radars and brought more Luftwaffe interceptors up to attack us from bases along the Flemish coast and the Frisian Islands.

Our B-17, however, was badly wounded. We were losing altitude and speed. We had to let the rest of the aircraft go on ahead. We were now the straggler, the wounded aircraft that the Luftwaffe always made a point of destroying. Their bullets kept slamming into us. Then a cannon shell hit the number three engine — the inboard power plant on the right — where its streamlined housing or nacelle connected it to the wing. The shell severed the mounts that anchored the engine, and the huge Wright Cyclone separated from the wing, leaving a gaping hole. We were still over German soil, probably a little more than 300 miles from home, with the North Sea ahead and only two engines still running. We were firing back aggressively, but we were taking an unbelievable number of hits. I had no working instruments — no compass, no airspeed indicator, no fuel gauges — nor could I transfer fuel from the disabled engines' tanks. Reckoning from the position of the mid-day sun, I pointed the airplane in what I took to be the direction of the English coast. Damage to the airframe, however, including our smashed nose and the huge cavity where the number three engine had been, was causing a tremendous drag.

Our crippled plane droned on as the fighters continued shooting at us. Occasional gaps in the clouds afforded quick glimpses of the ocean. I could see whitecaps, and estimated our altitude at about 2,200 feet. We were still nearly 300 miles from England. My tail gunner was a compact fellow named Ray Provost. For the last two hours he had muscled his twin .50 caliber machine-guns back and forth in a determined frenzy, firing some 8,000 rounds at the Germans as they streaked by. He was exhausted. Worse, the cocking handle that reloaded his weapons was jammed, and the guns' breeches and barrels were so hot he could not touch them.

Tracer bullets began to flash past our nose, fired from below and to one side. I turned the airplane toward the attacker; the idea was to close with him and reduce as quickly as possible the distance between us, thus shortening the time he would have to shoot at us. I found myself facing a red-painted Me-109, the trademark color of Goering's Flying Circus. His guns raked the bottom of our plane from the ball turret to the tail gun, starting a peel of aluminum skin that continued along the entire belly of the fuselage, exposing the airplane's aluminum frame, from stem to stern, to the ocean below. One of his bullets struck the receiver of the tail guns and then fell into Ray's lap, spent. A second round hit the jammed cocking handle on his machine-guns, knocking it free and enabling him to fire them as the Me-109 passed. He hit it squarely at a range of only about 30 feet. The Messerschmitt exploded into flaming pieces of red metal that cart-wheeled down into the sea. The Me-109 was part of a final wave of a dozen coastal fighters. Like the others they came at us from every angle. One of them hit my number two engine, the inboard power plant on the left side, killing it and bending its mounts so that it dropped down from the wing at about a 20-degree angle. The control lines were severed, so I couldn't feather the prop, which along with the bent-down engine nacelle increased our drag and slowed us even more. We now had only one engine to carry us across some 150 miles of ocean.

My plane looked like a sieve. There were holes everywhere. Why we didn't explode or simply fall apart I'll never know. Despite our predicament, however, my gunners had stayed focused on the battle and were hitting their targets, sending three of Goering's fliers spinning down into the sea. Three others began to trail smoke from their exhausts and sped away. That left five still shooting at us. They kept up their attacks, but failed to inflict much more damage. Then, abruptly, they all ceased fire; apparently they had finally run out of ammunition. Then something strange occurred. Despite having lost at least four of their own, they circled us, waggled their wings, and waved, saluting us, before breaking off and heading back to their base. That is how things went sometimes in war back then.

All this time we had been on a westerly heading over the English Channel. Our one remaining engine was at full throttle, but the damage to the aircraft — the peeled skin, the sagging engine, the gap in the wing where the engine had ripped free, and our blunt nose — were creating so much wind resistance that we were gradually losing altitude, a few feet every minute. We flew on, hoping that our one remaining engine would have enough fuel. To lighten the load on that one engine, we threw overboard everything we could do without on the flight home, including our machine guns, ammunition and spent cartridges. Our radio compartment was a shambles, full of wrecked equipment, so we removed and threw out all of it we could pry loose. Once over water, Fitz threw out his secret Norden bombsight. Everything loose had to go. An hour passed. Then another half hour. The airplane droned on west. As long as it kept on flying, we were determined to head for home. The thought of ditching in the cold waters of the North Sea was extremely unappealing and downright frightening. That wounded B-17 seemed as determined as we were to make it back to England. Finally we spotted a faint low darkness on the horizon: England!

We were now only a few hundred feet above the waves. As we neared the coast, I could make out a wide beach bordered by a row of tall trees planted as a windbreak for a grain field just beyond. I considered putting the bomber down on the beach, but my rudder and elevators were not responding, and I feared that if I tried to bank the plane in its damaged condition, to turn parallel to the strand, I might not be able to level it out, and we would catch a wing and flip. The key to surviving a crash-landing was to keep the airplane on an even keel. I decided to try to coax the plane over the treetops and put it down in the ploughed field beyond. As we approached the shoreline, still sinking, I saw that the treetops, perhaps 75 feet high, were now about 15 feet higher than we were. If we flew into them it would be catastrophic. I pushed the yoke forward, putting the airplane into a shallow dive to gain air speed, adding just enough momentum to allow me to pull up and, in a sort of ski-jump motion, vault the treetops which brushed loudly against the bomber's belly and wings. At that instant, our one remaining engine began to miss. It was out of gasoline.

The engine quit, and we bellied into the barley field, sending up a huge plume of red dust. Because the bottom of the airplane had no skin, the red dirt blasted into the crew spaces. I mistook it for smoke and believed the plane had caught fire. I shouted at the crew to get out and heard a chorus of voices affirming that they were on their way. Joe unbuckled himself from the copilot's seat and darted into the narrow crawl space behind our seats, an escape route too small for me. My only way out was a small side window. I squirmed into it and wriggled out, certain the airplane was about to explode, and I fell onto the wing. When I looked at the porthole later, I could not fathom how I had been able to get my 230 pounds through it. I looked around for the others, shouting at them to get out of the airplane and stand back. I was still under the impression that the red dust had been smoke when I became aware of a little blonde-haired girl, nine or ten, standing beside the airplane and gazing up at me with bright blue eyes big as saucers. Before I could say anything to her — I was as surprised as she was — she turned and ran away. No wonder. I guessed she probably thought we were Germans.

We didn't know where we were. Since 1940 the British were so fearful of an invasion and so certain one was imminent, that they had removed all the directional signs from the roads in hope of hampering German troop movements. Gradually, however, local folk began to appear at the edge of the field. Some tramped through the barley sprouts for a closer look. They told us we had come down near the farming hamlet of Rackheath, which meant nothing to any of us. Later when we found out that this hamlet was close to Norfolk, we knew where we were. Someone had summoned the Royal Air Force who said they would send a lorry to pick us up. I regretted the damage to the barley field until someone told me that the beach, which had looked so inviting, was sown with land mines. If I had put the airplane down there, we would have blown ourselves to pieces.

The people who streamed out from the village were jovial and kind, full of warmth and hospitality. It felt wonderful to be alive. After the adrenaline rush of the last few hours and our delight in having survived, the enormity of our good luck began to sink in. Not only had we survived, but we had managed to find our way back to within several miles of our base at Framlingham. I gazed at the wreckage of the B-17 that despite so much horrific damage was able to fly its last 500 miles. The Boeing's back was broken; it had cracked in two at a point behind the ball turret where a cannon shell had smashed through some key structural members. Most amazing of all was that we had not suffered a single casualty, let alone a serious injury. Our two waist gunners, Bill Cochrane and J.L. MacNeil, had a few scratches, but despite the thousands of bullets and shells that came our way and the crash-landing, no one had been seriously hurt.

It was well into the evening when the lorry from the RAF arrived. We said farewell to our airplane, piled into the truck, and waved good-bye to the townsfolk of Rackheath as we were ferried back to Framlingham for a late supper generously supplied by the mess crew in appreciation of our successful return. We had missed the usual post-mission interrogation, nor was I asked to turn in our regular written mission report. On our absence, our report was filed by someone else, and it barely covered the fact that we made it back to England.

After dinner, Fitz and I walked back to the Officers' Quarters, and found Basey DeWolf sitting on his bed with his back to us, sobbing and shaking. He had been drinking. In his hand was a stack of five-pound notes, poker winnings, including his take from the game the night before the Kiel mission. Fitz and Basey had a pact that in the event one of them should fail to return from a mission, their combined poker winnings would be divided, half going to the survivor and the other half split between the survivor and the lost airman's mother. Basey, in his cups, his speech slurred, was sorting his stash into two piles. "One for Fitz's momma, and two for Basey DeWolf... one for Fitz's momma, two for Basey DeWolf..." Fitz walked up behind him, grabbed him by the collar and threw him across the room, feigning outrage that he had caught Basey splitting the pot prematurely. Basey happily threw himself at Fitz and they grappled for a moment in jest, then embraced each other warmly. We were grateful beyond words that we had survived. The next morning, every member of my crew showed up ready to fly again.

At breakfast, however, we learned the depressing facts about the raid on Kiel. It had not gone well. Of the 76 B-17s that started out, 16 soon aborted their flights for various reasons and returned to base. Twenty-two of the remaining 60 airplanes were lost in combat — a casualty rate of 37 percent, the worst for American bombers so far in the war. Ten of those were from the 95th Bomb Group. The greatest losses were in the 94th, whose airplanes had been spread out the most. Changes in the command structure inevitably followed. Curtis LeMay was made CO of the 4th

Bombardment Wing on June 18, 1943, and promoted to Brigadier General on Sept. 28, 1943, and to Major General on March 3, 1944. Curtis LeMay reinstated his combat box and replaced and transferred the colonel who had commanded the ill-fated 94th. On September 16, 1943, "Uncle Ugh" Kessler was promoted to 13th Bombardment Wing Commander. I became commander of the 334th Bomb Squadron. Several weeks later, Bob Cozens was designated Squadron Commander of the 335th. I had flown to Kiel as a First Lieutenant; a few weeks later, I was wearing the "railroad tracks" of a captain.

June 26, 1943

> Colonel Kessler is to become General Kessler, as he will be promoted to be Commander of our 13th Bombardment Wing, a much bigger job. He's still one of us, however, and spends a good deal of his time with us. He is one of the finest men I've ever been associated with. I admire him tremendously. He claims we are the best outfit in this theater and the records bear him out. It's all due to his efforts and the training he put us through back in the States. He had marvelous foresight, for we are so far better equipped to meet the situations that confront us than the other Groups that it isn't funny. As long as he is up there the 95th has nothing to worry about; he'll take care of his boys.
>
> I turned my crew over to my copilot, little Joe Noyes, a youngster of nineteen and I'm certainly proud of him. He has done a swell job. The other day I flew with Bob when we went into the Ruhr and Little Joe flew off our wing. He really stayed in there all through a tough fight and every time I looked over he was laughing at me. He is my boy and I'm mighty proud of him. He is so little that he sits on a parachute and THREE cushions to see out the window. He is the favorite of the whole group. To look at him you would think he was about fourteen! If I have done nothing else in this war, I have turned out a damned good pilot in Joe Noyes.

It was some months before we learned what had become of Harry Stirwalt's navigator, Bill Brown, the Yale swimming team captain who was last seen plummeting toward the Baltic Sea, his parachute unopened. It turned out that he had fallen some 20,000 feet before pulling his ripcord, and by virtue of his conditioning and swimming skill he managed to survive in the chill ocean waters until he was picked up by a German fishing boat. He would spend the next two years in a German prisoner-of-war camp, the only known survivor of the explosion that had claimed Harry Stirwalt, my first student and friend Al Wilder, and General Forrest.

> ...We have had several wonderful missions in the past two weeks on which our bombing was exceptional, as the papers no doubt have said. It is also pleasing to us that we haven't lost a crew since June 13, which is the day I landed in the grain field. I'll never forget that day as long as I live! I'll never see a fiercer battle than that one!

Some memories fade over the years, but I had never forgotten the sight of that wide-eyed little girl in Rackheath who scampered away from the wreck of our bomber in the moments after our crash-landing. I had not seen her again in the several hours we lingered in the farming village before the RAF hauled us back to base. There were so many people I met back then who had drifted away, whose addresses had been lost, or simply forgotten. Then, one afternoon in 1993, the telephone at my home on the San Francisco Peninsula rang. I answered and heard a British-accented female voice ask if this was "Captain Conley." I said, "well, not anymore," but confirmed that I was indeed Harry Conley. "Weren't you the pilot of the plane that landed in our field in 1943?" I was silent for a moment — stunned. It was the little girl, now in her mid-sixties. Her name was Daphne Dennis. The excitement of that summer afternoon — our "invasion of Rackheath" she called it — had stayed with her, and as she went through life, marrying and raising children, she had from time to time wondered what had become of me and my crew. She had noticed our airplane's nickname, *Blondie*, from the nose art, and had written down its serial number. Years later, her inquiries to the Royal Air Force were referred to the U.S. Army, then passed along to the Air Force, where someone did her the favor of tracking down my telephone number. Within a few moments of my picking up the telephone, a half century of life was set aside and we were back together in the barley field at Rackheath on that June day. Later, she wrote me a letter with her recollections of that day.

Norwich, Norfolk, England

21-3-99

Dear Harry,

Just a line, before I go off to our "Coastal Watch", as I promised you to tell you "my memory."

Mum, my little brother David and I had left Norwich for a week to have a break in the country, to get away from the air raids and to get some decent sleep! I was 11 years old at the time, and playing in the farmyard, and was offered a horse ride by the farmer's son. David came with me on his bike, and we hadn't gone far before we heard this airplane which even I realized was in bad trouble. The noise was horrendous, and I remember thinking how close it was, when it crash-landed in the next field — in fact, just over the hedge. I think my horse shied, or I fell off, my first instinct being to get on the ground, and my next thought was to go and see what happened.

I went up to the airplane, and heard someone say, "Can you open the door, honey? I think it's jammed." But I couldn't reach it to try to open it. And then the crew came out — some through the door and some through the front windows.

A number of people had arrived by then, and someone — I guess it was you, Harry — said that everyone must stand well back, because you still had fuel on board and there could be a fire. At that point I fled, being very afraid of any more explosions or fire. In fact, I left my little brother there and had to go back after him.

All through the years I've often wondered what happened to the crew. Were any injured or killed, and it's strange to think that all these years on, the mystery is solved.

I still have a piece of "Blondie," though — a ring made by the farmer's son from a piece of the window. It had two "diamonds" in it (pieces of broken milk bottles, I think) which have long disappeared.

Lovely to talk to you yesterday, Harry, and I look forward to seeing the photos. Give my best to your wife and family.

Regards, Daphne

(Editor's Note: As a recognition of his leadership, flying skills and devotion to his crew's safe return to their home base from the Kiel mission, June 13, 1943, Captain Harry M. Conley was awarded the Distinguished Flying Cross.)

CHAPTER 6

THE REGENSBURG SHUTTLE

Following the loss of *Blondie II* after the Kiel mission, we were issued a new B-17G, which became *Blondie III*. The "G" was the latest model of the B-17 and it had a newly-designed gun turret under the nose. The German fighters had found that the most vulnerable spot on our B-17s was the nose, and they were making the most of it by concentrating their attacks diving head-on into our formations of B-17s. To counter this threat the ingenious engineers at Boeing figured out a way to beef up the firepower coming from a B-17's nose by placing two .50 caliber machine guns in a movable turret under the nose. This proved to be a significant improvement in the so-called "self-defense" capability of the B-17. The greatest technical improvement that increased our defensive capability, however, wasn't in the bombers at all — it was the development of external fuel tanks for our fighter planes, so they could accompany us on long range missions into Germany. But that latter development didn't really help us yet in mid-1943, but rather in 1944, when our P-47s and P-38s were equipped with wing tanks so they could protect us on long range missions, and the P-51 came into its own as a truly long-range, top-notch fighter.

Because I had been promoted to Squadron Commander of the 334th Bomb Squadron in the 95th Bomb Group, *Blondie III* was now piloted by "Little Joe" Noyes, who had been my copilot. Now when I would fly a mission, I would fly as a Command Pilot in the copilot's seat of the lead aircraft. Colonel Kessler was to become General Kessler, and the Commander of the 13th Bomb Wing, a much greater responsibility. He, too, would occasionally fly as either a Command Pilot or as an observer on bombing missions for the Wing.

My new assignment as Squadron Commander was welcome, but it came with a lot of new duties and responsibilities to which

I had to adjust. One of the most vital, I soon discovered, was the maintenance of the morale of the men in my squadron. The losses we had experienced in the Kiel raid had unnerved many of our crewmen. The 95th Group lost ten crews, 100 men, in that battle. The empty beds in the barracks when we woke the next morning were very hard to take; the sudden disappearance of their friends drove some of our men into emotional instability. My own crew, luckily, was composed of some naturally strong and stable men. But now I had to concern myself with the emotional stability of all the men in my command. Each man's own emotional reactions to loss and fear needed to be carefully observed, delicately balanced and controlled. So I in essence became a "sort of" chaplain as part of my command duties. My door was always open, 24 hours a day, to all the men, and they responded by coming in to talk with me. They talked some about their fears, but mostly they just talked about their families, their sweethearts, their buddies, their hopes for the future, and on and on.

One man who "lost it" emotionally could quickly infect others in his crew and his barracks. If one man broke down, we had to pull him out right away and send him to the Flight Surgeon for evaluation. We couldn't let him stay with the others and bring them all down with him. I remember once when we came back from a mission having lost three crews. But one member of one of those three crews didn't go on that mission because he happened to be on sick call. Before I went to bed I suddenly remembered that one man, and went to his barracks. I found him sobbing uncontrollably in a barracks of empty beds. I got him out of there quickly and took him to the Flight Surgeon. He was evaluated and then reassigned elsewhere to a ground job. In the course of all these conversations with everyone in my squadron, I really got to know and respect a great many more good men. This was quite helpful to me as I had to make judgments about promotions and replacements.

Another little job I picked up was being the squadron's outgoing mail censor. I had to read the outgoing mail for everyone in the squadron before it was packed up and sent back to the

States. During the war all mail written by servicemen was censored to ensure that no sensitive military information — data about troop movements, the strength of forces, losses in combat, new weapons, etc. — leaked out that might aid the enemy. In the course of that job I came to know a side of Private First Class Francisco Gonzales that I had not known or appreciated before. Private Gonzales was a young Hopi Indian lad, probably about 18 years old, although he looked like he was about 14. Small in stature, he was quite handsome, pleasantly charming and very attracted to the gals and vice versa. To me it seemed as though he had never been off the Reservation before he joined the Army. Assigned to be an Assistant Cook, he was minimally educated, and appeared to be quite unsophisticated and naïve. He performed his duties to the satisfaction of the Mess Sergeant, but he had no idea about military discipline or what was required of a soldier. For instance, he had a penchant for taking off whenever he thought it would be a good idea. He first came to my attention at Rapid City when he was brought in to me by the MP's, having been found AWOL (absent without leave) on a train in Montana headed west. His reasons always seemed good and logical to him. That time it was because he was homesick and wanted to see his mom. Another time, also while we were at Rapid City, it was because he hadn't been feeling well and he needed to visit his medicine doctor. But we never really got after him badly; his charm and work performance kept him his Pfc Stripe. When I got to censoring his mail, I discovered — perhaps I was even a bit envious — how socially active he had been. He was writing identical letters romantically professing his everlasting true love to a half dozen or more young ladies, once every week. He had girlfriends in Rapid City, Spokane, Ephrata and wherever we had been stationed. Every one of these letters was identically formally signed, "Francisco Gonzales, Pfc," with his Army serial number. That was apparently how he had come to identify himself. Of course, we just sealed up those letters and sent them on their way. As far as I know, Pfc Francisco Gonzales, Assistant Cook, kept sending those identical letters to his many girlfriends throughout the war.

As a new Captain and Squadron Commander, I noted in the table of organization for the Air Corps that my job called for the rank of a Lieutenant Colonel. That really struck me worth a good chuckle, since only a year earlier I had been an Aviation Cadet.

Again, I wrote about our off-duty experiences because I knew that was what my parents would want to hear, rather than some of my harrowing experiences in combat.

> ...Bob Cozens and I went to London last week for a couple of days and had a swell time. Did a lot of shopping and saw a marvelous musical review and a swell movie. The review, *Best Bib and Tucker*, was by far the best I've ever seen. We had been trying to get seats ever since we have been here and at last succeeded. The movie was Saroyan's *The Human Comedy*; it was truly wonderful, one of the best I've ever seen.
>
> The highlight of the trip, however, was the wonderful beds we slept in at the Strand Palace Hotel, just like home! Then we really indulged ourselves until ten o'clock and had breakfast in bed two mornings. Not that I ever liked doing that at home, but it was such a change from the routine around here.
>
> When in London I managed to get a Dunhill pipe for Dad which I forwarded to him already. They are scarcer than hen's teeth around here as they make only two dozen per day. You have to be at Dunhill's at the precise moment that they are brought in to be able to get one. It is really amusing to see the pomp and ceremony that takes place. First off, Dunhill's is quite a swanky place. The pipes are brought in at eleven thirty each morning. By eleven there is quite a crowd lounging about examining the various merchandise, casually, with one eye on the stairway. At precisely eleven thirty the little man in a frock coat comes down the stairs with the pipes and everyone makes a dash for the pipe counter. The little man proceeds across the floor to the aforementioned pipe counter and ceremoniously hands each pipe to the clerk who carefully attempts to lay them out on counter. But they never reach the counter as everyone makes a grab and they are all gone. It is really a funny sight. I managed to get two — one for myself and one for Dad. Hope he enjoys it. I'll bring him some more when I come home.

Our June 13th mission to Kiel was still very prominent in my parents' minds, as well as my own, so I had received a letter from them expressing their concerns. I had to send them a message of encouragement to let them know that neither my body nor my spirits were damaged by that "hair's breadth" escape.

June 30, 1943

>Just to reassure you, neither I nor any other member of the crew was even shaken up by the landing [Ed.: in the barley field on June 13 after the Kiel mission], and with the exception of Tom McArthur and Bill Cochrane, the two wounded men, we were none the worse for our "Sunday outing." Mac and Bill are now back flying, so their wounds weren't too serious.
>
>As for the ship breaking in half on landing, well, she was almost shot in half by 20 mm cannon fire and had a tremendous hole right through her, and that is where she parted when we landed. I have some pictures of the remains, but I am not allowed to send them through the mail. You'll just have to contain yourself until I get home.
>
>That was *Blondie II*, hence the remarks about her short career. *Blondie I* also hit the scrap heap a while back. She suffered from the same trouble, 20 mm cannon fire. It is fairly common around here. *Blondie II* made three trips before meeting her doom. *Blondie III* is now in active service and has made several trips avenging her ancestors. She is flown by my old crew with little Joe Noyes, my former copilot, at the controls. So far she hasn't been scratched in several encounters. Let's hope she continues that way. When I go along now I ride with Bob Cozens in the *Patsy Ann II*; and *Blondie III* is on my right wing.
>
>We had a happy surprise today. A couple of our boys who were shot down over the Continent a month ago yesterday came walking in. Of course, how they got back is a great secret, but it is happening every day. They will get a promotion and be sent back to the States.

July 3, 1943

>This air-sea rescue operation they have over here is really marvelous. On our last outing, which I led, three of my crews landed in the Bay of Biscay. Within eighteen hours, all thirty men were picked up and all are safely here now.

Now as a Squadron Commander, I had other new responsibilities including, I found out, answering for failing to complete a mission as planned.

July 10, 1943

Today I led a raid on a very important target in a famous city. Unfortunately, after fighting our way into the target we could not bomb because of heavy cloud layer. So we had to turn around and fight our way out again and bring our bombs home. As I was responsible for the direction of the raid, I had to go to Bomber Command this afternoon and explain the situation and my subsequent decisions to the ranking officers. It was not my first visit and all came off smoothly. It requires quite a performance. You have to get up before the Bomber Command Staff, all generals and colonels, and on a map that covers the entire wall, take your notes, explain the entire mission from takeoff to landing using your notes. So far I have been lucky and the three raids that I directed came off smoothly. The inability to drop my bombs today is not considered my fault.

Took a brass hat from Washington along on the ride today. You should have seen him duck behind the armor plate when the fighters came in!

Our good luck still holds. We have only lost one crew in the last month.

July 20, 1943

You certainly seem to be duly impressed by our experiences of June 13th. True, it was a rough situation for a few minutes, but my boys and I thrive on that. So the whole gang was ready to go again the next day. Not one man had any nervous results. They are a tough lot, that crew of mine! The crew is practically still intact, except for Fitz, my Bombardier who is now Group Bombardier, and me. Since June 13th, the boys have been on seven outings without incident. Little Joe has proven to be one of our best pilots.

The other day a couple more of our boys lost about seven weeks ago came walking back to our base. We also know of about a dozen more who are on their way and will arrive shortly. You will be amazed when I get home and am able to tell you how many of our American airmen shot down over the Continent get back here to England.

As far as my next promotion is concerned, I won't have the necessary service time to become a major for another several months. I don't worry about rank. That all takes care of itself. As far as Bob Cozen's Captaincy is concerned, it has never caught up with him. So we have to put him up again over here and he should get the "railroad tracks" in a few days.

As far as my safety is concerned while riding with Bob, he is for my money the best pilot in the Eighth Air Force, so don't worry. Anyway, we take turns flying on those missions. Hell, I can't just sit. I have to keep my hand in this flying business.

My letters had to be worded very carefully to avoid violating the rules of security and alert the censors of all our mail. But I was able to allude to facts — places and people and incidents — that my parents knew and understood to give them the general idea of what I was trying to tell them.

July 26, 1943

Please excuse the lapse between my last letter and this. But, as you no doubt have gathered from the newspapers, we have had an extremely busy week. Yes, busy and successful. We have enjoyed three days of extremely accurate bombing.

I was lucky enough to get in on two of them, one being the longest raid ever made in Flying Forts. We were in the air over twelve hours and practically reached the Arctic Circle. (Ed.: bombing submarine pens in Norway.) We certainly took them by surprise that day.

The raid yesterday was back to my old stomping ground of my last flight with my old crew. We went in with real force this time. I've never seen as many B-17's as there were in that vicinity yesterday. We ranged over the area for two and a half hours going about two hundred miles east of that notorious place and then coming back over it again. As usual up there we were well received, but we came through unscathed.

Today the boys were back in that vicinity and we lost one airship. I did not go. Unfortunately, the ship that was lost was carrying three of my old crew, two gunners and the engineer. I feel very badly about it. However, when last seen, the ship was under control, so I feel certain that they got out safely.

Along those lines, I heard through channels that three other of my boys who were knocked down about six weeks ago are safe in Switzerland and living the life of Riley. It is absolutely amazing how many of our boys get out and back home. Some day I'll tell you the story. It's far better than fiction.

I was still the young warrior in my heart, and I wanted to be in the thick of the fight with my own plane and crew.

...When we retraced the steps of *Blondie*'s last flight, I flew my own ship for a change, as we did not have another lead pilot in the Squadron and Bob Cozen's has been grounded for a few days. It sure felt good to get in there behind the stick again and hear all my old boys' voices on the interphone — just like old times!

Today it has been exactly a year since I graduated from Flight School and became a Second Lieutenant. A lot of water has gone under the bridge in that time. In the past year I have flown better than 1,300 hours in B-17s alone. That is a lot of time, and classifies me as a veteran in this game now. We get our seasoning in a hurry over here. A year ago I never dreamed in my fondest hopes that I would have my own squadron of B-17s in an outfit that is the cream of the Army Air Forces.

Along those lines, tomorrow Secretary of War Stimson is coming to visit us, so we all have to dress up and look pretty. I've been invited to eat at his table with the Colonel, and all the Generals will be there — lots of rank in attendance!

Yesterday a Group Commander, who was my squadron C.O. in the 391st rode along with me to observe the activity. It was his first raid. Like all the other novices, when the flak and fighters hit us, he ducked. I laughed.

The air combat was getting more and more fierce as we entered the second half of 1943, and most of the details were "confidential" as far as correspondence was concerned.

August 3, 1943

In your letter of the 23rd you certainly hit the nail on the head. You said that you hadn't heard of the Eighth Air Force for a while, "so it must be the lull before the storm." Boy, you were really psychic. We started our blitz on that day and we're still going strong as you no doubt have seen in the papers.

In the past week the B-17's have knocked down over 500 Jerry fighters, and we now go anywhere in Germany that we choose. Places that two months ago would have been impossible, we now just sail into. We were within 90 miles of Berlin one day last week.

One of the things that really impressed me was the ingenuity and capability of our British allies, and in particular their skills at retrieving our airmen downed in the English Channel after being shot up badly in a raid over Continental Europe.

August 13, 1943

A couple of days ago I had to go down to London to identify another one of my boys who made his way back to England after going down over the Continent. Now, with the exception of Harry Stirwalt's crew in the plane carrying General Forrest, and two other boys who we know are prisoners in Germany, all of the 334th boys who went down are either back here in England or in a neutral country awaiting transport back here. That is, with the exception of one of our crews that went down yesterday; we believe that they are floating in their rubber boats in the North Sea. We've had several radio position reports from a crew out there and believe it to be ours. We've had several crews from the Group fished out on different occasions. During that last big week of operations, they fished 178 boys out of the North Sea! The Air-Sea Rescue setup the British have is really marvelous. It's unbelievable how close they go to the enemy coast. They picked up one crew eight miles outside the harbor of LeHavre, France. They dropped them a motorboat by parachute from a bomber that had a fighter escort. The boys climbed aboard and rode home to England.

When I was in London the other day I saw Churchill's airplane and the King's ship as well. Boy, they are really something inside. We flew down and landed at the King's own field right in the center of town, just a few minutes from Picadilly. It was some layout.

August 17, 1943, was a day I'll never forget. The 95th Group was assigned the first of many "shuttle missions," in which we would fly from England, do a bombing run, and land elsewhere;

then we would refuel and rearm and fly back to England on another bombing run. One of our objectives was to prove to the German High Command that we could bomb anywhere in Germany and not be stopped by geography or the Luftwaffe. The target area, Regensburg, Germany, contained Germany's largest aircraft manufacturing plant, the main manufacturing facility for Messerschmitt airplanes, particularly the Me-109 fighters. About 90% of Germany's Me-109s were made there. Regensburg is located at a broad curve of the Danube River between Germany and Austria. The Danube is a major river and that curve is a distinctive landmark, making it easy for us to spot our targets from our high bombing altitudes.

This raid was also our first massive attack on Germany's aircraft production industry. It was to bring into Germany the most powerful force of American daylight bombers yet in the war. Colonel Curtis LeMay's (Ed. note. Curtis LeMay was promoted to Brigadier General on September 28, 1943; and Major General on March 3, 1944) 4th Bomb Wing, was assigned to bomb Regensburg and shuttle off to Africa, while the 1st Bomb Wing was to turn to the north and bomb Germany's critical ball bearing factories at Schweinfurt. That would be 376 bombers in total hitting Germany on the same day! It was really the beginning of the end for Germany, as our bombings severely decimated the mass production of Me-109 fighter planes, the backbone of the Luftwaffe's defense of Germany. The intent of these simultaneous missions was to split the German fighter force, making them less effective against either of the American forces. The overall mission of the Eighth Air Force was to destroy the German Luftwaffe so that the Allies could have air superiority over Europe in time to allow the Allies to land troops the following summer. This raid was a crucial and, as it turned out, successful step toward our achieving that objective. It was also the longest bombing mission over hostile territory so far in the war.

It was a spectacularly clear day on August 17. After we assembled our bomb groups into formation over England, we flew across the Channel at about 25,000 feet and could see the Alps

Lt. General Ira C. Eaker (later General) USAAF. Commanding General 8th Bomber Command, and later 8th Air Force, 1942-1943. In 1944 he became Commander-in-Chief of the Mediterranean Allied Air Forces.
Col. James Parton, USAF
Gen. Eaker's ADC

General Adolf Galland, Commander of the Luftwaffe's Fighter Arm on the Western Front.
Hans Hoehler

Fritz Blitz *dropped its bombs on Bremen as I took this picture from my command pilot seat. Fritz Blitz was unfortunately shot down a few weeks later over Regensburg with the loss of all 10 crewmen.*

Regensburg on the Danube River. Note the accuracy of the bombing pattern.

The Messerschmitt factory in Regensburg.

Col. John Gerhart was on board the Patsy Ann III *as an "observer" on the Regensburg shuttle mission.*

The Patsy Ann III *with Bob Cozens piloting and Harry Conley in the right seat as Command Pilot, as we dropped our bomb load on Regensburg, August 17, 1943.*

After bombing Regensburg we flew south over the Brenner Pass, Italy, where we enjoyed the beautiful view of the Alps without any fighters or flak.

A crippled Fortress lands in Bone, Africa, after bombing Regensburg.

Patsy Ann III *rests in Africa, while undergoing repairs from flak and fighters encountered over Regensburg. When we landed in Bone, we had no brakes and at the end of the runway we ground-looped creating further damage.*

A partial Regensburg crew on the ground at Bone. Pilot Bob Cozens standing, second from right; Bombardier Basey DeWolfe, standing at Coz's right; me with sun glasses, kneeling on right.

Nine men on this crew disembarked on arrival at Bone. Where is the Tail Gunner? Gone! The gun position and gunner were sliced off by the wing of a bold German fighter over Regensburg and survived.

several hundred miles to the east. Having clear visibility on our bombing run meant that we could very accurately place our bombs on their targets, which would make our mission successful. But it also meant that the Germans could see us very clearly, too, and they could, and did, easily deduce where we were headed to do our bombing. At any rate, we became aware rather quickly that the Luftwaffe knew on this day where we were going, and they were ready for us in full strength.

We were briefed to cross the Dutch coast and fly into Belgium, which we did. As soon as we entered Belgium we were attacked by fighter aircraft. Adolf Galland, who was Germany's leading ace pilot of World War II, was the head of the Luftwaffe's fighter force defending Germany; and he had called in all his fighter groups from the fronts in Russia, Norway and Italy to stop us. We flew with 146 bombers, after the few early aborts in our 4th Bomb Wing left our formation. To defend their airspace, the Luftwaffe flew over 600 fighter planes, probably their greatest number in the whole war. They called in the Me-109s, the Ju-88s, the FW-190s and every airplane they had that could shoot at us to try to keep us away from Regensburg.

From the time we entered enemy airspace, we had no friendly fighter protection, because our fighters still did not have the range necessary to go into Germany and return. As soon as our fighter cover turned back, the German fighters started to close with us at very short range. They boldly flew within a few feet of us as they attacked from all angles. So there we were, a group of B-17s with only ourselves to protect us. We had learned to fly extremely close formations as the best defense against fighter attacks. Nevertheless, all our planes received damage from these attacks on this mission, but those B-17s were marvelous; they would keep on flying with damage that you'd think would cause them to fall apart.

Adolf Galland, commander of the German fighter aircraft in World War II, was a true professional military airman and he developed a method of attack that was quite difficult to stop. These German fighters would line up along side of us parallel to our direction of flight and just outside our gun range in single file; next they would speed up and go out in front of us; then they would turn directly into our aircraft, six abreast, firing their guns all the time, trying to split up our formations. As they approached us, they rolled out in a "split S," passing us upside down and dropping down rapidly away from our guns, thus avoiding the bullets from our tail guns. It was hard to get a good shot at them when they did that. The air was so clear and visibility was so good that we could observe the whole panorama of their fighter tactics. After two passes through our formations they would go back down to the ground, refuel and rearm, and come back again to join the queue alongside us, preparing for another attack. We could see them doing this, but we couldn't do anything about it as we had to continue on our bombing mission.

We lost a lot of good men and machines both before and after our bomb run over Regensburg. There were times when all we could see in the sky were airplanes going down in flames and many, many parachutes — white parachutes carrying American crewmen and yellow parachutes carrying Germans. At the height of the air battle we could see the air around and below filled with these parachutes. It was an AWESOME sight, one that will probably never be seen again! We had lost 14 B-17s before we even reached the IP, leaving 132 B-17s to bomb the Messerschmitt factory complex. The fighters continued their attacks even after we had released our bombs.

I think we endured over two and a half hours of attacks by fighters as we approached our targets. Their attacks were at their worst during the bomb run, when we gave the control of the aircraft over to the bombardier and we weren't able to do any evasive maneuvers. We had our orders from Colonel Curtis LeMay that once we reached the "IP," the initial point of the bombing run, we had to fly straight and level to ensure the accuracy of our bombing. Our squadron was lucky — at least I can say our B-17, the *Patsy Ann III*, was. We made it; we dropped our bombs and got away. Our squadron started off with 18 aircraft; two dropped out early for mechanical difficulties, leaving 16 of us on the bomb run.

We lost four, and 12 aircraft made it to Africa, and later back home.

I was actually flying in the right-hand seat as the Squadron Commander of the 334th Bomb Squadron. Bob Cozens was my pilot. Standing right behind Coz and me was Colonel John Gerhart, our 95th Group Commander, riding as an observer. Colonel LeMay, Commander of the 4th Bomb Wing, was the Mission Leader; and he was in the lead aircraft of the 96th Bomb Group. As we flew towards our target, Regensburg, the 1st Bomb Wing became delayed by weather conditions at their home bases, causing them to be over three hours behind us over Germany. This delay virtually nullified the planned effect of dividing the Luftwaffe fighters. We received the full brunt of all the fighter forces that Galland could muster. Then later that day the 1st Bomb Wing mission of 229 bombers was also attacked in full force by the Luftwaffe as they flew toward Schweinfurt and returned home to England.

After we dropped our bombs, we turned south toward Italy instead of returning home to England. This maneuver truly surprised the Germans. Most of the fighters then left us, although a few squadrons followed us for a while to try to down a few more of our B-17s. Then they, too, left us. We crossed the Alps and regrouped over Lake Garda in Northern Italy, east of Switzerland. We reformed into our tight formations there again as we anticipated major fighter opposition coming up from Italy. At Lake Garda there was a large Italian airbase, but the Italians didn't take off to attack. They had no taste for war with the American Air Force. As we circled widely over Lake Garda in the process of forming up with all our surviving aircraft, we passed over Switzerland, Austria and Italy. The Italian anti-aircraft guns were silent when we passed over them, but when we circled over Switzerland, the Italians sent up a huge barrage of flak overhead aimed so that they would never hit an American plane. They appeared to be going through the motions, just firing away so as to make a show of trying to get to us but making it impossible to hit us. The actions of the Italians made a profound statement about their state of mind about the war at that time. For me and my crew, this was the first realization of the disinterest of the Italian armed forces in fighting the Allied forces on behalf of the Germans.

We didn't encounter any German fighters there at Lake Garda, or for that matter anywhere in Italy either, because they had all been ordered up to Germany early that morning to defend Regensburg and Schweinfurt. Nor did we see any Swiss fighters rising to greet us or to defend their neutral air space. So we had a free ride all the way down the boot of Italy and across the Mediterranean to Algeria. We flew on to an Allied airfield in Bone, Algeria, near Constantine, where we landed.

In Algeria we found out from reports we received after we landed that we had been quite successful in our bombing mission, hitting the required targets and really decimating the Messerschmitt factory buildings. Photographic records from our aerial reconnaissance following our bombers really proved the effectiveness of American precision daylight bombing. The results were clearly seen. The clear skies aided enormously in making this raid probably the best exhibition of bombing so far in the war.

As we were all landing at Bone we noticed that one of the B-17s in our group had only nine crewmen disembarking instead of the ten crewmen required in a B-17. Where was the tenth crewman? When I went over to that plane and talked to the pilot, he explained that his tail gunner was expelled over Belgium in the first wave of attacks by German fighters. This B-17 was one of the planes in our formation following behind mine the entire way with us through the bombing mission. One of the German fighter aircraft, in charging through our formation, sliced off the tip of the tail of that B-17 that contained the tail guns and the gunner. His wing cleanly missed the bomber's rudder and elevators. When that happened, the gunner was literally thrown out of the tail at 25,000 feet. Fortunately, he had his parachute on and wasn't badly injured, so he made it safely to the ground. And the plane was able to continue flying its mission with a damaged tail and no tail gunner. Funny thing though: that gunner got back to Horham before we did.

Upon our return to Horham, we heard his story. After the gunner landed on the ground and gathered up his parachute to hide it, a Belgian farmer ran over to him and guided him toward some trees. They came to a canal lined with willows, whose branches came down to the water. The farmer indicated to him to hide in the water under those branches. The farmer told the American to stay hidden in the willow trees up to his neck in the water, which he did for the rest of the day. That evening, the farmer came after him in a rowboat and picked him up. The farmer then took him to a nearby Belgian village, where he was turned over to the underground. The Belgians had a strong underground working; the gunner was put into the flow of downed Allied air crewmen. He was transported to Paris and sent on over the Pyrenees Mountains to Spain and then finally back to England in less than the three weeks it took us to return.

We had another big surprise upon our landing at Bone. Because our mission had been originally planned to be three weeks earlier, but was delayed because of bad weather over Germany, things had changed from the way they were planned. In that time period, the Allied forces that were supposed to meet and refuel us had moved on to pursue the retreating Germans and Italians. This was when General Rommel and his "Afrika Corps" were retreating eastward towards Egypt. When we landed at Bone it was really quiet there. No one came to welcome us or acknowledge our arrival in any way. We found a big marble headquarters building virtually empty with only a small housekeeping group housed there. Curtis LeMay was really visibly upset when he called General Tooey Spaatz, then Commanding General of the 12th Air Force, yelling into the microphone, "Hey, Tooey! We're at Bone. Where the Hell is everybody? Goddamnit! There's no one here to service our aircraft!" He was shouting so loud into the mike that I'd be willing to bet General Spaatz could have heard him even if the radio hadn't been working! The Army didn't leave us any tank trucks, but instead we found there were a series of gasoline dumps of 55-gallon drums and some hand pumps, plus a couple of GI trucks to use for ground transportation. Here it was the middle of August in the Algerian desert with the daytime temperatures well over 100 degrees, and we had to load these 55-gallon drums onto the trucks, drive them to our planes and refuel their gas tanks using hand pumps. Very hot work! Then, to make things worse, after we filled all but about 50 of the B-17s with hand pumps, we discovered that some of these drums contained kerosene, which wouldn't work in our engines. At that point we couldn't identify which planes had received any of the kerosene. So, we had to empty ALL the aircraft fuel tanks out on the ground and refuel from drums that we knew contained gasoline. It took us all of three weeks to complete this refueling project.

At Bone we hired as many local Arabs as we could to help with refueling. The Arabs who worked for us there in Africa didn't have much they could do with our money when they were paid. Then some of our ingenious Americans discovered that the Arabs liked our mattress covers, which they made into clothes by slitting the sides and making a head hole. Well, our quartermaster's supplies contained lots of mattress covers. So our guys requisitioned mattress covers by the hundreds and traded them to the Arabs for fresh eggs, chickens, watermelons and other Arab staples.

The deserts were strewn with war debris, the remains of burnt out tanks and trucks and so on. And there were scores and scores of Italian prisoners of war. Every time the Americans sent out a work detail with, say, a hundred prisoners, they would come back with a hundred and fifty prisoners. They all wanted to come to us where they could get something to eat. No one guarded them. In fact it would have been impossible to drive them away. They couldn't do enough for us. Among them were many good cooks, and one of the things they cooked for us was Italian-style French bread. When we headed back to England on the second part of the shuttle, we loaded up our planes with loaves of French bread, which everyone at Horham really enjoyed.

Several of our planes were badly "wounded" and too damaged to make it back to England; so we had to patch them up as much as possible and send them on to Marrakech in Morocco where the

American Army had established a major depot for parts and service. Those of us that could continue on the "shuttle" loaded up with bombs and ammunition, and proceeded on a bombing mission over France, and then home to England.

While our shuttle aircraft were being refueled at Bone, one of our crews traded a bunch of mattress covers for a donkey and a cart from one of the local Arabs. When their plane left for England with us on the shuttle return flight, they brought the donkey and cart with them. I remember looking out the window at that plane and I could see the donkey with an oxygen mask over his snout; his large ears were quite visible. They successfully got the donkey and cart safely back to Horham, where they later gave donkey cart rides to many of the local children. The donkey cart became an important part of the base transportation system in lieu of bicycles, taking men from one place on the base to another. The donkey wasn't really well acclimated to England's cold and wet weather, however, and it died that winter. To honor the donkey who had performed with such gallant service, the men put an American GI uniform and special dog tags on his body, loaded him onto one of the B-17s, and dropped him somewhere over Germany. I can just imagine what those Germans must have thought when they found a dead donkey in an American uniform on the ground after a bombing raid!

Both the Americans and the Germans had very high losses resulting from the two raids on Regensburg and Schweinfurt on August 17. Combined losses of the two divisions that day amounted to 60 aircraft downed with their 600 crewmen, and more than 100 aircraft damaged, many beyond repair, but we brought down some 400 or so of the enemy's fighters. Yes, the losses were about 20% of our bombing force, but that was "better than par" as our losses were generally 18 to 25%. The losses by the Luftwaffe were critical for them, because they had committed the major part of their air forces to defending Regensburg and Schweinfurt and had lost a very large percentage of them. It seemed certain that Hitler's air defenses had received a crippling blow. This must have been very hard for the German people, as they had been pumped up by

Hitler's propaganda machine to believe that the air defenses over Germany were invincible.

The losses of bombers caused the Eighth Air Force to build up its strength as quickly as possible before confronting the Luftwaffe over Germany. It was not until October 8 that a bombing mission was next scheduled over Germany, and that mission used a large force of P-47s equipped with wing tanks for protective cover. After these two missions on August 17, the one thing that came out of these battles was the firm determination by the leaders of the Eighth Air Force that we had to proceed quickly to equip our fighter planes with extra fuel tanks so that they could cover our long-range bombing missions. And that action was carried out during the succeeding six months.

Note 1. The excellent results of the Regensburg mission and the manner and discipline with which it was performed were commended in the first of three Presidential Unit Citations for the 95th Bombardment Group (H). This Citation reads as follows:

HEADQUARTERS EIGHTH AIR FORCE
Office of the Commanding General

9 February 1944

GENERAL ORDERS
NUMBER 35

CITATION

The 3rd Bombardment Division (H) (then the 4th Bombardment Wing (H)) is cited for outstanding performance of duty in action against the enemy, 17 August 1943. This unprecedented attack against one of Germany's most important aircraft factories was the first shuttle mission performed in this theater of Operations and entailed the longest flight over strongly defended enemy territory yet accomplished at that date. For four and one half hours, the formation was subjected to persistent, savage assaults by large forces of enemy fighters. During this bitterly contested aerial battle, 140 fighter aircraft were definitely destroyed and many more damaged. In spite of desperate attempts by the enemy to scatter the bombers, the Groups of the 3rd Bombardment Division maintained a tight defensive formation and coordinating as a perfectly balanced team, fought their way to the assigned target at Regensburg. Though weary from hours of grueling combat, the bombardiers released their bombs accurately on the target and wrought vast destruction on an aircraft factory of vital importance to the enemy's war effort. The high degree of success achieved is directly attributable to the extraordinary heroism, skill and devotion to duty displayed by members of this unit. Their actions on this occasion uphold the highest traditions of the Armed Forces of the United States.

By command of Major General DOOLITTLE:

> JOHN A. SAMFORD,
> Brigadier General, USA
> Chief of Staff

Note 2. In addition, Captain Harry M. Conley was awarded the Distinguished Flying Cross. The citation was as follows:

> For extraordinary achievement while serving as Commanding Officer of a B-17 Group on a bombardment mission over Germany, 17 August 1943. In spite of intense anti-aircraft fire and extremely heavy fighter opposition, the formation made the deepest penetration thus far into Germany, bombed a target of vital importance with highly successful results and continued on to bases in another theater. During one of the greatest aerial battles of the war, lasting over three hours, approximately one hundred and fifty enemy aircraft were destroyed. The courage, skill and determination displayed by Captain Conley on this occasion reflect the highest credit upon himself and the armed forces of the United States.

CHAPTER 7

MISSION TO MUNSTER

Following our return to our home base at Horham from our long shuttle mission, we enjoyed a little "down time," giving me a chance to write my parents and tell them what little I could about my recent adventures.

August 28, 1943

Since I last wrote I've traveled some 4,000 miles. Yes, we had our "summer vacation;" at least we had a change of scene. Of course we combined business with pleasure and left a few "calling cards" both on the way down and on the way back. The results were most gratifying! In fact, the best we ever had. We really hit Adolf where it hurts. We also pulled a fast one on him by keeping right on going after we dropped our eggs, over to Africa.

We met around 400 fighters and for two and a half hours the battle raged. Boy, it was terrific, even worse than Kiel, I think. However, except for the ship, Bob Cozens and I came out OK.

Had a wonderful time in Africa. Got to see a lot of old classmates who are flying down there. They certainly have a picnic. Just to show you the difference, our operational tour up here is 25 missions, while down there they have to go 65 missions. In the Pacific it is even more.

I talked to a boy in London who had just returned after being shot down over the Continent. He gave me word of nine of our "missing" boys; he walked into a bar in a little town in France and met all nine there. According to him, they will all be back shortly.

Major Dave McKnight, one of our colorful Squadron Commanders, was at a "pub" in London one evening, and he happened to meet a Vicar of the Anglican Church. The Vicar was in London visiting with some Bishops and other high-ranking members of the Church of England. He apparently liked Dave, and the two became, as people often do over a toddy or two, fast friends. Before the evening was over, the Vicar told Dave that his

Parish was in Northern Scotland in Aberdeen on the River Dee, and then he invited Dave to visit there and to bring a few of his friends.

This was shortly after the Regensberg Shuttle mission, and when Dave brought this invitation back to us at Horham, we were ready for a refuge from the war, at least for a few days. So John Gerhart, Bill Lindley, Dave McKnight and I loaded up one of our war-weary B-17s that we used for local transportation and flew it up to Aberdeen. We took off in the afternoon and landed in the early evening. An RAF patrol base was there in Aberdeen with some aircraft that patrolled the coastline, and it was quite adequate for landing our B-17. We were greeted by the Vicar who welcomed us and invited us to stay at his rectory. We did, and we had a fine meal, after which we spent the evening helping the Vicar get rid of a large decanter of scotch whisky. He told us we really should go about 50 miles east of Aberdeen up the valley of the River Dee to see the beautiful and bucolic hills of Northern Scotland and a little village called Ballater. It was not far from Balmoral Castle, the retreat of the British Royal Family.

The next morning we boarded a bus, the only form of transportation up through the River Dee Valley. We felt like we had gone to another world, a world in which there was no such thing as war. It was truly beautiful and green with the winding River Dee and all the small farms. The bus was full, with lots of interesting local people. Apparently this bus was also the mail and package delivery for all the farms along the way because the people got on and got off, and the bus driver stopped frequently and delivered the mail and parcel post. We must have stopped at a hundred places on our fifty-mile trip. But this was a real vacation for us. We weren't impatient; we were there to enjoy the rest and scenery.

Ballater was a quaint Scottish rural town. The people there hardly seemed to know there was a war going on. There was no rationing. They raised all their produce and livestock. There was no regular transportation in or out of the town. These folks actually lived very well, like kings in fact. We stayed at what you would call a "bed and breakfast," but they call an "inn." The townspeople greeted us warmly and made us all very welcome. They were all very friendly.

They had a golf course there. Now I used to be a "scratch" golfer in college, so I readily accepted an invitation from two old Scotsmen for a round of golf. I thought I was a pretty good golfer. Well, they taught me a thing or two about golfing in the rough! These fellas were real golfers! They knew every hill and dale, every tree and bush and every blade of grass on that course. But, we had a lot of fun as they showed the visitor how it was done.

We stayed there about four days, and then returned to Horham and the war. But we made numerous retreats back to Ballater during our two years in England, regarding it as our private little spot of "R&R" (Rest and Recuperation).

My letters continued to give my parents an idea of what I was experiencing that I could share with them.

September 1, 1943

> Just came from a very good variety show up in the enlisted men's mess hall. Adolph Menjou and his troupe of entertainers were here for the evening and put on an excellent performance. We get these shows about every week and the boys enjoy them tremendously.
>
> Among the enclosures is my latest photograph. Notice the coat and necktie. It's one of my escape pictures that we carry in case we have to bail out over enemy territory. Think I'd pass for a Frenchman?
>
> Also enclosed is a picture of Regensberg after we finished with it. Boy, that place is really a wreck! Not a bomb dropped outside of the target area; consequently, not a building in the target area was left standing, as the damage assessment photos taken the next day showed.

We were, of course, continuing to fly our bombing missions, although now I flew only when it was my turn as Command Pilot. This tended to cut down on my accumulation of mission credits toward the magic number of 25 missions for completion of a tour of duty in the European Theater of Operations. Everyone watched their credited mission totals very carefully, because after 25 missions a man could stop risking his life for his country in the air over enemy territory. But my own career path had led me to such a position of responsibility so quickly that I was beginning to question whether or not I really wanted to end my combat role at 25 missions. And now it was beginning to look like the Allies were starting to get the upper hand.

> ...To date I have completed 12 missions. Bob has 13 to his credit. For a while there they were getting pretty strict and the Squadron Commanders rarely got to go. But lately they have relaxed a bit and I've sneaked a couple in. As I told you, 25 is the tour of duty in this theater; however, I won't get to come home then anyway. I'll probably have to take a job in Bomber Command, from what I hear. For the Regensberg raid, Bob and I were both recommended for the D.F.C. (Distinguished Flying Cross). What will come of it I don't know. Also, the papers on my Majority have gone in and should be through in about two weeks.
>
> We still lose quite a few planes on our missions. But now when we send three forces in at the same time only one will be attacked. They don't have enough fighters to hit all of them. Sometimes now we never see an enemy fighter, while at other times we catch them all. Also the flak is getting more accurate all the time. They should; they certainly get a lot of practice.

General Hap Arnold was a distinguished hero and leader, and he delighted us with a visit to honor the 95th Group's achievements.

> September 3, 1943
>
> Remember when I was home last, that one of our friends forecast that I would someday meet General Arnold? Well, I met him today and am going to a dinner for him tonight. We had a big flag waving today over the success of the shuttle mission to Africa. He was the guest of honor.

Not everything was upbeat. Sometimes our missions put us under risks that weren't all the doing of the enemy.

> September 12, 1943
>
> Yesterday we went on a long raid. We didn't get back until midnight last night. We bombed in daylight but returned in darkness.

It was our first experience with night operational flying. Personally, I don't care for it. Too many airplanes too close to you without any lights of any sort. They really black these countries out over here. We couldn't see a light anywhere. To make matters worse, we flew through a terrific storm in total darkness. It was almost as bad as that night crossing over the South Atlantic.

One of the essential elements of survival was having to rise above the loss of people close to us. The losses of our compatriots was something we just had to accept and live with and move on. It wasn't something we could dwell upon. One of my saddest moments was when I had to confront the fact that the young man I had trained and nurtured into becoming a good B-17 pilot had become a "missing in action" statistic. But I still had hopes for him and several other members of my old crew.

> ...We lost Little Joe Noyes and my old crew yesterday. No one saw them go down. They just disappeared out of the formation and were never seen again. It is rough; they only had three more raids to go before returning to the States. I hope they went down in the water. If so, the British Air-Sea Rescue will get them. So far they have never failed us. We have had eleven crews go down at sea and all have been picked up within 48 hours.

Then there were also some updrafts in the flight through life. Bob Cozens' Captaincy finally came through. Naturally it was cause for great celebration.

September 26, 1943

> I have lost Bob from my squadron. He is now Commanding Officer of the 335th Bomb Squadron. The Air Executive from our Group was given a position in Bomber Command; so the C.O. of the 335th was promoted to Air Executive. It's a swell break for Bob. He moved from the 334th area to the 335th area the other day. It seems strange not to have him for a roommate after so long together. Isn't it remarkable how our paths have paralleled one another! I know of no other similar cases in the Service. I'm having a devil of a time replacing him as lead pilot for my outfit. Pilots of his caliber don't come in dozen lots. However, we are both on the Group Staff now

and are definitely fair-haired boys around here from the looks of things.

But it wasn't long after that when I received a pleasant surprise: promotion orders for me.

October 7, 1943

>Just a line to let you know that I am well. My Majority came through a week ago, dated October 1st, but I received it only three days ago. So now I wear the gold leaf instead of the railroad tracks.
>When I think back that just a year ago I was a spanking new Second Lieutenant, I realize that the 95th has been pretty good to me. Of course, I know that I have given my best efforts, yet there is a certain satisfaction in receiving the proper recognition.

My duties as a Squadron Commander and my new rank as a Major brought with them the responsibility to visit various different Army Air Bases in England on business.

>...Now I have an airplane at my disposal at all times. Any time I want to go anywhere — London, Scotland, Oxford — I just take off. No worries about expenses or time. It is a wonderful feeling. I make the 120 miles to Oxford in around thirty minutes.

Life in the Army Air Forces wasn't all flying around the English countryside, however. Our bombing missions were continuing at an increasing frequency with ever-increasing numbers of American bombers on each mission.

>...Yesterday we made a really long trip to Danzig. We went by way of Denmark and at low level, too. Not too much opposition. A very enjoyable trip. It was the first time since we began operations in this theater that we didn't have to use oxygen. It is certainly a good deal more comfortable than flying at 25,000 feet and above at temperatures of minus 35 degrees and lower and have to wear a damned oxygen mask. However, it isn't every target that we can afford to approach at such a low altitude. On this trip the flak was practically negligible.

Bombing submarine pens at St Nazaire, France. The bombing pattern shows how the Eighth totally blocked the locks, rendering useless this facility.

Bombing the locks at the submarine pens at Antwerp. Another excellent bombing pattern.

A German Me-410 passes very near our right wingtip. Note the hole in our right wing from his 20 mm cannon fire. Immediately after this photo was taken, Big Fitz got him with his machine guns and he exploded from a bullet into his high-pressure oxygen tank, almost taking us with him.

Our bombing pattern at Munster, showing how accurately we hit our target within the old city walls, October 10, 1943.

A German ship convoy near Emden.

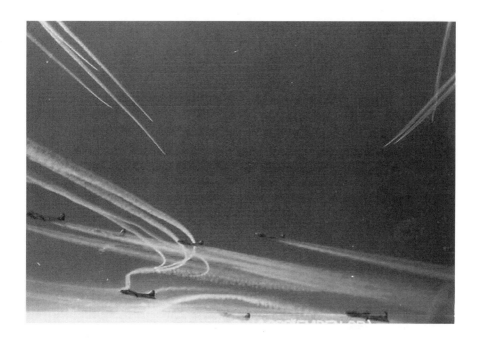

Bandits (German fighter planes) over Emden in September 1943.

Curtis LeMay would have liked to have seen this tight formation of B-17s.

B-17s of the 95th Bomb Group (H) on a mission.

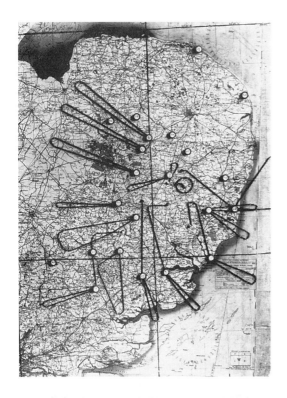

Map of East Anglia showing the takeoff and letdown patterns and the bunchers used by the 93rd Combat Wing.

It was always good to see a "Little Friend" like this P-47 come alongside.

Captain Kenneth Kimborough, officially an Intelligence Officer but unofficially our home-maker away from home.

Ken Kimborough's touches with a Nissen hut at Horham.

One Sunday morning, the 10th of October in 1943, the alert came, not the previous evening as was the usual thing, but that morning. It was a most unusual day and a most unusual mission. We all trooped out to the pre-mission briefing, and Jiggs Donohue, the Group Intelligence Officer, told us about our target for that day[3]. I'll never forget it! For the first time we were going to bomb civilians on purpose! Our target was Munster in Germany along the Rhine River and the hub of Germany's main manufacturing area, the Ruhr Valley. Vast coalfields underlay the Ruhr Valley providing the fuel to produce Germany's steel, so this area had grown over the years as the major industrial center for the country. The city of Munster was the transportation center for all these manufactured products; as it was at the conjunction of the Ruhr River and the Rhine River, it had also become the railroad hub for the country.

Munster itself was a very old city with its core surrounded by a large stone wall dating from medieval years. Outside the walled old city were the manufacturing plants as well as the affluent suburbs. Inside the walled city lived the workers, the blue-collar folks who worked in the factories and train yards. In the very center of the old walled city was the Munster Cathedral, a beautiful structure built many centuries ago. What Jiggs told us, to our amazement and consternation, was that our aiming point on this

---

[3] Major F.J. "Jiggs" Donohue briefed the Group as follows: Munster is a vital rail junction between Germany's northern coastal ports and the heavy industries and the munitions plants of the Ruhr Valley immediately to the south of your primary target. Through Munster's marshalling yards, each day and each night, roll hundreds of tons of armament and war material produced in the Ruhr Valley and destined for all points north, west and east.

However, unlike all previous military and industrial targets attacked to date by the Eighth Air Force, today it will be different — very different — because today you will hit the center of that city, the homes of the working population of those marshalling yards. You will disrupt their lives so completely that their morale will be seriously affected, and their will to work and fight will be substantially reduced.

Should the primary target be obscured by cloud or industrial haze, the secondary target is Hamm, located in the Ruhr Valley itself, and as a last resort, any industrial town in Germany.

Sunday was to be the center of that historic walled city. We were to bomb everything inside the old walls into rubble including all the workers' homes!

Up to this time we had been given targets that were primarily factories or military installations. We were rudely awakened to the realities of war when we were told we had to bomb this city of civilian workers, their homes and their church. But it had been decided at the highest level of the Allied Command that we had to bring the war to the working people to demoralize them, to get them to start pressuring their government to end the war. Several of our pilots, speaking for themselves or for their crews, said for the first time that they had problems reconciling this bombing objective with their moral senses; but Jiggs explained the thinking of the Allied Command. He told them that we had, up to now, carefully avoided bombing civilians; but now we had to carry the war to the German people to make them realize the horrors of the war that their leaders had brought on all the other peoples in Europe. They had to be made to understand that they had become the victims of their militaristic leaders, and that they must face the reality that they could very well lose this war. By the end of Jiggs' briefing, we were all ready to proceed with this mission to Munster.

The day dawned with clear skies, and they were forecast to remain very clear all the way into Germany, so the assembling of the 13th Bomb Wing, including our 95th Bomb Group, was relatively easy. We had been told in the briefing that we shouldn't expect to encounter particularly strong fighter opposition because the Luftwaffe wouldn't be expecting us to head for a population center or to be taking off as late as we were on a Sunday morning. Wrong! As soon as we crossed the English Channel we saw a great many fighters assembled on the ground waiting for us to fly beyond the range of our friendly fighter protection. At this time we still had very limited fighter support. A few American P-47s equipped with disposable wing tanks for additional fuel accompanied us part way, but even with the fuel to extend their range, they could not go all the way to the Ruhr Valley with us. As soon as we neared the Ruhr Valley most of our fighters had to turn around and the Luftwaffe rose to meet us in force!

As a Squadron Commander, I climbed into the Command Pilot's seat, on the right hand side, in the lead aircraft, nicknamed *Holy Terror*, and piloted by Captain Roy A. Thompson. I was leading the "high" squadron. Bill Lindley was "Group Lead," flying at the head of the 95th Group Lead Squadron. Colonel John Gerhart was Mission Commander, flying with Bill Lindley. Bob Cozens wasn't flying that day.

This was to be the 25th mission for Basey DeWolf, Bombardier, who was flying with John Adams, a good pilot, just off my right wing and leading our "low" squadron. I had selected this mission for Basey, and Colonel John had approved it, because we were told that it would be a "milk run" without strong fighter opposition. That turned out to be a major miscall. As we were approaching the target their plane got shot up badly. It started billowing smoke and I could tell they were in serious trouble. Adams gave the order to bail out, and everyone but Basey rolled out pretty quickly. Basey was the last to leave the burning plane. He opened his chute early and floated down waving his "V for victory" hand sign. He and the rest of the crew ended up as prisoners of war in one of the Stalags.

The German fighters swarmed up from their bases like hornets coming out of their nest. Me-109s and FW-190s by the hundreds lined up and flew parallel with our formation just outside of our firing range; then they turned and came head-on at us, six abreast, firing all their guns, diving straight down between us in their attempts to break us out of our close defensive formations. When I say they flew through our close formations, I mean they were really close, within a few feet of our wingtips! Those Germans were good pilots, and they used their skills to the maximum. They tried to frighten us into moving apart and loosening our tight formations. They scared us, all right, but we held our formations tight and kept our "combat box" that allowed us to use all our guns to defend the whole Squadron. And because we were the lead Squadron, we got hit first.

This mission turned out to be one of the greatest air battles of the war! We were vastly outnumbered by these attacking fighters. Somehow, the German intelligence operation must have been able to get an advance notice about this mission. Adolf Galland, the Luftwaffe fighter chief, had brought over 250 of his fighters from all over Europe to converge on about 90 B-17s in our 13th Bomb Wing. Galland was a real professional military tactician; many of his methods of using fighter aircraft for their greatest effectiveness in battle are being taught today in our own Air Force. We were really getting hammered, and it lasted for over an hour. Several of our B-17s were getting mortally wounded and going down. Our 13th Combat Wing eventually lost 25 B-17s that day. Every one of our planes experienced battle damage. It was a bitter and prolonged battle. The anti-aircraft guns blazed away and the German fighters flew through the flak to shoot at us. When we got to the IP we had to fly straight and level to maximize the accuracy of our bombing; then it got particularly bad. We were vulnerable, and the German fighter pilots knew it. So they pressed their attacks even harder.

Big Fitz, who had been my Bombardier, was in the nose of one of the B-17s in my Squadron. The Navigator, Harry Meintz, was behind Fitz manning the two side firing 50 caliber machine guns against the onslaught of fighter attacks. We had passed the IP and Fitz was busy guiding the plane toward the position where his Norden bombsight would tell him to release our bombs. A shell came through the side and hit Meintz on the elbow, blowing off his right arm just below his biceps. Fitz, intent on his job of sighting in the target, never saw him get hit. Harry Meintz never cried out or said anything aloud to Fitz or anyone else in his crew. He just reached over with his left arm and grabbed the microphone cord and used it to make a tourniquet around his right arm stump. He stemmed the blood flow, and then he continued firing his gun with only his left arm. He also diligently continued notating in his navigational log. It wasn't until we had dropped our bombs and were headed home that he signaled to Fitz that he'd been hit and needed some assistance. Fitz was astounded! There was blood all over the inside of the nose of the plane. Fitz then took the necessary steps to aid him. For his heroic conduct, devotion to duty, and self-discipline under the most severe circumstances, that valiant Navigator later on received a high award with a medal.

Munster was definitely the roughest raid we had experienced up to that time. Our 334th Squadron lost three planes and crews out of our sixteen on the mission. But the 100th Bomb Group, flying last in our 13th Combat Wing, lost 12 B-17s! Only one airplane in the 100th Group made it back!

The Munster mission was the one that got me a Purple Heart. The Jerries were attacking us with their new air-to-air rockets, a very potent weapon that was fitted with a time fuse. When these rockets exploded they really raised hell with whatever they hit. One of them burst just outside our cockpit, taking out three of the four windows, the cockpit roof and most of the instrument panel. A large chunk of very hot metal struck me at the base of my neck on the left side. It felt as if someone had hit me with a baseball bat! Fortunately for me, the spinning fragment hit me flat and didn't penetrate; it could have torn off my head! Anyhow, I instinctively reached up to the hurting spot on my neck, and in doing so, touched that hot metal and dislodged it so that it went under the collar of my heavy flight jacket. It slid down inside my flight clothes and burned a streak all the way down to my waste band, where it lodged for the rest of the flight. I had a very stiff neck, a big burn blister at my belt line and a few other painful burns for the rest of the mission, but that was all. Right after I was hit, I looked to my left to see that Roy Thompson, the pilot, was OK; he was covered with shards of plexiglas, but otherwise none the worse for wear.

When we got back to Horham and I rose up out of my seat, the damn thing fell out my pants leg. I picked it up and walked to the dispensary to get my burns treated. It was about the diameter of a silver dollar and twice as thick. Well, I put it in my pocket, and I subsequently used it as a paperweight in my office. I kept that piece for years! I figured that that was the baby with my name on it. From then on, all I had to worry about were the ones addressed "To whom it may concern!"

Well, we dropped our bombs, using the old town center as the aiming point, and we did a whale of a good job! Virtually all our bombs landed inside the walls of Munster! The clear skies gave us great daylight visibility at 3 p.m. when we dropped our bombs, and the photos taken afterwards very clearly showed our accuracy in the pattern of bomb damage within the walled city.

So much for working for the General. After dropping our bombs we were working for ourselves, getting home. Flying the plane home without any instruments was a bit of a challenge, but we stayed close to the formation and made it without any further problems. Fortunately, the fighter attacks were sporadic on our return flight. Bill Lindley's Lead Squadron led us home and we were joined by the remnants of the 390th Bomb Group, which had lost eight B-17s, and the sole survivor of the 100th Bomb Group.

Not one of our ships returned from Munster without at least a dozen holes in it. That was really an air battle on a gigantic scale and the Germans were out to stop us at any cost. They didn't succeed in stopping us, and it cost them very heavily. Our 13th Bomb Wing had over 50 German fighters confirmed downed!

After this mission to Munster, the 95th Bomb Group received a Presidential Unit Citation for its discipline under extreme fire and its accurate bombing. Bill Lindley and John Gerhart both received the Silver Star, and I, a Distinguished Flying Cross, for our leadership in maintaining discipline and keeping our formations flying tightly together. Dewey Johnson, the Lead Bombardier, and John Gerhart both received the British Distinguished Flying Cross.

A few days later on October 14, Bob Cozens' Squadron led a Third Air Division mission of 142 B-17s to Schweinfurt. Accompanying them were 149 B-17s from the First Air Division, so the total mission comprised 291 Flying Fortresses, along with four groups of P-47 Thunderbolts. Unfortunately the P-47s were not able to go the entire distance with the bombers, which had to fly several hours over German territory unescorted. As soon as the P-47s turned back, the Luftwaffe hit them hard with wave after wave of fighters. Even worse, as they neared the target area the flak was really fierce. The Germans put up a box barrage and they had to fly through it to get to their target. This is always an uncomfortable few minutes, to say the least. It doesn't do any good to take evasive action, so our bombing crews had to screw up their courage and just plow through that flak to drop their bombs. Nevertheless, the many tons of high explosives and incendiaries wreaked heavy damage on the ball bearing factories in Schweinfurt. But it cost us dearly: 60 bombers and crews lost and 138 more bombers damaged, some beyond repair. Bob and his crew made it back OK. It was, however, just one more example of the need for long-range fighter cover for our bombing missions.

Note. The Presidential Unit Citation reads as follows:

WAR DEPARTMENT, WASHINGTON, D.C.
4 OCTOBER 1944

As authorized by Executive Order No. 9396, superceding Executive No. 9075, citation of the following Unit in General Orders, No. 138, Headquarters 3rd Bombardment Division, 23rd May 1944, as approved by the Commanding General, United States Army Forces in the European Theater of Operations, is confirmed under the provisions of Section IV, Circular No. 133, War Department, 1943, in the name of the President of the United States as public evidence of deserved honor and distinction.

The citation reads as follows:

The 95th Bombardment Group (H) is cited for outstanding performance of duty in action against the enemy in connection with the bombing of an important target at Munster, Germany, on 10th October 1943. The 95th Bombardment Group (H) led the 3rd Bombardment Division and the 13th Bombardment Wing (H) in the air, on this highly successful five hour operation which involved a flight of 520 miles at an altitude of 24,000 feet. During the period of no friendly fighter support, the Group was subjected to the violent and concentrated attacks of approximately 250 enemy fighters, chiefly FW

190's, JU 88's, Me 110's and 410's. Choosing the 13th Combat Wing as a focal point, the waves of attackers, after shooting down all but one of the aircraft in Low Group and eight of the aircraft in the High Group, concentrated on the 95th Bombardment Group (H). Twin-engined enemy fighters, firing 20-mm and 37-mm cannon and rocket projectiles, attacked in Staffels of 12 to 15 aircraft each. Losing five aircraft to this concentrated opposition, the Unit maintained a cohesive formation throughout the attacks. The 95th Bombardment Group (H) is officially credited with the destruction of 41 enemy fighters, 5 others probably destroyed, and 19 damaged. Beginning at Dorsten and continuing through the target area, the Group also encountered extremely intense and damaging anti-aircraft fire. Ten of the remaining aircraft in the Group were damaged. Rallying the remaining aircraft of the Lead Combat Wing, the 95th Bombardment Group (H) led a 6-minute bombing run in a highly effective formation, dropping its bombs on the main point of impact. Flying directly through the anti-aircraft barrage, which grew increasingly heavy as the bomb release point was reached, the Unit took more than the usual amount of time on the turns, so that the following Groups which were also undergoing vicious fighter attacks, could rejoin the formation and receive the benefit of defensive firepower. The bombing results were superior to those of any other Bombardment Group participating in the operation. Of the 102,000 pounds of bombs released by this Unit, 36 percent fell within 1,000 feet, and 64 percent hit within 2,000 feet of the assigned aiming point. The bombing pattern was excellent. Testimony to the highly successful bombing of the target was the award of the British Distinguished Flying Cross to the Lead Bombardier (Captain Dewey Johnson) for his work on the mission. After the bombing, the Group led the Division's forces to the Rally Point where friendly fighter support was met. As a result of the savage enemy opposition, 51 of the Unit's personnel are missing in action, and 4 were wounded.

Distinguishing itself by courageous resolution in overcoming vicious enemy fighter attacks and heavy anti-aircraft fire, the 95th Bombardment Group (H) displayed extraordinary valor, audacity, and courage under fire. By heroic strength of purpose, it led the way over the target to carry out its mission successfully. This Unit's personnel performed its task with coolness, skill and self sacrifice in the face of unusually determined and damaging enemy fire. The extraordinary devotion to duty and disregard for personal safety displayed, above and beyond that of all the other Units participating in the same operation, resulted in a vital blow at the German war effort. The outstanding valor and bold, vigorous heroism displayed on this occasion presented an inspiring example for other Units of the Army Air Forces.

BY ORDER OF THE SECRETARY OF STATE FOR WAR:
G. C. MARSHALL
Chief of Staff

In addition, the following Memorandum was issued by General Curtis LeMay:

From: 3rd Bombardment Division Headquarters
To: Commanding General, U.S. 8th A.A.F. Headquarters
Subject: Remarks to conclude summary of the mission to Munster 10/10/43

(1.) On this mission the heaviest losses to date were sustained by the 3rd Division, the result almost entirely of enemy fighter opposition. No new weapons were used by the enemy, but an analysis of their tactics indicate that greater effort was concentrated on the lead combat wing, and more especially on the Low Group of that Wing. This completely disrupted one Group of the bomber force. It is not likely, however, that the plan reduced the losses of the enemy to an appreciable extent.
(2.) Despite the heavy opposition, the remainder of the Groups of the formation bombed with great effectiveness, completely obliterating the assigned M.P.I. Such results under adverse conditions prove that hard training and good air discipline pay dividends.
(3.) Another change in enemy tactics is that their fighters are now waiting to strike until the escort of the bombers has turned back. This will require a more comprehensive system of diversion in the future.
(4.) Flak was again the cause of a few losses, the aircraft being hit and forced out of formation where enemy fighters could easily concentrate on them. Crews are reporting certain areas to be defended by especially accurate anti-aircraft gunners. A record of these districts is being kept and an effort will be made to avoid these areas in the future or to warn formation leaders of their location prior to each mission.

(s) Brigadier General Curtis E. LeMay

CHAPTER 8

A TRAGIC DAY AT HORHAM

We certainly didn't "stand down" for long after our 95th Group's missions to Munster and Schweinfurt. It was soon back to business as usual. After all, we had a very important job to do over there in Europe.

October 19, 1943

> We have been quite busy both with operations and training new crews. I've had particularly bad luck and lost five of my crews during the past ten days or so. As you have undoubtedly noted in the newspapers, we have had some terrific battles in our last couple of outings.
> Cliff Cole, 95th Group Operations, who was shot down over Holland about three months ago, turned up in London today. He phoned to say "Hello" and is coming to see us tomorrow. He couldn't say much over the phone, but he'll have quite a story to tell. The last I saw of him was near Rotterdam when he had half of his right wing blown off by flak. We gave them all up for dead. It just shows you can never tell. Also recently received news that two other of my crews who went down over Germany about eight weeks ago are all safe and are prisoners.

We did, however, squeeze in some time to get down to jolly London.

> ...Yesterday Bob Cozens and I went down to London for the afternoon to get a fitting on our new uniforms. We flew down and it only took twenty minutes. We stayed for dinner and by the time we took off for home it was pitch dark. And believe me, with this blackout over here it really gets dark. Well, at any rate, there were only the two of us in a B-17 and we didn't have any of the special navigation equipment that we use in our combat ships. Consequently it took us two and a half hours to find our home base. We must have circled the vicinity for an hour and a half before we contacted them

by radio, and they turned on the field lights for us so that we could locate the damned place. It was quite an experience. Anyway, it gave me a chance to get in a couple of hours of instrument flying which I needed to keep my hand in. We could have landed at several other fields in the vicinity, but we had plenty of gas and decided to wait this one out.

I acquired a new addition to my "family", a really fine wire-haired terrier puppy. I figured that he had the makings of a real champion; only three months old and already of top conformation. He was full of life, and he seemed to fill a void for me in my quarters now that Bob had moved to the 335th Squadron. The boys in our parachute department made him a specially designed oxygen mask so he could fly with us.

> ...As I write this, Pete, my pup, is sitting here on my big chair and watching every move I make. He is really good company and no bother at all. He just follows me wherever I go. He loves to ride in my Jeep and even in the airplane. He sits up in the glass nose and watches the ground with great interest. He is really a beauty — one of the best looking wire hairs that I've ever seen.

The 95th Bomb Group was about to celebrate completion of its first year, and that meant a party. This time there would even be girls there! That made all of us young men sit up and take notice.

> ...Friday will be a year since the founding of our organization. We have a great party planned. Luck was with us and less than a week ago a brand new hospital unit right fresh from the States moved into quarters less than ten miles from us. So we will be honored by the company of seventy American nurses. I only hope the poor girls won't be shocked by the rowdy rat race that will transpire. Ever since we have been organized we have had a reputation for the wildness of our parties. This should be no exception.
>
> As for the girls, I have met lots of nice girls, both English and American. We have parties on the post every other Saturday evening. On alternate Saturdays the 100th Group have their festivities. As they are only four miles from us, we go to their parties and they visit us. Between the nurses from the big hospital nearby and the young ladies from Norwich and Ipswich who attend, we have a plentiful supply. I

am also acquainted with several in London whom I see when I go down there. Nothing very exciting, but lots of fun.

As autumn turned into winter, the weather continued to be a problem as far as flying was concerned. Nevertheless, we in the 95th Group were constantly building up our forces, along with all of the other Allied armies in England, in anticipation of eventually driving the Nazis out of Europe.

October 30, 1943

> Things have been quiet with us over here. The weather has been terrible for operations. The notorious English fog has set in and we haven't been able to see across the field for over a week. The respite has been a welcome one and well used, however.
> We are doubling the size of our Groups and a good deal of work has to be done to provide quarters for the new crews. Now instead of nine crews in my Squadron, I will have eighteen. We are gradually building up to strength as rapidly as we can provide quarters for the additional men. We should be complete around the first of December.

Occasionally my letters home reflected something personal that gave me a chuckle as I read them many years later.

> ...Also a minor tragedy has occurred. Last night I lost my NEW hat up in Norwich. It was the one you got for me in San Francisco and just sent me. Bob Cozens and I went up to meet a couple of B-24 boys for dinner. We put our hats and coats on the rack at the hotel along with about 60 others. Apparently in the shuffle, someone just got the wrong hat. As it is almost impossible to track down my chapeau, I need a new one. While you are ordering it, Fitz, my Bombardier, asked if you would be kind enough to order one for him, same size as mine. Please also order the hat emblems. Thanks a lot!

As I mentioned earlier, the American Red Cross was truly the U.S. Serviceman's friend in England.

November 10, 1943

    As I write, I am at the Red Cross Club in London. Bob Cozens and I have just come from dinner after seeing the premiere of *This is the Army*. We thoroughly enjoyed it. Besides being a wonderful show it was doubly enjoyable because of the presence of all the distinguished British and American notables. We were extremely fortunate in getting seats. The show has been sold out weeks in advance. However, we arrived in the city only last evening. We got in touch with this woman at the Red Cross, Mrs. Geraci of Alameda, California, who has been wonderful to the 95th boys. How she did it, I don't know, but today she produced two seats, third row, center.

It was truly amazing how many of our boys downed over enemy territory or into the frigid waters of the English Channel came back to us. And those who didn't come back, because they were either imprisoned in POW camps or out of communication with the underground folks, would often get word back to us. I still held out hopes for my former copilot, Joe Noyes, as well as the other members of *Blondie III*'s crew.

November 14, 1943

    Regarding boys who have gone down, of the twenty-one crews that my squadron has lost since we have been in operations, I have sixteen accounted for. The other five are too recent to have heard from as yet. The others have either made their way back to England or are prisoners of war in Germany. As yet I have heard nothing from Joe Noyes, but in the next few weeks we should hear if they are prisoners. The other three boys from my crew who had gone down previously are all prisoners.

My mother mentioned in one of her letters that she was saving all my letters. I thought that was silly; but now I'm quite glad she did.

    ...Don't save my letters for me. I have no desire to keep them. However, I do wish to keep the pictures I have sent home.

My job as Squadron Commander turned out to be one that was putting a dent in my ability to get my 25 credited missions. And my additional responsibilities were so interesting and challenging that I began to doubt that I would really want to leave them after I finally made my 25 missions. I had to let my parents know what was going on with me as regards the length of my tour of duty.

> As for my tour of duty, it is still twenty-five missions, no matter what the rank. It takes quite a while to get there for me as I am one of the five Command Pilots, including Bob Cozens, in the Group, and we alternate the leads. However, it will progress quicker now as this week we are doubling the size of the Group. Instead of nine crews, I now have eighteen crews and airplanes in my squadron. Henceforth, we will put two groups, 95A and 95B, in the air on all raids. That will mean that I will get to go twice as often. Hot dog!
>
> To be very frank with you, I'm not very anxious to go home. I want to stay here and see this thing through. All Hell is going to break loose over here one of these fine days and I want to be here to see it. When it is over on this side, I'd like to go back to the States for a while and then go on out to the Pacific and do another tour in that theater. Undoubtedly, my experience will be of value; so they might as well make the most of it. However, we'll cross those bridges when we come to them.
>
> My hat arrived in good shape, and it is swell. I keep it anchored to me with a big chain! When Big Fitz received his, he said for me to thank you for your trouble; he really appreciates it.

On November 19, 1943, the 13th Bomb Wing was taking off on a mission, and this was one of the missions where I, as Squadron Commander of the 334th Bomb Squadron, was alternating with Bob Cozens as Command Pilot for the 95th Group's missions; he went on the mission and I stayed at Horham. I was, however, in the tower watching the planes take off. With me in the tower were Dave McKnight, who also wasn't scheduled to fly that day, and his Squadron Flight Surgeon, "Doc" Imes.

As I had mentioned before, we loaded these B-17s with as much fuel and as many bombs as possible, pushing their capability regarding weight maximums to allow for getting them off the ground at takeoff. So we watched them as they gained ground speed and finally rose over the end of the airstrip and became airborne. After they were safely in the air, they made their first left turn to begin the pattern for attaining assembly altitude. It was quite clear that morning, and the dangers of running into other airplanes were not worrisome. Because this day's mission was deep into Germany, these planes were really loaded to their maximums. We could see them becoming airborne way down at the farthest end of the runway. My 334th Squadron was the last of our 95th Bomb Group to leave on the mission. By 8:30 in the morning they were all up in the air but a few, and we were getting ready to relax and go back to our desks to do some paperwork until the time came to sweat out the return of our boys from bombing Germany.

The plane then making its takeoff run was piloted by Lieutenant Kenneth B. Rongstad, one of our newer pilots, a cocky blonde kid with a lot of confidence in his flying skills. At this stage of our build-up of forces in England, we were absorbing and training a great many new pilots and crews, and we were concerned about them as they proceeded on their first few missions. Ken Rongstad, however, was well regarded by most of us as both a good pilot and as a responsible captain of his crew, although certainly not as experienced or as well-trained as pilots who had arrived earlier. As Rongstad's plane lumbered along gaining speed nearing the end of the runway, it just barely rose off the ground and apparently started its bank to the left. But it was still too close to the ground! The plane stalled and its left wing hit the ground. The plane spun around and crashed! It started burning right away.

I ran and jumped in my Jeep and drove as fast as I could over to the crash. I could see that Dave McKnight and Doc Imes were also driving madly over there to the end of the runway to help the crew. I parked as close as I dared and ran to the plane, which was now burning well and igniting ammunition, like very loud popcorn going off inside. I was one of the first to get near the crash. I was less than 50 yards from the burning wreck when — WHOOOM! — the whole thing exploded big time! It literally blew me back flat on my backside! I got up again and approached the burning wreckage; I tried to drag a couple of the boys out of there, but they were all dead, and the heat of the fire was so great that I couldn't get anyone out anyway. Lt. Rongstad and his whole crew were killed.

As Squadron Commander, one of the duties I reserved for myself was to write to the families of the men in my Squadron who were killed. I had always felt that it was important for me to soften the blow of the loss of a son in action in my Squadron. I had learned firsthand about the need to help parents with their grief when I had to take the body of my roommate, Errol Crowe, back to his parents after he was killed in a flight training accident. So I wrote to Lt. Rongstad's mother; however, she wrote back to me insisting that he could not have been killed as he was too good a pilot. I had to write back to her, again explaining what happened in the crash and that no one in the crew could have possibly lived through the explosions and fire. She continued to refuse to recognize that her son was killed. She insisted that he couldn't have been killed; it must have been somebody else in the cockpit of that plane. We had to exchange several more letters, until she finally stopped corresponding with me. She certainly stayed in denial of her son's death for a long time, and trying to reason with her was pretty difficult for me.

There was a farmhouse about forty yards from the crash, and inside it was the farmer's wife, eight months along in her pregnancy, along with her two-year-old daughter[4]. Thank God neither she nor her daughter were physically hurt, and the severe trauma did not disturb her pregnancy. Her home was demolished around her with the force of the explosion and pieces of flying debris. Doc Imes took her to the base hospital for examination, and she was apparently unharmed. Her husband, the farmer, had been out in the fields when the plane crashed. He came running across the fields when he saw the crash in what appeared to be his back yard. He was immensely relieved when Doc Imes walked her out of the shambles of what had been their home and loaded her in his

---

[4] The farmer and his wife, I later learned, were named Harold and Iris Tydeman. Also in the cottage on the side away from the explosions was their horse handler, Victor Gooderham; he, too, was not injured beyond a few glass splinters.

field ambulance. She eventually gave birth to another daughter, and the family moved into a home nearby. And, of course, the American Army compensated her for her physical losses, but I doubt that she and her husband ever wanted to live that close to an airfield again.

Note

One of the original crew of Ken Rongstad's B-17, Staff Sergeant Louis A. Godek, who wasn't flying with his crew that particular day, later wrote about Lt. Ken Rongstad in a manner that reflects the respect and loyalty that the crews of B-17s had for each other and especially for their pilots.

> For the records of the 95th, I would like one and all to know that our pilot, Ken Rongstad, was a gem and an extraordinary commander. We formed our crew in Moses Lake, Washington, and then went to Walla Walla, Washington, before that long hop to Bangor and the Great Northern Circle via Labrador, Greenland and Iceland to Prestwick, Scotland. There we received our assignment to our Group, and were able to talk to many people about combat experiences and received first hand information which later proved very helpful to us. We made it to Horham finally, and while checking in at Administration, we watched the Group returning from a mission, including firing off red flares to indicate they had wounded men aboard. That was an interesting introduction to air warfare.
>
> The 334th Squadron was to be our home, nestled up on the hillside above the 13th Wing Headquarters.
>
> Our combat training started immediately, and it didn't take Lt. Rongstad long to figure out that we were going to be flying over a lot of water and we had better know how to get out of a plane quickly if we ever had to go down. We were at the plane day in and day out practicing what we thought were the best techniques learned from both American and British sources, augmented by ideas of our own. The ideal time we strived for in evacuation was under two minutes; and on land we managed to get there. Ken was a stickler and everyone knew their position and responsibility. This was a MUST: practice every day, while waiting for that first trip.

After a few aborts, we finally climbed aboard an old clunker aptly named *Spare Parts*, and took off on what was to be our first mission, a very interesting trip to Daren, Germany! We had a lot of enemy company just going there and by the time we got to the target we had already lost one engine, and by the time we turned to go back home we lost another. Before we knew it the last engine went and we were on our way down just off the coast of Holland. One of our squadron crews followed us down carefully, to avoid flying through our jetsam, so as to report our position, and it did look somewhat hopeless for us. Ken Rongstad brought that dead bird down as easy as pie atop the crest of a wave, and after the second bounce and settling we were cleared out of that plane in less than 30 seconds. She stayed afloat for almost ten minutes even though she was in two pieces, broken at the ball turret. The ditching was flawless. We didn't get a scratch and the only sour happening was that the raft on the starboard was not tied down and started to drift off. Sgt. Louie Mirabile swam after it and caught up with it as it neared the tail section. Then Lt. Joe Spicer, our Bombardier (who before that day had never swum a stroke) swam to it and climbed in with Louie. The rest of us, all eight, climbed into the other raft. We figured out how to crank the Gibson Girl (a hand-cranked signal beacon narrow in the middle to fit between the knees). And we learned how to stay warm in the cold North Sea in waves that were probably 20 to 30 feet high. We also learned about frustration when a British Sutherland seaplane found us only to be able to wag his wings because of the high waves.

Anyway, THIRTEEN hours later, some 20 miles north of the place where we ditched, a British Rescue Vessel found us. Thanks also to the flares we were able to shoot up overhead with our Very Pistol! They picked us up and transported us into Yarmouth, where we were given the treatment. There we got to thank a real spunky Captain by the name of Gable who managed to take good care of us and get us back to Horham.

The morning after our return we were headed out to Wilhelmshaven, that great trip where we had to descend all 29,000 feet down through solid overcast. We made it home and immediately the following day we got to experience a trip to Blackpool for a rest period. At this point we knew we had a pilot who was going to take us there and back. Upon our return from Blackpool we were scheduled for a trip to Norway. On this mission I had my hands frostbitten pretty badly, even though we were only at 10,000 feet. Anyhow, when we landed back home, I was given a trip to the hospital, which is where I was when this saga (the crash at Horham) started.

When I was finally well enough to return to active duty, I was "adopted" by the Squadron CO, Major Harry Conley, and I flew mostly with his crew or when he commanded. I did some instructing during the off days. The ditching procedures devised by Lt. Rongstad were so highly thought of after our report that they became standard procedures.

CHAPTER 9

A CALIFORNIA HORSE IN ENGLAND

In mid-June of 1943, Curtis LeMay, then a Colonel and Commander of the 4th Bomb Wing, moved his headquarters into a grand old Georgian mansion situated on a rolling 23,000 acre rural estate of woods and fields near Ipswich, Norwich and Cambridge. Located in the heart of Suffolk, where the U.S. Army Eighth Air Force and the Royal Air Force were to ultimately have almost 100 air bases as the Allied forces built up their strength, Elveden Hall was (and still is) the ancestral home of the Earl of Iveagh, who in those days was Samuel Guinness. Elveden had come into the Guinness family in 1894, purchased by the 1st Earl of Iveagh following the death of its builder, the Maharajah Duleep Singh, ruler of the Punjab. Because of the war emergency the British Government had taken over its 200-odd rooms, and the Earl and his family had moved to a much smaller if no less handsome Georgian house on the property.

Among the Guinness family holdings, of course, is Guinness Stout ale, and Elveden reflected the clan's social position and affluence. The Hall — really more like a palace — was the centerpiece of a picturesque estate more than one and one-half times the area of Manhattan Island. Most of it was pastureland. One of the largest landholdings in Northeast England, it was famed as a hunting resort frequented by generations of British aristocracy. Three reigning kings — King Edward VII, King George V, and King George VI — had sojourned there, coming like most visitors in pursuit of its vast population of game birds.

Elveden Hall became a central meeting place for USAAF commanders and their staffs. Colonel LeMay held his trademark post-mission critiques there, meetings attended by many members of the mission's flying crews, all of them asked to speak their piece about the day's events. As new bomb groups came into the nearby area of East Anglia, their crews joined in these post-mission critiques. Based on the fliers' observations, LeMay developed and refined his battle procedures. It was a superb and inspired management technique.

In September 1943, LeMay was made a Brigadier General, a rank we called "Buck General," and was assigned to form the Third Air Division, which would include the new 13th Combat Wing consisting of the 95th, 100th and 390th Bomb Groups. As a Squadron Commander in the 95th, immediately after I'd return to Horham from a mission, I would climb into a Jeep or a truck for the twenty mile drive to Elveden Hall for those debriefings. Afterwards, we senior officers would stay for evening cocktails, and the Earl often stopped by to join us. We found him a charming fellow, and we got on well. He invited us to roam the woods and fields with a shotgun, and in our off time quite a few of us did. England was then on strict food rationing, however, so we were asked to check in with the estate's game master when we returned from the hunt to turn our birds over to him. In exchange for our take he would give each of us a maximum of two cleaned birds, cold-storing ours for the upcoming weekly sale at a nearby public market where local folk purchased the estate's wildfowl as a welcome supplement to their restricted diet.

In his late thirties or early forties, the Earl of Iveagh was a Major and a paratrooper in the British army. His army unit was stationed nearby, so he was able to come back to his home estate almost every evening. While the authorities had requisitioned his estate house, the Earl's land and livestock operation remained under his supervision. Despite his wealth and titled status he was an exceedingly friendly fellow with a lovely wife named Elizabeth and two beautiful children with flaxen hair who were about four and six years old. Affable and unaffected, he asked me to address him simply as Sam. Sam and his generous family became particularly close and friendly with John Gerhart, Grif Mumford, and me; and we were often invited to dine with the Guinness family in their home. We, of course, reciprocated and invited them to dine with us at Elveden Hall. It was, after all, really their home. Prior to 1939, the Earl's life had been largely given over to managing his farmland and livestock, in particular Guernsey cows, and to keeping abreast of the latest advances in agricultural science. On learning of my experience with cattle in California, he began to quiz me about American livestock and farming techniques that might be applicable to his estate.

His interest peaked, however, when he discovered that we shared an affection for horses. He modestly allowed that he played "a lot of polo." A lot indeed; he was rated an eight-goal player, which made him a world-class competitor. He was eager for me to have a look at his horses, of which he was quite proud and kept in a lovely stable. When we toured the paddock I saw that his pride was justified, for they were all fine horses. He pointed to an especially good looking, light framed thoroughbred I put at about 1,100 pounds, proclaiming it his "number one polo pony." About 15.3 hands high with good conformation, he had a lustrous sorrel coat and a white blaze, and seemed exceptionally alert and intelligent. Sam let me admire the horse for a moment before delivering the punch line. "He came from your part of the world. He's from San Mateo, California." I was astonished to say the least! Then Sam explained to me that he had acquired this horse, albeit indirectly, from Charlie Howard, a socially prominent and wealthy Buick dealer based in Burlingame, California. In the 1930s Burlingame was a gentrified semi-rural village on the San Francisco Peninsula a few minute's drive north from San Mateo along the eucalyptus-lined *El Camino Real*, the 18th century Spanish highway road linking Old California's 21 Franciscan missions. Charlie Howard, the owner of the famous race horse, "Seabiscuit," was a respected and renowned polo player, and the horses from his ranch were widely regarded as among the finest to be had anywhere in the world. People came to San Mateo from far and wide to buy them, the Maharaja of India among them.

Sam, however, had gotten this horse from Aiden Roark, another topflight polo player, who had purchased it from Howard's stable. Aiden Roark was world famous, as was his Irish father, Pat Roark, a ten-goal polo player in Great Britain. Once a year, Aiden

Roark (who went on to become an American citizen and marry the Berkeley-bred, first-time female Wimbledon tennis champion Helen Wills) traveled through California, stopping at San Mateo and Monterey to buy trained horses for sale in Britain. Due largely to Charlie Howard's father, Lin Howard, San Mateo had become an important place on the map of world polo activity before the war, and remained so for several years afterward. Lin Howard had been a renowned breeder and trainer of fine polo horses, and partnered with Bing Crosby to establish the Del Mar Race Track near San Diego, California. In addition to the San Mateo training center that son Charlie managed, Lin had a sprawling horse breeding farm in Mendocino on the coast about 60 miles north of San Francisco. He selected the best young horses from his breeding stock and trucked them to San Mateo for training. What made his ponies so attractive in addition to their good bloodlines was that they were invariably high-quality "finished" bridle horses. They had been trained according to methods developed in the early 1800s in *Alta California* when much of what is now the Golden State was a rural province of Mexico, and its Spanish-Mexican citizens, known as *Californios*, were legendary for their astonishing horsemanship.

Because they were in fact trained by a genuine *Californio*, an elderly *vaquero* named Fernando Michel, Charlie's horses thus made excellent polo ponies. Though Fernando was esteemed among breeders and horse people as one of the finest trainers on the West Coast, in those days he was not unique; other trainers with a similar heritage used Old California methods with similarly excellent results. "Go ahead and ride him," Sam told me. "See how you like him." I shook my head in wonderment at encountering, here in the English countryside, a horse reared where I had learned to ride as a boy. "He's a very lovely, sensitive horse," Sam assured me. "Try him and see what he can do." Soon I was mounted on a horse in my Army uniform. I felt as though I had somehow magically reverted to civilian life. As I barely touched his side with my spur, Sam's California horse moved easily across the Guinness lands some 5,300 miles and a world apart from where both of us had been introduced to the unique *Californio* relationship between horse and rider. I thought of Fernando Michel and the tradition he represented.

Fernando worked exclusively for Charlie Howard at Charlie's elaborate two-story stables in San Mateo, and hewed to the traditional Old California skill and precision of horse training. He usually trained some 20 horses simultaneously, assisted by helpers who groomed and saddled them and cleaned the barns. Fernando, however, was their exclusive trainer and only rider. Beginning at daybreak, he rode and trained each horse for about 20 minutes, then dismounted, turning the animal over to an assistant and immediately mounting another until he had completed a session with each of the ponies. Typically he was done for the day by noon, and you could walk into the center of the beautiful big U-shaped stables and see him sitting, relaxed, studying the horses in their stalls, their heads out of the top half of their Dutch doors.

When you looked at them you saw that all were "bitted up" in *Californio* style bridles. With their necks properly arched they learned to give to the bridle and flex their necks, an important element of their training. These horses all had spade bits, which gently touch the pallet and made them unusually responsive to the lightest and most subtle movement of the reins, probably the key element behind Fernando's reputation for turning out finely trained horses — so responsive, it was said, that they could be ridden with silk threads in their mouths. Although the Spanish spade bit appears to be a lot of iron to put in a horse's mouth, heavy and potentially hurtful, in the proper hands it is a very gentle and subtle tool for transmitting a rider's instructions to his horse. The training of a horse with the spade bit was an art in which Fernando was indeed an artist. Fernando's success burnished the reputation of Charlie Howard's stable and attracted buyers from all over the world.

Not surprisingly, when I commenced my ride on Sam's horse, he instantly came to life and his *Californio* training became immediately evident. Responsive to the slightest signals, feather light on the bit, he responded perfectly. I tried turning him on his hindquarters, and he did that exactly right. I demonstrated him doing spins on his hindquarters, first to the left and then to the right. Sam was astonished. "I never knew he could do that!" he exclaimed. I ran the horse down the field and asked him to do a quick stop, *vaquero* style. He came to a square sliding stop, bringing his hindquarters down toward the ground with his feet firmly planted, gouging two lines in the turf as his four hooves slid across the ground, leaving him in perfect position to change direction quickly as a *Californio* horse would when he turned a cow. It well-qualified him for the *vaquero* game of *once*, the Spanish word for eleven, represented by the two lines left in the dirt after such a stop was made.

A herd of Sam's prize Guernseys was grazing nearby, providing an opportunity to try this horse at working cattle. I asked the horse to sort out a single cow, and then chased the cow down the fence at speed, overtook him and turned him against the fence. We, the horse and I as a team, were sorting or "cutting" the animal from the herd and pinning him to the fence using the classic maneuvers of a *Californio vaquero* horse. Fernando's former pupil performed perfectly, responding to my signals and controlling the cow with alacrity and evident pleasure. I demonstrated these maneuvers twice again to show Sam the speed, agility and lightness of signal of his polo star. Sam, grinning broadly, expressed his amazement at observing his horse's hitherto unrevealed abilities.

Our shared love of horses made us friends and riding buddies. He invited me to come out to Elveden to ride whenever I had time between bombing missions or was summoned to meetings there by General LeMay. An accomplished horseman, he was especially able to appreciate the arcane abilities of his *Californio*-trained animal, possessing skills rarely if ever seen among horses in England then. Sometimes when he and his wife had guests, Sam would ask me to come over from Horham to demonstrate the horse's cattle working skill for their friends. Though my bombing missions were increasing in frequency, we managed to get together quite often, and somehow even found the time to take the horse to several major exhibitions and shows in Norwich, Cambridge and London. Under Sam's auspices I rode him in the famed "White City" show grounds to demonstrate his cattle working abilities in front of an appreciative audience of Britons unaccustomed to cutting horses and "cowboying."

Sam, horseman that he was, really wanted to learn the arcane skills of *vaquero* reinsmanship, to become worthy of being called, in Spanish, a *reinadero*. He worked with me to learn how to make his horse perform these *vaquero* moves and skills and became quite capable of making his "Number One Polo Pony" look like what he really was, a finished *Californio*-style bridle horse. We rode together across his estate while I gave him instructions in reining his horse, just as I had been taught in California. Sam soon became proficient enough in *vaquero* skills that he was able to demonstrate his horse himself in exhibitions.

Perhaps it was over cocktails — and perhaps in part because of them — that Sam and I cooked up the crowning event in this horse adventure in England. We decided to put on a three-day Western Rodeo right there in Norwich. It all started when some of the guys had heard me telling about riding Sam's horse, and so they went and talked to the Recreation Officer in the 93rd Bomb Wing. The Recreation Officer got in touch with me and remarked that there were a lot of Airmen in the Wing who were rodeo enthusiasts and wanted to see my *vaquero* horse demonstration. Recreation Officers were always searching for fresh ways to entertain the troops. He asked me to stage a horse demonstration like the ones I was doing for British audiences. Before long we were planning a classic Western rodeo that quickly expanded into a three-day event. We asked the Red Cross to send us clothing and equipment from the States. I wrote down what we needed and, being the Red Cross, they got it: Western saddles, chaps, spurs, hats, lariats and so forth. Sam enthusiastically threw himself into the project, lining up 25 thoroughbred polo horses for the riders in various events, five "Suffolk Punches," big work horses raised in Suffolk which we used as the world's largest bucking horses, and some 60 of his cattle for cutting horse and roping events. For a rodeo arena he secured the use of Norwich's soccer field. Norwich was the largest town in nearby Norfolk County, with about 100,000 inhabitants, and the soccer field grandstands could seat 55,000 spectators. We hadn't thought about it at first, but it soon became apparent that the local force of American Airmen, most of them ground crewmen, included a good many professional rodeo cowboys. After asking around, we found that we had about 60 seasoned competitors. The residents of both Norfolk and Suffolk Counties came in droves; over the three days, some 75,000 people attended — a sell-out performance. Sam was in his newfound glory as an apprentice *Californio*, personally demonstrating his "number one polo pony" by performing splendid *Californio* reining work and riding him like a genuine *vaquero*. For the citizens of Norwich, our Authentic Western American Rodeo was the highlight of the summer of 1944.

But we were, after all, still at war, and the war continued to take its toll. The brief respite of my riding days together with Sam Guinness, the 2nd Earl of Iveagh, came to an end at the end of 1944. As the Allied invasion of Europe bogged down in France in November, 1944, Sam and his unit of paratroopers were called into action there in the Battle of the Bulge. Late that December I went back to the States on my long-awaited Christmas leave and we were out of touch. It was not until I was reassigned to the Pentagon in January when I heard from John Gerhart, who was discussing his own reassignment with General LeMay's office, that Sam had been killed in December when a V-1 Flying Bomb hit his temporary headquarters in Belgium. Those of us who had gotten to know him were particularly saddened by the loss of such an extraordinary fellow. John diligently passed on our condolences to Lady Elizabeth. Following Sam's death, Elizabeth and their children moved from Elveden to live with her family and I never again rode their beloved California horse.

CHAPTER 10

LEARNING SOP'S THE HARD WAY

When we of the 95th Bomb Group arrived in England in April 1943, there were few established standard operating procedures (SOPs) for combat. We had no idea in the world what to do or how to do it. We had to learn by doing. We basically knew how to fly our B-17s and we had received some instruction in formation flying, although we hadn't really experienced formation flying the way we had to do it in battle. This was a new kind of war with new weapons, and there weren't any manuals of SOPs in existence. We had to develop procedures as we went along, trial and error, learning from our mistakes.

One of our most disastrous lessons learned the hard way took place at Alconbury, one of our first temporary bases after we arrived in England. As we were preparing for one of our early missions in May of 1943 we were loading fused bombs into our B-17s, which was our procedure then because it was fast and easy to fuse the bombs on the ground where we could readily reach them. Unfortunately, someone apparently dropped one while loading it onto an airplane. The result was a horrific explosion — or series of explosions — and we ended up losing 19 men and 15 planes, plus 30 more men wounded and several other planes damaged but repairable. I was about a quarter of a mile from the original explosion, with my crew playing poker, and we experienced the building and ground shaking repeatedly with every explosion. We hit the floor, not knowing what the hell was going on. When the explosions stopped, we went out to see what happened and to assess the damage. It was gruesome! The accidental detonation of a bomb caused a chain reaction with all the nearby planes and fused bombs. Fires and debris and dead and injured men were all over the field. What a catastrophe! That was the last time we loaded fused bombs! We immediately changed procedures, and from then on we loaded our bombs without fuses, letting the crewmen screw in the fuses after we were airborne. It was more difficult to set the fuses when the bombs were in their bomb racks, but it was certainly much safer. This was a very tragic and expensive lesson.

Colonel Curtis LeMay was an innovator from his early days in Eighth Bomber Command as Commanding Officer of the 305th Bomb Group, and as a result a number of Col. LeMay's bombing procedures were adopted by other Bomb Groups of the Eighth.

Later, when Col. LeMay commanded the 4th Bomb Wing, and the 3rd Bomb Division, this pattern of leadership by LeMay continued and many of our procedures in the 95th Bomb Group and other Groups were developed when he required us to meet together with him after each and every mission to critique the missions. Many of the flight personnel in the Division who went on the missions, pilots, navigators and bombardiers, had to attend. There at these post-mission meetings we were all treated as equals regardless of rank, and we were asked to say our piece about what we did that worked and what we did that didn't work. This was one of the greatest things that Curtis LeMay did to resolve many of the problems we had, both foreseen and unforeseen, early in the war. From the suggestions made in these meetings our procedures continued to develop.

One of the first things we learned was that we should never leave the skies over the British Isles at an altitude under 20,000 feet. We had found that the German 88 millimeter anti-aircraft guns had pretty good accuracy up to about 20,000 feet, and below that altitude we became easy targets for them. The 88 millimeter gun the Germans used as their primary anti-aircraft weapon was probably the greatest gun in the war. It could shoot straight ahead as an anti-tank gun or a shoreline defense gun defending the Normandy beaches, and it could rise vertically and be an excellent anti-aircraft gun. The higher we could be when we approached the French coastline, the greater were our chances of not being hit directly by these 88 millimeter shells. Usually our missions headed

The 95th drops its bombs.

Colonel John Gerhart.
Official Army photograph

The 95th Bomb Group assembles for takeoff from Horham Airfield.

The 95th Bomb Group personnel assembled for this photo for Life Magazine *as part of our celebration of having completed 200 missions.*

Life Magazine

across the English Channel at 25,000 to 28,000 feet to keep away from those 88 shells. Our B-17s flew very well at these altitudes.

The B-17 was a damn good airplane; it was the best airplane in the war, no question. It was reliable and stout. You can see that even the airplanes of today still utilize many of the design features of Boeing's B-17. It was the first four-engine airplane used in any quantity by the Army, starting in 1935. The other airplane we used was the Consolidated B-24, a four-engine high wing airplane with twin tails; it was supposed to have performance characteristics better than the B-17. It was designed in 1939 to be the most advanced heavy bomber in the world, with greater fuel capacity and range, more speed, and capability to carry a larger and heavier bomb load. But for flying close formations at altitudes over 22,000 feet, there was no comparison. The B-24 was designed with a "Davis Wing," a very different design principle than the one used on the B-17; it had to fly "on the step" like a speedboat with its nose depressed and its tail elevated in order to maintain its altitude. When it lost speed, its tail would come down; in order to regain speed, it had to lose altitude and get its tail back up. We always climbed our B-24s to 500 feet above the desired altitude so we could drop down to the right altitude while maintaining our airspeed in a tail high position. A B-24 didn't fly with ease or grace; it lumbered through the air reluctantly. All these characteristics made the B-24 very difficult to fly in close formation. The B-17, on the other hand, flew level straight ahead and maintained its altitude. When you'd see a B-17 flying, it was graceful and beautiful; it looked like it was reaching for the sky. And as far as being able to take punishment, the B-17 would fly as long as you had the control column in your hand. I've flown them home with one, two or even three engines gone. Trying to do that with a B-24 would be much more difficult. When Colonel John Gerhart formed the 93rd Combat Wing, he was assigned some Groups having a total of 500 B-24s. He sent all those planes back and insisted on B-17s; and he got them. Those B-24s were reassigned either to the Second Division, which used all B-24s, or to the South Pacific where they didn't have to fly the close formations we did.

An interesting sidelight was that all the newly manufactured planes we received were equipped for use both in the South Pacific and in Europe, and these were two very different types of aerial warfare. As they were being manufactured in quantity and their ultimate destinations were not known when they came off the assembly line, they were all similarly equipped. Equipment we didn't need only cut down the fuel and bombs we could take on our missions, so we needed to get rid of anything extraneous. Therefore we established at Bovingdon just outside of London a modification center for all incoming aircraft. There the equipment for use specifically in the South Pacific was removed before the plane was ready for our use. Something we didn't need and couldn't use was LORAN equipment designed for long-range navigation over the ocean, something vitally needed in the Pacific Theater of Operations. In the South Pacific they had to do the same thing with equipment designed for European warfare, such as all our deicing equipment, electric flying boots and the like, since our bombers there didn't need to fly at high altitudes like we did in Europe. The need to establish such a modification center for new aircraft was something we had to learn as we went along.

Another thing we learned as we started flying these new B-17s was that each one seemed to fly differently from the others, even though they were all supposed to be the same. We found that the quality of production varied with different manufacturers. Boeing's B-17s were well-made and they all flew well. Some of those of other manufacturers were not made with as much care and as a result did not fly as well. They all came with documentation of their quality control and, in particular, their finished weight. That was very important because we put that into our calculations about how much weight we could carry in fuel and bombs and still get off the ground. And we pushed that weight limit to the absolute maximum! When we started having some planes run off the end of the runway and into the soft soil beyond the perimeter track, we realized that the weight data we were receiving from the manufacturers were not correct. We then added to the SOPs for Bovingdon to weigh each plane before turning it over to us. It surprised us how much these weights differed. One manufacturer acknowledged that they weighed only one out of every 100 aircraft made! The guys at Bovingdon were also finding "stuff" in the wings and elsewhere in these planes — tools, parts, Coke bottles, lunch boxes, old work clothes, and so on. That stuff could cause unanticipated weight variances. So as an additional procedure they had to go over the hollow places in all these new planes and remove such excess items.

After a few of our "escapees" returned from France where their planes had been shot down, they let us know that our bombing had not been nearly as effective in destroying trucks, tanks, and buildings as we had thought it was from the aerial photographs. Under the protection of the French Resistance, they were able to roam surreptitiously around the environs of Paris quietly taking intelligence photos. They showed us photos taken on the ground that illustrated how our bombs were only blowing piles of dirt up on top of our targets and not destroying them. The Germans were able to recover their equipment merely by digging away the dirt. Well, what we had been doing was setting the time fuses on our bombs to detonate a few seconds after impact. The objective was not to just put a hole in the roof of a structure but to penetrate the roof and destroy everything inside the structure. However, this delay in detonation was also causing our bombs to burrow down into the earth before exploding. Their delayed detonation therefore blew all the covering dirt upward covering the target instead of damaging it. When we figured that out, we changed our procedure for fusing our bombs so they would detonate instantly upon contact. Then they would explode downward as soon as they touched something like a building roof or a piece of military equipment, exploding directly at their targets. That made a tremendous difference in the amount of damage done to the enemy.

Our SOPs to assemble our airborne forces and fly together into combat had to evolve, as well, from our experiences. At first we went on missions as a Group, usually with four Squadrons of 16 bombers. Then as our air forces grew we went on missions as a Wing, consisting of four or more Groups. By the middle of 1944 we were, on occasion, assembling missions of 1,000 to 2,000 airplanes all headed for the same target areas. The logistics of getting all these aircraft together to fly in formations to the same destinations became very involved and detailed, especially with England's tricky and unpredictable weather conditions.

Our Command Center, located at High Wycombe, Buckinghamshire north of London, was the origin of all our detailed battle plans, which were then relayed to us by our Intelligence Officers, including Jiggs Donohue, Intelligence Officer of the 95th Bomb Group. Our airfields were located mostly in East Anglia, about four or five miles apart. Horham in Suffolk, for example, was the base for the 95th Bomb Group; and the 100th Bomb Group was about four miles away at Thorpe Abbotts. East Anglia is low, rolling farming country, open and relatively level with a few small scattered forests, ideal for aircraft landing fields. Also, it is closest to the North Sea and the coast of Holland. It was loaded with almost 100 military airfields, both British and American. Aircraft from all these various bases had to take off at night at close to the same time on a specific heading, even in heavy fog or clouds, at one minute intervals and climb at a rate of 500 feet per minute up to a specific altitude, holding very carefully to specific compass headings and following certain homing beacons, called "bunchers," located in several known locations around the British Isles. Upon reaching a buncher, each plane had to make a 180° left turn at a new heading toward another buncher while continuing to gain altitude at 500 feet per minute. This "laddering" would continue until the assembly altitude was reached, usually around 25,000 feet and usually over East Anglia, as this most eastern portion of England was the closest to the English Channel and the coast of France. The clouds over all the British Isles were often quite thick and very high reaching 20,000 feet or more, adding greatly to the riskiness of the assembly process.

Assembling these large formations of airplanes was probably the worst part of the mission, worse than the flak, even worse than the Luftwaffe. Doing it in bad weather made the dangers even greater. Sometimes the fog was so bad that we had to be led by a blackout-lighted jeep out to the runway for takeoff. When we got to our takeoff positions on the runways, our navigators had to align our compasses with the painted lines and heading markers on the tarmac to ensure that we would take off into the heavy blinding fog in exactly the right direction. Once we were off and into the clouds, we had to fly purely on instruments very precisely as instructed no matter what, and we hoped every other plane to our left and to our right kept to its course as well. These other planes were taking off from fields only four miles away on both sides of us on parallel flight paths. Our timing had to be accurate to 30 seconds! It was pretty sporty! In the deep blackness of the fog and clouds we couldn't see a thing until we popped out of the clouds. Nevertheless, frequently we'd be flying along in the blackness and suddenly — WHOOMP! — we'd fly through somebody's propwash. But we'd never see anything. We just had to keep on flying as directed. Unfortunately, we lost quite a few planes in midair collisions as we flew blindly through the clouds up toward the assembly point.

Our navigators had to know exactly how many seconds it took for our planes to make a turn around each buncher. As the planes assembled into squadrons, and then into groups and then into wings, the timing of the turns became longer; and the navigators had to calculate these timing changes as planes joined up with the formations. If a formation didn't get started properly at exactly the right timing or if it got off timing during assembly, that formation could get into trouble interfering with other formations on the same mission. The calculations of the navigators had to include factors for bomb loads and fuel weights, which were specific to each mission. For instance, short distance missions could take less fuel and thereby be able to carry more bombs; and the longer missions would have to carry more fuel and less weight in bombs. Nevertheless, each bomber never carried less than ten 500 pound bombs on any mission.

Once we would reach our cruising level, the skies would be getting light with the dawn. We could look down on the beautiful clouds below and we'd see airplanes popping up through the clouds here and there. The clouds below looked like a sea of cotton, sprouting little airplanes as they emerged from below. It was a truly magnificent sight as the sun's morning rays started to shine on the cloud tops! After popping up out of the clouds, we started the assembly process by flying a dog-leg to the left. Then the lead planes of each Squadron and Group would send up specifically color-coded flares to signal the other planes to assemble with them. As planes assembled, the dog-leg paths we flew would have to get increasingly larger to give room for additional planes to join up. Meanwhile our navigators had to keep advising us pilots about the time, in seconds, required to make our turns to maintain our formation's timing. Then the numbers of aircraft would increase until a Wing was assembled; then they would all move together in formation to cross the Channel. By the end of 1944, the number of airplanes flying together on these missions was so great — sometimes more than 2,000 heavy bombers — that it would take two hours or more for all of them to pass over a specific spot on the ground! Never again will the world see anything like that number of planes in the sky!

All those airplanes created a new cloud deck with their "contrails," condensation from an atmospheric reaction to the heat of the engines' exhausts. You can see contrails frequently these days when just one jet flying high overhead on a clear day leaves its contrail across the sky. Well, try, if you can, to imagine the combined contrails of thousands of planes all flying at the same time in the same direction. We really made clouds that actually blotted out the sun! And, of course, those clouds were just one more hazard we had to fly through!

By 1944 our combat missions grew so large — hundreds of miles from front to back — that communication and control became much more difficult. So, we had to develop a new procedure! The RAF had a small fighter-bomber, the DeHavilland "Mosquito." Its body was very light, made of plywood and it had two large Rolls Royce engines that made the "Mozzie" the fastest piston-engine aircraft of the war. It was really fast! Although it was designed for two, a pilot and a navigator/bombardier, we took out the second seat, then we also took out the guns to make more room for fuel. Our 93rd Combat Wing was able to get hold of several Mosquitoes, initially designated for use in aerial reconnaissance. This hot little airplane became the "Mission Command Center," piloted by the Mission Commander. I had many occasions as Mission Commander to fly my Mosquito over the lead bombers on their way into Germany and then to circle around over the target area, keeping track of the various Wings and Groups as they hit their targets and turned around. I was in radio contact with the Flight Leaders that were near and over the target area. Because those lightweight unarmed Mosquitoes were so fast they could fly away from the Germans' Me-109s and FW-190s. They looked a lot like the Germans' Me-410 twin-engine fighters.

Those characteristics really helped me out once. I was flying in my Mosquito over the target area, and when I discharged the last Squadron on the mission I then headed home to the west, right into the setting sun; and it was blinding me. As I was flying west right over Frankfort, suddenly I saw an airplane passing directly in front of me headed north. It was an Me-109, and it was part of a whole formation of German fighters headed to attack our bombers. They must have mistaken me for a Me-410, but they were flying all around me, taking evasive action to avoid collision. There were airplanes going every which way. They were ducking me. I was unarmed and in real danger! As soon as I figured out what was happening, I thought to myself, "I better get the Hell out of here, and FAST!" I pushed my throttle forward and put the nose down to gain speed. Three of those Me-109s peeled off and took out after me, but my Mosquito quickly outran them. Thank God for those Rolls Royce engines! I kept going as fast as I could, and I think I set a record flying from Frankfurt to the Cliffs of Dover in an hour and five minutes! Those little Mosquitoes proved to be successful as Mission Control Centers for our very large missions. Again, using them for this purpose became a procedure we developed as we went along and as the need developed. I have never heard anyone talking about the war mention how our Mission Commanders were able to control vast groups of airplanes using an RAF fighter plane. The British used them to take bombs up to 3,000 pounds all the way to Berlin on their night raids.

To add to the complications we encountered as we were taking off on our missions in the blackness of the heavy fog and clouds, the RAF was returning from their night bombing missions and landing. They didn't fly in formations as we did. Sometimes they were descending as we were ascending in nearby air space. I tell you, it was worse than combat! These RAF pilots would often head for the first possible landing field they could come to in East Anglia, especially if they had incurred damage or had wounded crew aboard, and those fields were often the ones we were taking off from at the same time! Our ground support folks always welcomed these RAF guys warmly as comrades in arms, and helped them repair their planes sufficiently to fly safely to their own bases. But our food was so good they often didn't want to leave. We had a much better mess than the British did, and they knew it. Sometimes they would stay two or three days, enjoying the good fellowship and food we provided. They'd use any excuse they could think of to land on our fields and enjoy our excellent mess and hospitality. Every now and then the RAF would come by, making a sweep of our bases to make all their crews go to their home bases. All this was done in a very friendly manner, of course.

We also learned early on in the air-to-air war with the Luftwaffe that we had to stay in our tight formations for the best defense against their attacks. Any stragglers were sitting ducks for those German fighters. And especially during the early part of the war, those Luftwaffe fighter pilots were good. They really benefited from their experience gained in the Spanish Revolutionary War and in the German invasions of Poland, Czechoslovakia and Russia. In 1944, when we had pretty well destroyed the Luftwaffe, they put up less experienced pilots and it was clear that they weren't nearly as talented as those earlier pilots. But we still had to maintain our tight formations to utilize the B-

17's guns to our best advantage. We used to say, "There are no foxholes in the sky." That was true. We couldn't duck down and get out of the line of fire. We had to stay in our good defensive formations.

Our "combat box" formation had been designed by Curtis LeMay and developed during the early missions. As I recounted in some detail in discussing the battle of Kiel, when General Nathan Bedford Forrest arrived on the scene he redesigned our formations. We practiced his new formations for two weeks, and we just knew that our old "combat box" formation would provide better combined firepower for defense from fighter attacks. Several of our pilots appealed to him to let us use our "tried and true" combat box formations, but General Forrest was certain that his new formation was better. When we used the new formation on the Kiel mission, the results were disastrous! General Forrest's plane, piloted by Harry Stirwalt with my good friend Al Wilder riding as Command Pilot, went down in flames killing him and all but one of the crew aboard. We lost a lot of aircraft on that mission, and we survivors cussed the changes made to our combat box formation. Trial and error! We went back to the defensive formation that had been developed under Curtis LeMay and stayed with it for the rest of the war in Europe.

Then there were some procedures we developed to correct problems we had no idea would ever occur. We started to find on our missions that some of our bombers couldn't drop their bombs because their bomb-bay doors were stuck tight. They just wouldn't open over the target as we flew over at 28,000 feet or so. But then when we returned to the base, the doors worked fine. Well, as we prepared for our missions starting with the 11:00 p.m. briefings to the 4:00 or 5:00 a.m. takeoffs we had all consumed quite a bit of coffee, and by the time we were airborne, many of us had to relieve ourselves of "used coffee", which we did over the bomb bay doors. That worked fine at lower altitudes, but up there over 20,000 feet that urine froze solid and locked up those doors! Naturally, when we descended to warmer temperatures, the doors thawed out and worked. This was figured out in the post-mission meetings of the flight crews. An order went out instantly to change this procedure, making it "verboten" to relieve oneself over the bomb bays, and we stopped bringing home our fused bombs! Trench helmets, like the infantrymen wore, and chamber pots became standard equipment for in-flight relief.

Another change that was determined very early at our post mission briefings had to do with an original design feature of the B-17. Each of the plane's 50 caliber guns had, just under it, a chute for the spent cartridges to fall out of the plane. Well, when we got into missions with many B-17's flying in close formation firing 30,000 to 50,000 rounds of ammunition, we were dropping literally tons of spent cartridges, many of them on our own planes in our airstream, doing considerable damage to them. This became a serious problem. We were starting to do more damage to ourselves than the Germans were! So we modified our planes to cover over these chutes and keep all those cartridges inside the airplanes. Unfortunately when we got into those heavy attacks by German fighter planes we fired our guns a lot, and we filled the body of the planes with spent cartridges. It became hard to move around when we were waist deep in empty cartridges. But we made it work that way, and we brought all those cartridges back home with us. It was better than expelling them onto our own airplanes and causing much worse problems!

By the end of 1944, we had our SOPs down pretty well. It did us a lot of good to be able to make corrections and changes as necessary to meet the needs of our missions. The ability of our commanders and our maintenance and support staffs to hear our comments and to act quickly on them was part of the great teamwork that helped us win this war and bring peace to Europe.

CHAPTER 11

BOMBARDIERS

Bombardiers were a unique bunch of guys, and they really made the lives of us pilots interesting and challenging. Pilots were the aircraft commanders, the "captains of the ship" so to speak, but the bombardiers were in charge during the bombing run. They had the Norden bombsights and they had to keep the aircraft proceeding at the right speed, altitude and attitude until "Bombs away!" Then the pilot took charge again with the objective of getting us all home in one piece.

Earl T. "Basey" DeWolf was a bombardier with Bob Cozens in the 334th Bomb Squadron in one of our original crews. He was kind of an owl-shaped fellow, a lean, long-bodied guy who should have been quite tall except that he had short legs, making him about 5'9"; he was sort of a unusual looking guy. He teamed up with my bombardier, "Big Fitz", who was quite tall, just a real big fellow. Together they looked like Mutt and Jeff, the old comic strip characters. They were quite a pair, because they were always in trouble. Coz and I spent a major part of our entire careers trying to keep those two guys from getting court-martialed or jailed.

Basey DeWolf had quite an entrepreneurial bent. As mentioned earlier, when we were stationed at Rapid City Army Base before we went to England, we were restricted to the base. However, the Base Commander had printed special ID badges, "Pass Cards" to cover the few times when one of us had to leave the base. Well, Basey got hold of one of these Pass Cards, took it into town and had duplications made up, which he then sold at $5.00 each to everyone in the 95th Bomb Group. Of course, almost everyone in the Group bought one, and we could go in and out of the base as we pleased.

Basey's idol was Winston Churchill. He copied Churchill's manner of greeting people by holding up his hand in a "V for victory" sign. You could count on it; Basey DeWolf would always greet you with his hand held up in a "V for victory" sign.

Basey even used it in his "grand exit" over Germany. It was in October 1943, and we were on approach to Munster. This was Basey's 25th mission, after which he would be allowed to go back to the States. By then, both Coz and I had been promoted to Squadron Commanders, and we no longer had our own crews. Basey was assigned to John Adams' crew leading our low squadron for the October 10th mission to Munster.

As Squadron Commander, I was flying as Command Pilot in the right hand seat, so I could see Adams' plane on my right, with Adams in the left hand pilot's seat and Basey in the nose of the plane, giving me the "V" sign, when he noticed I was looking. We usually tried to assign the men who were getting close to 25 missions to the "milk runs," the easy missions, but we picked the wrong one for Basey DeWolf. The Munster mission turned out to be a hell of a mission; it was one of the great air battles of the war. Germany had a powerful fighter force then, and I think they turned every one of them on to us. Well, as we neared the IP, I saw that Adams' plane had been hit and was on fire. The crew, as I could see them, were all getting ready to bail out, except for Basey, who gave me the "V for victory" from his position in the nose. He apparently didn't know his plane was on fire. The fire in their aircraft was spreading, and soon I saw nine crewmen bail out. Basey was still in the nose, giving us the "V for victory".

When we had to bail out at bombing altitude, usually about 25,000 feet, we were supposed to free fall down under 10,000 feet, and then pull the rip cord to release our parachute. Two good reasons for this: first, it got us out of the way of the enemy fighters as well as our own planes, and second, it got us as fast as possible to an altitude where oxygen was not needed, since we had no oxygen with us after leaving the plane. We were at about 24,000 feet on this bombing run and the flames were starting to cover Adams' plane. Finally I saw Basey unbuckle his seat belt and head for the bomb bay to bail out. He jumped, but instead of going into a free fall, he released his parachute right away. The last time I saw DeWolf, he was floating down from 24,000 feet, giving the "V for victory" with planes flying all around him.

Anyway, when we returned home to Horham, we reported what we knew about Adams' plane and crew. About two months later, we got a postcard through the Red Cross from Basey saying, "Just a note to tell you that we are all safe here in Stalag 18. Wishing you an early Merry Christmas. We are making Christmas cheer from Red Cross raisins." How he got this card out of the German prison camp, I couldn't imagine. So he and the full crew had made it alive. Then we didn't hear any more, until about six months later when he showed up! Right there at Horham! What happened was that he was probably the only man in the Allied Air Forces that the Germans sent home as an incorrigible! The Germans kicked him out of the prison camp on a prisoner exchange. Apparently what he had done was to commit so many practical jokes on the prison guards that they desperately wanted him gone.

Exchanges of prisoners of war, particularly those who were wounded and needed considerable medical attention, was a standing procedure between the Allies and the Germans. To my knowledge, Basey DeWolf was the only man ever exchanged as an incorrigible.

One thing Basey did was to get a piece of thin wire and string it about a foot high across the entrance to their barracks; so when the Commandant strode through the doorway to make one of his regular "spit and polish" inspections, he fell ass over teakettle. Why didn't they just shoot DeWolf? Well, they were afraid to do that because we had so many German prisoners the Commandant was pretty circumspect to avoid giving us a reason to treat their boys badly.

The next thing he did involved a knothole in the false ceiling in their barracks. The German guards made it a practice to examine every nook and cranny in these prison areas for tools, weapons or signs of planned escape efforts. If they saw a knothole in the ceiling, they'd put an arm or a finger up there and feel around to see if anything was hidden there. One day, Basey hid up above that false ceiling, and when the guard put his finger up through the knothole, BANG! Basey hit it hard with a piece of pipe, causing extreme pain for the guard. This time they put him in isolation for a while. Apparently, he was always doing pranks like this to annoy them.

As you probably remember from the movie, *The Great Escape*, the Allied prisoners were often secretly digging tunnels to get out. Basey secretly dug a hole under his bed, and he took all the dirt out in his pants pockets and dumped it outside. He made his excavation down and then out about 10 or 12 feet towards the perimeter fence. But he then dug a big hole and filled the hole from the "honey bucket". He camouflaged the top of the hole with paper so that it looked like the floor of his tunnel. At the next inspection, he made the entrance to his tunnel more obvious, so it was discovered. Two German guards dived into his tunnel and then went PLOP! PLOP! into the hole. The next time the Germans had an opportunity, they sent Basey back to England.

Since he had completed his 25 missions, he was sent home, and I didn't see anything of him until much later in my civilian life when I went through Barstow, California, which had been Basey's hometown. I looked up as I drove through town and saw a big banner for a municipal election proclaiming: "ELECT EARL T. DeWOLF — SHERIFF — MAINTAIN LAW AND ORDER." I did make contact with him then, and, yes, he was elected Sheriff. Much later on, he became a real estate developer in Laguna Niguel, on the Southern California coast.

And then there was "Big Fitz", the bombardier on my original crew. His real name is Wayne R. Fitzgerald. He was quite tall, about 6'6", I believe, and quite handsome in a boyish way. He was an All-American basketball player for the University of Michigan before the war. Wherever he was, if there were any women around, he would find them! He had a girlfriend who lived nearby in Ipswich while he was in England. She was a big buxom blonde gal and he used to call her "Two Tons O'Honey."

Of course, I've already told you about Big Fitz finding two Indian girls in Rapid City, South Dakota, for him and Basey DeWolf. And you remember the time in Dakar when he hit the

Army MP Major over the head with an empty champagne bottle. And then there was the time Big Fitz found girls in the Medina in Marrakech. Well, here's another memory I have of Big Fitz.

In the Winter of 1943, when it was raining — it was always raining in England, it seemed — we were having a dance party. We used to get our girls for our parties from the corps of nurses at the general hospital nearby in Ipswich. The Head Nurse counted 'em in and counted 'em out. They would bring them in and take them home in big Army trucks. Well, as the dance ended and we all took our dance partners back to the truck, we had to pass a big ditch full of rainwater. Everybody was saying goodbye. Big Fitz and a gal, a tall bony gal, about 6 feet tall, we called "Nursie," were walking, arms around each other along the bank of this ditch, which had about two feet of water in it. Fitz decided to give her a big kiss; he did, and bent her over backwards, and, since he was pretty well-gassed by then, they both fell over into the ditch. As they climbed out of the ditch, covered with mud, Nursie discovered she had lost her false teeth in the mud. So there they were, the two of them, on their hands and knees in the ditch, feeling through the mud for almost an hour looking for her teeth, which they never did find.

Then there's the time in June of 1943, just after we of the 95th Bomb Group had moved into our new base at Horham, when Fitz came within a hair's breadth of embarrassing the United States Eighth Air Force in front of Winston Churchill. Lord Beaverbrook, the British Minister of Aviation in Winston Churchill's cabinet, had been delegated to make a courtesy call on the newly arrived USAAF groups in England, and he came to pay his respects to the 95th Bomb Group. It was sort of a diplomatic mission, welcoming us to Horham. John Gerhart, the Group Commander, had delegated the duties of shepherding Lord Beaverbrook around the base to Bob Cozens and me. We were to act as his aides and make him welcome at our new base. The Lord, who also happened to be the owner of the *London Times* and many other publications in Britain, arrived in a limousine with his chauffeur, and we, John, Coz and I, in our best dress uniforms, greeted him warmly. His appearance was perhaps a bit stuffy-looking, dressed as he was in a business suit with the standard derby hat, but he instantly revealed that he was a warm, personable, just plain nice guy, and we were delighted to show him around the base and take him to lunch in our Mess. With Coz and me as his guides and aides, he visited with John Gerhart and all the members of the senior staff; and then he joined us all for dinner. Coz and I got many opportunities to chat with him, and as he was about to leave he thanked us for our hospitality. Then as we were escorting him to his car, he said, "Now when you get to London, let me reciprocate. If you have a little time, please give me a call." Then he reached in his pocket and handed us his cards with his private telephone number. He was aware that we would occasionally have a few days between bombing raids, when our planes would have to be repaired and maintained, and would be allowed to go into London for "R&R." It was a sincerely warm and generous offer; and the next time we had a respite between missions Coz, Big Fitz and I went to London to accept Lord Beaverbrook's hospitality.

When we arrived at our hotel in the latter part of the afternoon, we called Lord Beaverbrook's private telephone number. His secretary put us through to "His Lordship," and he answered, saying how happy he was to have us call him. He said, "As long as you are here, there is something you might find interesting happening tomorrow. We could meet you for lunch at Claridge's at noontime." Now Claridge's is a world-famous hotel in London, and their dining room was the place where the British cabinet ministers met informally for lunch. Well, we of course said we'd be delighted. In the course of discussion, we mentioned that we were planning that evening to try to get to a performance at the Palladium of Irving Berlin's musical review, *This Is the Army*, with Irving Berlin personally performing. But this was still in the afternoon, and Coz and I decided we wanted to go shopping in London. Fitz said he didn't want to do that and he went out on his own. When Coz and I returned to the hotel, there was an envelope from Lord Beaverbrook awaiting us with a nice note and three tickets for prime seats at the Palladium for the Irving Berlin show.

Well, Fitz never came back to the hotel, which didn't surprise me; so Coz and I went to the show and really enjoyed it. Fitz never did come back to the hotel.

The next day Coz and I went to Claridge's to have lunch with Lord Beaverbrook without Fitz. Claridge's is a very unassuming-looking place, with a conservative awning over the entrance, a doorman in front and a revolving glass door opening into a rather small lobby with a bar at one side. As you enter the hotel you can see a door opening into the dining room just off the lobby. Coz and I, in our freshly pressed dress uniforms and shined shoes, came through the revolving door into the lobby, and there was Lord Beaverbrook with several other distinguished-looking gentlemen. He greeted us warmly and introduced us around to several other cabinet ministers and some other high British officials. They were all standing around the bar having an aperitif before lunch, so we joined them. One of these gentlemen standing there with Lord Beaverbrook was Winston Churchill and another was Anthony Eden, Foreign Secretary.

As we stood there exchanging pleasantries I couldn't help being concerned about Fitz, who knew about our planned meeting there, but hadn't yet put in an appearance. So I kept one eye on the front door for him. Then I edged around so I was standing near the revolving door, where I could see the back of the doorman. Suddenly I saw the doorman flying backwards after opening a taxi door. Then I hear a loud voice yelling, "Outa my way, you blimey limey!" It was Fitz, pushing the doorman as he got out of the taxi. His uniform was disheveled, his tie askew, his tunic unbuttoned, and I could see he had already had too many drinks. He reached in and pulled a red-headed gal out of the taxi dressed in a close-fitting black velvet floor-length evening gown, and they headed into the revolving door. I quickly moved to the revolving door and pushed it hard, capturing the two of them in it and bringing them all the way around and back outside. The doorman was still there with his mouth agape holding the taxi door open, so I shoved the two of them back into the taxi and closed the door. Then I reached in my pocket and pulled out a bill — I think it was a twenty pound note.

I stuffed it in the cabbie's hand and told him, "Here, take them as far away from here as this will pay for and drop 'em off!" Then I turned around and reentered the lobby. As I approached the standing group, Lord Beaverbrook turned to me and asked quietly what the commotion was all about. "Oh, it's nothing. Just some GI out there with a problem, and it's handled," I replied. Fortunately, no one in the lobby knew what happened. Anyhow we went on into the dining room and had a very nice lunch.

The "happening" that Lord Beaverbrook had invited us to turned out to be a debate that afternoon in the House of Lords, with Churchill speaking as one of the debaters. The cocktails and lunch were the "warm-up" for that debate. After lunch we all went from there to the House of Lords, and Coz and I were the only visitors there. We had a great time with Lord Beaverbrook listening to Churchill and observing the rituals of a debate in the House of Lords. It was a totally different world for us. We observed the Lords firing questions at Churchill, to which he responded in his eloquent manner. Today I have no recollection of what the subject of the debate was; it was the unique process of British governmental proceedings that stayed in my memory.

Afterwards we went to dinner with Lord Beaverbrook at the famous Simpson's on the Strand, where they served us some of their fabulous beef. Then we went back to our hotel, and the next morning we returned to Horham. Incidentally, I had occasion to call Lord Beaverbrook to thank him and talk with him a couple more times, but I never saw him again. Fitz finally showed up back at Horham in time for our next pre-mission briefing.

Fitz also made an impression on our new Commanding General of the Eighth Air Force. It was General "Jimmy" Doolittle who paid us a visit at Horham as part of his getting around to see and meet the members of his new command. Jimmy Doolittle was, among other notable achievements, the leader of America's first bombing raid on Tokyo, a raid immortalized in the book and movie, *Thirty Seconds Over Tokyo* by Ted Lawson. Doolittle and his raiders had taken off from an aircraft carrier in the Pacific with a squadron of B-25 twin-engine bombers, bombed Tokyo, and landed in China. His courageous and daring action was a fabulous morale uplift for America, as it happened at a time when the Japanese forces seemed to be winning all around the Pacific Rim. The then Col. Jimmy Doolittle was awarded the Medal of Honor for leading the Tokyo raid. So, of course, we had a party for him with our senior officers.

We had all consumed more than sufficient alcohol, but we were still chatting amiably at the bar of the Officers' Club. Big Fitz was leaning back on the bar smoking a big cigar as a group of us were standing with him, and Jimmy Doolittle was standing next to Fitz explaining to Fitz his strategy for winning the war. Now, Jimmy Doolittle was about 5'5" tall, and Fitz towered over him. And as Jimmy stopped talking to see if we got what he was saying, Fitz took a big puff on his cigar, which by then had an ash on it over an inch long, and said, "Well, General, we hope this all pans out." With that he flicked his cigar, and the ashes spilled all over Jimmy Doolittle's tunic. "You sonofabitch!" the General exclaimed as he jumped backwards. And then he laughed as he brushed himself off. He was really a neat guy, with a great sense of humor. Of course, it was Curtis LeMay who had introduced us all to the pleasures of smoking fine hand-rolled Cuban cigars, and those fine cigars were noted for holding their ashes intact until they became quite long. It was one such cigar that Fitz was smoking that night.

Another story involving Big Fitz and some top brass came about because of the 95th Group's distinguished record. Being one of the leading units of America's active participants in World War II, the 95th Bomb Group flew the most missions and was the most decorated unit in the Eighth Air Force. As a result, we were given the most attention by high ranking Allied officials and other notables. Important Government people were constantly visiting us.

When we had the celebration of our completion of 200 missions, we were allowed to "stand down" and have no missions for three days while we had one hell of a party. Glenn Miller and his whole band were there. So were Bing Crosby and Dinah Shore. It was the day after that party that Glenn Miller got in an airplane and disappeared; there has never been a trace of him since. His last performance was at Horham for the 95th Bomb Group.

It was a warm August evening at Horham on the third day of our 200th Mission Celebration. The Inspector General, a Lieutenant General of the Army Air Forces, was visiting us and he had turned out to be a stiff "by-the-book" type of guy. That night, Col. John Gerhart held a dinner party for him, attended by the senior officers of the 95th Bomb Group. Because of the warmth of the evening, the party was held in the garden adjacent to the Officers' Club. Of course, we were all in our Class A uniforms and had polished our shoes and buttons for the Inspector General. We started off with our pre-dinner cocktails as we discussed the procedures for the inspections the following day. All the windows were open in the Officers' Club since it was such a warm and humid night, so sound traveled well; and the sounds of the guys in the 95th on their third consecutive evening of celebrating were being heard all over the place. In the Club's barroom Big Fitz was dancing on the bar. Dave McKnight, another one of our colorful fellows, stripped down to his T-shirt. Big Fitz did the same. Then their dancing got wild, and Dave leaped through the window into the garden, where John Gerhart's party for the Inspector General was going on. He charged through the party and ran smack into the Inspector General and knocked him over, and then kept on running. Big Fitz chased him and he, too, dived through the window and ran right over the General again. The two of them just ran through and didn't stop. Well, that certainly surprised the Inspector General and embarrassed John Gerhart. As Queen Victoria was known to say, the I.G. was "not amused." He packed his bag and left the next morning without doing any further inspections. No, there were no repercussions from that outbreak.

When he finished his 25 missions, Big Fitz went home, but he and I maintained quite a correspondence. At one time after he was back in the States, he told me had three girlfriends in various parts of the United States, all of whom were engaged to him. Fitz was stationed in Florida when he came back to the U.S.; so in 1945 when I was reassigned to the Pentagon in Washington, D.C., I called him and he came up to Washington to visit with me for a weekend. At that time he kept talking to me about Jane Ann, the girl who lived next door to Fitz when he grew up in Michigan. He was just certain that she would be the right girl for me. She was a WAVE Lieutenant in Naval Intelligence stationed in Washington so he had me meet her. It's quite a long story for another time, but Fitz's evaluation was right; later on I married Jane Ann, and Fitz, who had introduced us, was at my wedding.

Finally, Fitz settled down and married a lovely gal, Peggy, whom I later met and have known now for many years. He's been married now for over 50 years, and he's a "born-again Christian" and the most conservative fellow you could imagine. He certainly changed from being the biggest and loudest hell-raiser in my crew!

Fitz was one of only three of us who were members of the 100 men in the original 334th Bomb Squadron who went to England in 1943, and survived the 25 mission tour of duty without being shot down or killed. The other two were Bob Cozens and I. We were the lucky ones.

CHAPTER 12

BILL PRATT, NAVIGATOR

This is a story about a lesson in compassion that I learned in the midst of war. It is about a Navigator in my 334th Bomb Squadron named William C. "Bill" Pratt. Bill came to me as a replacement in June 1943, shortly after the Kiel Mission that had created a lot of vacancies in our crews. The United States Army Air Forces replacement crews generally came to England by ship to ports on the western coast of England, where they disembarked and were transported to London and then disbursed by rail to our various bases. Our replacements were always instructed to get off the train at a little town by the name of Diss, about 70 miles north of London. These trains normally arrived with our replacements at 11:00 p.m. The replacements were met by our "lorries," two-and-a-half ton Army trucks, and brought over to our base at Horham. They arrived with only their hand luggage, and the rest of their stuff came in later. Normally we tried to give these replacements some practice missions over England for a week or two to teach them what we were doing.

But when Bill Pratt came in one evening, I, as a newly appointed Squadron Commander, was hard pressed to fill up my crews. I needed a Navigator and a couple of gunners to fill up a crew of ten men for a B-17. So I just took Bill and a couple of other men right off the train at Diss and used them to fill up my duty roster for a B-17 for the next bombing mission. They didn't even get a chance to find their quarters and unpack their hand luggage. I had the duty Sergeant find them flight clothing and usher them into the mission briefing that started about 2:00 a.m. and lasted until about 4:00 a.m. The mission that day was to Strasbourg, France, on the Rhine River. At this time we were still doing our bombing missions without fighter escort, as this was before our fighter planes became equipped with wing tanks for the extra fuel needed for long missions. When we got to Strasbourg the target area was covered with bunches of clouds. We were still pretty green then and we circled the target area waiting for openings in the clouds. That was a deadly thing to do. When we circled, we set ourselves up as targets for anti-aircraft fire. In the meantime, the German fighters started buzzing around us like a bunch of nasty flies. Our making a circle cost us about three or four airplanes out of the 75 that came on the mission. As we continued to circle, the concentration of fighter attacks increased and became very heavy.

I was riding at that time in the right-hand seat as Command Pilot with Coz, who was piloting the plane. Lou Reno was piloting the plane off my right wing, and Bill Pratt was his new Navigator. We were experiencing some really sporty combat, as these were the days when the Luftwaffe fighters were flying right at us through our tight formations. I remember looking over and seeing Bill Pratt in the nose of the plane next to me, and a Me-109 flew right between us! Things were hot and heavy, but we got home.

The next day we were put on alert again for a mission to Frankfurt, Germany. I thought the crews that we had put together for the Strasbourg mission had worked well together and would continue to work on this new mission. As Squadron Commander, though, I only went on every other mission, so I was to stay on the ground for this day's Frankfurt mission. We went off to the usual briefing, which went on until about 4:00 in the morning. Shortly afterwards the Squadron took off. All our planes were on their way to Frankfurt. No problems.

I left the flight line and went over to John Gerhart's office to do some administrative work with him. After we were together a while, the telephone rang. It was the control tower. They told us that Lou Reno, who was a good, competent pilot, one of our best, had radioed in that he was aborting the mission and returning to Horham. This was extremely early in the mission. They had just attained altitude, crossed the Channel and started to penetrate enemy airspace, when Lou turned his plane around and headed back home. Lou had further reported that all four engines were operating. John and I decided we'd better get to the tower to see Lou's plane in and find out what had gone so wrong as to cause them to abort. We saw his plane approach with all four engines working, and he landed without any apparent difficulties. As we approached the plane, all ten crew members came out, all looking perfectly all right. So I asked Lou Reno, "What was the problem?" He said, "I don't know. As soon as we got across the Channel, this new navigator, Pratt, just fell down on the floor and lay there, absolutely RIGID! I didn't want to start out on a bombing mission without a man in the nose to do my navigating; so I decided to abort and come home. The minute I turned the ship around and headed home, the man came to and acted perfectly normal".

Well, one of the problems we had had at that time, especially after the Kiel mission where we lost so many men, was the extremely sensitive morale of our crews. If there was one fellow in the barracks that was shaky, fearful or upset, then those feelings would go right through the rest of the guys in the barracks; and soon there'd be several crews in trouble. If we had anyone with any "nervous" problems, we'd get him out of there right away and send him to the flight surgeon for observation. Usually then we would "declassify" the man as unfit for combat and reassign him to a non-flying job.

So I went with Lou to talk to this fellow. He was a big, handsome fellow, about 6'2" tall. I asked him what his problem was, and he didn't say anything. Well then, I was a little brusque with him and I said, "Lieutenant, you just go report to the Flight Surgeon and he'll notify us as to what to do with you."

John and I went back to his office. Shortly afterward, Captain Bill Harding, our Flight Surgeon, called us about Bill, explaining, "Did you ever hear the expression, 'scared stiff'?" This young guy was literally scared stiff. He was absolutely paralyzed with fear. He's on his way back down there to talk with you."

In a few minutes he was at our door. I told John, "I want to talk to him." John replied, "Well, whatever you want to do, I'm with you." This big, tall kid came into the office with a hang-dog expression on his face. "I'm so embarrassed! I'm terribly sorry about what happened. I've never had anything like that happen to me before. I was just terribly frightened. After seeing those fighter planes fly right at us yesterday with their guns blazing, I became extremely frightened that I would be seeing more of that today." With tears in his eyes, he went on, "Please, I know you want to reclassify me. But if you would just give me one more chance, let me fly and I promise you it will NEVER happen again!" I looked him in the eye, and quietly studied the sincerity that I saw in him as I thought about what to do. So I said, "OK, Pratt, get a drink and go to your quarters and have a good night's sleep. I'll see you tomorrow."

Then I went back to the office and pulled out his personnel file. Bill Pratt had been a stock boy for Sears Roebuck in Rochester, New York. He hadn't been to college, but shortly after he had enlisted, he was nominated for Officer Candidate School, where he received excellent ratings. His father was a widower who had raised Bill and two younger children while working as a school janitor. I just had a feeling that there was more to Bill Pratt than what we had experienced in that second mission of his. I thought deeply about this situation and then I told John, "I'm going to give this lad a chance. I'm going to leave him on flying status." John's reply was supportive, which I really appreciated.

Well, that turned out to be one of my most rewarding decisions. Bill Pratt turned out to be an excellent Navigator. The fear never left him, but he overrode that fear with his resolve to be the best possible Navigator in the Squadron. He went through his 25 missions without ever again having the fear overcome him. And he was an outstanding Navigator. He turned in the best, most complete and precise navigation logs I had ever seen. He was truly successful. Ultimately, I appointed him the Chief Navigator of the Squadron. Always, though, he had to fight down the fear that was still there. Before his missions, he would often come and talk to me about anything and everything, except tomorrow's mission, just to get his mind off of his fears. And I would listen to him. And we would talk.

Later on when we formed the 93rd Combat Wing, I was appointed Chief of Staff of the new Wing. John Gerhart was the Wing Commander, and we needed a Chief Navigator to make all the flight plans for the Wing. Bill Pratt had become a Captain by then, and had his 25 missions and could go home. John and I decided to ask Bill if he would stay on with us and be our Wing Navigator. We talked to Bill and told him that we knew that he had always been fighting his fears about flying in combat, but we really wanted him to join us in this new organization. We offered him the new position of Wing Navigator, and we assured him that this job did not require him to fly in combat. He thought about our offer, and he expressed his genuine appreciation for being asked to take this new position. Then he said, "Yes, I'll join you. I know I could go home now, but I don't have anything important to do at home, and this I know is important. I want to do the job!" He stayed with us and soon became a Major.

Every time at our 93rd Combat Wing mission briefings, Bill would give the navigational briefings. And often he would fly with us on our missions, even though he was not required to do so. John Gerhart and I alternated in flying in the lead on missions as part of our command positions. Whenever either one of us was flying a mission, we'd find Bill Pratt waiting for us with his flight equipment, and he would accompany us. Before he'd go on a mission, he would walk the halls and talk with people, often with me, to keep his mind occupied and away from his fear. I once asked him, "Bill, why do you do this? You know you don't have to fly on our bombing missions. You are torturing yourself needlessly!" His reply was, "Well, if it's good enough for you fellows, it's good enough for me."

During the early first few months of establishing the 93rd Combat Wing, Colonel John and I had our living quarters and offices in Elveden Hall, where General Curtis LeMay and his staff were headquartered. So we often ate our lunches at the General's Mess there. One day as we were having lunch, Curtis LeMay came over to our table and asked me if I would fly him over to Liverpool for an afternoon appointment. That would be a short flight of only 190 miles, so I was quite ready and able to provide the General with transportation. After lunch we went over to Horham, which was about 20 miles away, and borrowed a B-17. Bill Pratt, wearing his new gold major's leaves, was there and asked if he could come along. "Sure, Bill," I replied, "if you'll be my navigator." Four of us boarded the plane: Curtis LeMay, who sat in the right-hand seat, Bill Pratt, who went into the nose as the navigator, and the Flight Engineer for the plane we were using. We took off and rose into a thick overcast at about 1,500 feet, preventing us from seeing any landmarks on the ground. Curtis LeMay relaxed in his seat in his Class A uniform smoking one of his characteristic cigars. About an hour along on the flight, it seemed like we should be getting close to Liverpool. I called down to Bill in the nose and asked him to give me a heading into the airport. Silence. I called him again for a heading. No answer. I started my descent and then called again to Bill, "Hey Bill, are you lost?" Immediately I got a loud and emphatic response in the interphone, "Hell NO, I'm not lost! I just don't know where I am!" I'm sure that was hard for him to acknowledge in front of the General, as he was very proud of his skills as a navigator.

As we broke out of the cloud cover, we looked around and got our bearings so I could adjust our flight path into Liverpool. Actually, we didn't have to make much of an adjustment as my dead reckoning had us pretty much on course. I wanted to show off my flying skills to the General by giving him a really smooth landing at Liverpool. As we started our approach, I noticed a wire fence at the edge of the field just before the runway began. I descended slowly under the overcast and made a nice three-point landing. It was a beautiful landing, right at the end of the runway. Then I taxied up to the headquarters building. Curtis LeMay thanked me, and I expressed my appreciation for his compliment. As we got out of the plane, I looked back and saw that I had about 200 feet of wire fence hanging onto the tail wheel of the B-17. I had dragged it all the way down the runway after hooking it on my landing approach. Curtis LeMay saw it, too, and just shrugged and said "Humpff!" He went on to his appointment and neither Bill nor

I ever heard another word from the General about the happenings on this flight.

Bill Pratt stayed in the Army Air Forces, and after the war was over in Europe, he transferred to the Pentagon. He became the Chief Navigator of the Army Air Forces and a full Colonel. At this point, Air Force Command Staff decided to do a very unusual thing with Bill. In the Army Air Forces then, and even in the Air Force today, if you are going to be a commander of troops, you have to be a pilot; you have to earn the wings of a pilot. So the Command Staff decided that he should go back to flight school as a full Colonel. Bill Pratt did and got his pilot's wings. The Korean War came on, and he became the Chief of Staff for General "Rosie" O'Donnell. Later he became a Wing Commander, and got his star, becoming General William C. Pratt. Eventually he retired as a General.

While on stateside duty after the war, Bill married a lovely lady, the daughter of a socially prominent owner of a large publishing company. The two of them lived happily together during Bill's continued Air Force career and retired together in Florida.

His whole career, his whole future, had been in my hands. If I had turned this kid down and not given him the chance he had asked for, he might have gone back to being a stock clerk. But I gave him the opportunity he needed to become a General. I took a risk with Bill, and he didn't let me down. This was certainly a lesson in compassion, and a growth experience for me, a particularly touching episode in my experiences.

CHAPTER 13

LEADERSHIP, OUR GREATEST ASSET

My wartime military service provided me the opportunity to meet and work with some of the finest men one could imagine. Many of these men were our commanders, and they were real leaders of men. I got to know and work with them as they moved up in rank in the Army Air Forces, and I admired and respected them. They turned out to be a powerful group of men who eventually became the top commanders of the U.S. Air Force for the next 25 years after World War II was over.

Alfred A. Kessler, the original commander of the 95th Bomb Group, organized us, trained us and took us to combat in England. He came out of West Point in the 1920's and was a definite "no nonsense" kind of a guy. Even though we called him "Uncle Ugh" quietly out of his earshot, we really did respect him as a thoughtful and conscientious commander. He was a demanding disciplinarian, but he was fair and a great leader for us. Uncle Ugh, then a Colonel, was designated to set up the 95th Bomb Group at the beginning of the war. He started by selecting some Army Regulars that he knew and then added a lot of pretty raw recruits. Many of us were just out of flying school. He did a great job of assembling a diverse group of very capable people and putting them together into a cohesive force. All of us were volunteers, and many were fine athletes. These young men were an outstanding group, and I was both proud and lucky to be a part of them. Many of them were outstanding leaders, too, and went on to positions of high responsibility.

Colonel Kessler was a very humane person with a large heart. It was clear that he cared about all of us under his command. That really showed right after the Kiel mission, when 100 of us — 10 crews — didn't come back. He actually cried, saying over and over, "These were my boys! These were my boys!"

On September 16, 1943, Al Kessler was appointed Commander of a new Wing, the 13th Bomb Wing, with the 95th Bomb Group being one of the three, and later four Groups in the Wing. He eventually was given his first star and made a Brigadier General.

Al Kessler continued up the command levels in the Army Air Forces. The last time I saw Uncle Ugh he was in Poltava, Russia as head of the American Air Mission in that Allied country. As the air war in Europe wound down, he became the Military Attaché to Sweden; then during the Korean War he spent some time in the Pentagon before being promoted to Major General and Commanding General of the Fourth Air Force at Hamilton Air Force Base just north of San Francisco, where he stayed until he retired in 1955. He returned home to Sacramento, California, where I talked to him once, but I didn't keep track of him after that. I heard, however, that he passed away shortly after he retired.

Succeeding Uncle Ugh as Group Commander of the 95th Bomb Group was John Gerhart. Although he was a product of the cadet program at the University of Chicago, he became a career officer and was a member of the original cadre of the Eighth Air Force. John was an outstanding guy, and a handsome good looking son-of-a-gun, like a movie star. He loved the women and the women loved him. He was a really fine leader of men, "a follow me" guy! He was probably about 35 years old when he was given command of the 95th Bomb Group, as he was about 10 years older than I.

John Gerhart liked to work with a Staff, so he set up a Headquarters with a Staff. One of the first men he added to the staff was a leading interior decorator named Kenneth Kimborough from Memphis, Tennessee. Actually, his Army job title was Intelligence Officer. This guy had a flair for making our officers feel comfortable in our Nissen hut living quarters. The first thing he did was to redecorate the mess areas with window drapes and wallpaper. He certainly had a talent, as he really kept us living in style. The Officers' Mess, which was in a corrugated-iron Nissen (sometimes called a Quonset) hut, was fixed up inside with indirect lighting and wallpaper. Kenneth searched out the personnel files to find people who would help him improve our living style. He found Sergeant Arthur Sondecker, officially a carpenter, who had been a sous chef for one of the leading Chicago hotels; so he became our cook. After Sondecker came with us, we regularly had tea, and sometimes we even had "high tea." He made cookies to go with our tea every afternoon. He prepared a lot of other special culinary treats for us. At night when we had our mission briefings, Chef Sondecker served us special delicacies. It was almost sinful when you think about it; if we made it back from our missions, we got treated like royalty back at the base. The 95th had the reputation for having the best mess anywhere in England, and guys from other groups were always finagling ways to get to come to our mess and enjoy the fine food served by our chef.

Kenneth Kimborough also set up a special cocktail party every evening for the senior officers. He was a fine gentleman, and his talent for making us all feel comfortable in the midst of a war was truly appreciated by those of us who got to experience that talent. Kenneth was quite enterprising, too. He used to borrow an Army truck every couple of weeks and take it to London and pick up empty bottles. After D-Day we could get champagne from France in barrels, but the bottles were scarce in France. So Kenneth got empty bottles for us to take to Allied bases in France and return with bottles filled with champagne. General Fred Anderson, Commander of all the USAAF fighters in the European Theater of Operations, had his headquarters in Reims, France, and he always kept us in champagne. Kenneth was mighty good at getting scotch, too, in barrels from Scotland.

Jiggs Donohue, another key man recruited by Uncle Ugh to be our Intelligence Officer and handle all our late evening/early morning mission briefings, arranged to get us bottled bourbon from the States. One of his old friends and law clients was an executive for Seagram's and provided the vital bottled "fuel." Jiggs arranged for it to be flown over to Scotland in Army transport planes by the Air Transport Command. We would pick it up by truck from the Air Transport Command at their base in Prestwick, Scotland.

All these things were really morale factors. John Gerhart also insisted that we all wear our "Class A" uniforms every evening for dinner. These niceties kept us all on our toes.

Whenever anything unusual was going on, John Gerhart was the leader. One incident demonstrated this. In the 13th Combat Wing, the 95th Bomb Group had a rivalry with the 100th Bomb Group. Whenever any large group of Air Corps guys had a party, there was always a big competition about getting enough women to come to the party so that all the guys could get a dance partner. In December 1943, the General Hospital, which provided all the nurses for our parties, told us that their nurses had all been promised to the 100th Bomb Group for their New Year's Eve party and they didn't have enough nurses to send any to our New Year's Eve party, unless we would postpone our celebration to the following weekend. A fine kettle of fish! We had to play second fiddle to the 100th! Late in the afternoon of New Year's Eve, which was to be the night of the 100th Group's party, John and his staff were sitting around having cocktails in John's quarters, commiserating about this unfortunate situation, and John came up with "I know what we'll do! Let's all go over there to the 100th Group's party. They will all be stoned by the time we get there, and we'll stage a fake fight! They'll get into it and we can take all the girls and have our own party!"

We were all half-crocked and it was only about four miles away, so we piled into John's command car and noisily drove over there. I'll never forget this trip! John was driving with his blackout lights on, and Dave McKnight acted as his co-pilot helping him navigate, "right rudder, left rudder, flaps up, flaps down," and so on. Bob Cozens, Bill Lindley, Grif Mumford, a whole bunch of us were there. John said, "Now, all of you go over there and mingle with everybody. Then two of you start a ruckus, but just between you two; don't pick on anybody else. When they all get started into it, I'll whistle (and he could whistle!) and everybody come out and get in the car, and we'll get out of there." Coz and I put on the first make-believe scuffle, right in front of the dais where the band was. All of sudden, the band's drummer came over to stop us; in the process, he took a swing at me. I ducked and hit him in the chest; then he staggered backwards and fell — right through the big base drum! Then everybody else got into the fight. They were all pretty well boiled anyway. So John gives the big whistle. We all put on a full retreat and got out of there. They were left having a big fight of their own. Their Group Commander was there, a fellow by the name of Chick Harding. He was quite a nice guy, and very well liked by the men in his Group. He tried to find out how the fight started, but no one there was able to tell him how it started or who started it.

The next weekend after New Year's Eve we had our rescheduled New Year's Party. John said to us, "somebody from the 100th Group is probably going to find out who started the fight last week, and they'll come over here and try to get even." Before our festivities started some guy heard there was a party going on and wandered in while we were still at the bar. He went up to the mike on the dais and announced who he was and said, "I'm from the 100th Bomb Group." Whereupon one of our guys came over and hit him! He was afraid that this guy was an emissary or maybe one of the lead troops. Anyway the stranger got out fast, and we ended up having a great party with no more "unpleasantness." Surprisingly, we actually got out of that incident unscathed.

When John became Commander of the 93rd Combat Wing and I was appointed his Chief of Staff, we had our quarters together with Jiggs Donohue in Elveden Hall, which was our Wing Headquarters. A fairly large room had been transformed into three rooms, side by side, for the three of us, with John's room in the center, which had large double doors opening out to a hallway; our common bathroom was just down the hallway, nearest Jiggs' room. To go in and out of my room, I had to go through the double doors into John's room and from there into my room. John's room, which had been the center portion of the original large room, had a beautiful fireplace and a sitting area in front of it, where we occasionally held small staff meetings.

Well, one afternoon about 4:00 o'clock I had just come back to my quarters after leading a very long mission to Leipzig,

Germany. I was pretty tired from having been up all the previous night planning and preparing for my mission, and then spending all morning and early afternoon flying the mission while dodging flak and fighters. I went to the bathroom and made myself a nice hot bath. I relaxed, and went into a sound sleep in the warm water. A couple of hours later I woke up and got out of the tub; I shaved, and then wrapped myself in a towel to go back to my room. When I got into the hallway, I saw, to my consternation, through the open double doors leading into John's room — my only way into my room — that John was hosting a cocktail party with some of the ladies of the local community of Norwich; he was doing his PR work. I peeked in and I decided to make a dash for my room while nobody was looking. I saw my opportunity and leaped through the double doorway. The only problem was that I had miscalculated the height of the door jam relative to my own height plus the height of my leap. The top of my head hit the door jam and the blow knocked me out.

When I came to, I was sprawled on the floor of John's room, my head hurt like hell, people were bent over me to see whether or not I'd killed myself, and I was bleeding badly from a major cut on top of my head. I realized that the towel around my middle had totally dislodged itself and I was exposing myself totally to the world — and the local ladies. Embarrassed? I certainly was! Lady Elizabeth Elveden, who was hosting the party, was nearby. She came and bent over me and covered me up with my towel; then she started using another towel to wipe away some of the blood I was generously spreading around. She was a qualified Nurse's Aide, so she knew what she was doing and wasn't put off by the blood or my nakedness. John worked his way through the crowd of people around me, took a look, and said, "He's OK! He's coming to. Get the man a scotch!" Someone poured a drink and handed it to John to give me. John took one look at the drink, and said, "Hell, I need this worse than he does!" Whereupon he tossed down the scotch. By that time I was able to sit up and someone then handed me another scotch. John picked up the phone and asked our Wing Flight Surgeon, Bill Harding, to come over from his nearby infirmary. I just kept sitting there on the floor with my towel wrapped around me, sipping my scotch. Bill Harding came right over and sat down in a chair behind me, and had me put my head between his knees. He quickly examined the bleeding cut, gave me a little local anesthetic, and, holding my head tightly between his knees, he proceeded to sew me up like the lacing on a basketball. He put eighteen stitches in my scalp, which he then covered with a bandage. All this time the party carried on, so I got up and went to my room to get dressed. When I returned to the party, the ladies were just leaving. After they left, John and I had a couple more scotches and went to dinner. All in all, I'd had a very full day. And John had provided a bit of unscheduled entertainment for the ladies of Norwich.

John Gerhart was such an outstanding leader that he received many promotions in the Army Air Forces. Later in his career he became head of NATO, and after the war, Commander of the North American Air Defense Command, headquartered in Colorado Springs.

I had the distinct pleasure of getting to know and work for Curtis LeMay. But before I worked for him in Washington, D.C., I had a friendly "run-in" with him in mock air combat. As our various groups were spread around all over England, those of us in the Wing or Division Staff needed to get around to visit our Bomb Groups in many different places. This would be somewhat difficult to do in a big bomber with a crew of ten, so we were given fighter planes to travel on our business from base to base. It was also the custom then for friendly fighters to "bounce" each other for fun and practice when appropriate and over home territory. One day as I was flying my P-47 between bases I spotted another P-47 slightly below me. So I decided to bounce him. I dove down and made a mock attack on it. Well, that P-47 did a fast maneuver and — ZOOM! — he was very quickly on my tail. I did every twist and turn and roll I could think of, but he stayed hanging tightly on my tail. I went up to about 12,000 feet, about as high as I could without oxygen — I hadn't put on the oxygen for such a short hop

— and I dove down into the trees and he hung onto me like he was on a towrope. Nothing I could do would shake him off me.

I looked at my gauges and saw that I was running out of gas, so I turned my fighter plane toward the field where I was originally headed and landed. I didn't look behind me. I just taxied over to park. Then I looked around and there on the taxi strip was a P-47 with its engine idling. The pilot pushed back his canopy and it was General Curtis LeMay, all dressed up in his Class A uniform. He waved to me to come over. I trotted over and jumped onto his wing so I could hear him over the engine noise. He put his arm around my shoulder and said, "Son, you'd better stick to bombers!" With that, he gunned his engine and blew me off the wing! Then off he flew. And, by God, every time after that when he saw me he would tell the story about the dogfight we had and how he blew me off his airplane.

When I was given the position of Squadron Commander and had to attend meetings chaired by Colonel Curtis LeMay, he gave me a wallet-sized card to carry with me. To this day I still carry that card. It is now a well-worn document in a battered plastic cover. In 1943, when Colonel LeMay gave these cards to all his officers in his newly formed Third Bomb Division, he told us that printed on this card were the standards he used in guiding his actions and objectives in his positions of command, and that these would be the standards he would expect us to follow as well. Here it is in its entirety as an example of the manner in which Curtis LeMay carried out his approach to command and to all his official relationships.

MY PERSONAL QUESTIONNAIRE

Do I sometimes give orders and fail to carry through?

Do I heckle my subordinates or strengthen and encourage them?

Do I use moral courage in getting rid of subordinates who have proven themselves beyond doubt to be unfit?

Have I done all in my power by encouragement, incentive, and example to salvage the weak and erring?

Do I know by NAME and CHARACTER a maximum number of subordinates for whom I am responsible?

Am I thoroughly familiar with the techniques, necessities, objectives and administration of my job?

Do I lose my temper at individuals?

Do I act in such a way as to make my subordinates WANT to follow me?

Do I delegate tasks which should be mine?

Do I arrogate everything to myself and delegate nothing?

Do I develop my subordinates by placing on each one as much responsibility as he can stand?

Am I interested in the personal welfare of each of my subordinates as if he were a member of my family?

Have I the calmness of voice and manner to inspire confidence, or am I inclined to irascibility and excitability?

Have I exerted myself to establish cordial relations with local civil authorities?

Am I inclined to be nice to my superiors and mean to my subordinates?

Am I open to my subordinates?

Am I interested sufficiently in the behavior of my subordinates when they are off duty?

Do I think of POSITION or JOB?

Am I carrying the good principles implied by these questions to every link in my chain of command?

Curtis LeMay's style of commanding was to be clear and concise in everything he said. He never said two words when one would do. He had a reputation for being a "hard ass" and that was probably true — he had to be strict and enforce the discipline necessary to maximize our fighting strength and accomplish our objectives — but he really had a heart of gold. Those of us who had the privilege to work closely with him got to know that side of him. He was always very sensitive about the morale of his enlisted personnel. One example of that sensitivity was that he often attended the Saturday night movies, one of the most popular diversions for the enlisted men, but he ordered that there not be any reserved seating, not even for him, the Commanding General. When he arrived late and all the seats were gone, he stood in the rear of the theater to watch the movie.

I was so fortunate during my wartime career. I was with such a diverse group of exceptional people. I was lucky to be in the first wave of the American military build-up. I was on the ground floor and got to meet the people who set up the strategies and plans to carry out the war effort. And of course, I was lucky to have survived my many missions. I really became a fatalist. But while I and my crews had to put our lives on the line on each of our bombing missions, we would come home to nice — really fine — meals, hot showers, clean clothes and warm beds. We really lived very well in England.

One of the most interesting missions I went on was one that had me spending a day with General George Patton. In July, 1944, Patton and his tank force broke out of Normandy and drove across France, eventually reaching Luxembourg in late 1944. When he did that he outran his supply train. So he called General Curtis LeMay and asked him if he could send him some fuel for his tanks. I was then Chief of Staff of the 93rd Bomb Wing, and Curtis asked me if I could respond to Patton's urgent request and take him some gas. Patton assured us he would guarantee the security of the airfield there in Luxembourg. We didn't have to worry much about the German air defense at that time because their fighters were all pretty well-decimated.

So we took a Group of 18 B-17s and fitted them with boards across the bomb bays and filled the spaces with 55 gallon drums of gasoline. We took our gas-laden B-17s and landed there in Luxembourg. General Fred Anderson, head of the American Fighter Forces in Europe, knew about the situation and provided us fighter cover while our B-17s were on the ground. With Patton's tanks and troops all around the airfield, it remained secure and we had no difficulties that day with the Germans. While his troops used hand pumps to refuel their tanks, George Patton and I played gin rummy. It took just about all day. I really enjoyed meeting Patton. He had an unusual high-pitched voice, but he was very much a dominant man, a leader of men, very much like John Gerhart in being a "follow me" guy. Although I don't recall our game scores, I do remember that we had a very interesting discussion about the progress of the war and, in particular, his current strategy, which was to move eastward, pushing the retreating German armies as rapidly as he could in order to capture as much territory as possible for the United States and leave as little as possible for the Russians. He correctly foresaw what later became the "Cold War" with Russia.

Sometime later after the war in Europe had ended, I saw General Patton again in Washington, D.C., with John Gerhart, who was a good friend of his. The three of us went out to dinner at one of Washington's best steak houses. John and I arrived first and were seated at our table. Then Patton made a dramatic entrance wearing, as part of his uniform, high military boots, cavalry trousers, and a pair of matched ivory-handled pistols prominently holstered at his sides. Flamboyant? Yes, but he was also a very pleasant conversationalist. We had a great time reminiscing and exchanging stories about the people and events we knew from the war, as well as discussing our thoughts about what would be happening next. He really impressed me with his sharp intelligence and the extremely broad scope of his interests. Our conversation ranged far and wide over many subjects until late that evening. I never saw him again, however, because shortly thereafter he returned to Europe and was killed in an unfortunate automobile accident.

CHAPTER 14

"BIG B"

Late in 1943 we in the entire Eighth Air Force were busy building up our strength in numbers of planes and crews, as well as ground support. As a Squadron Commander and senior staff member of the 95th Bomb Group, I was deeply involved in strengthening and training my squadron. During this time I was going on bombing missions over Europe as frequently as I was allowed. I wanted to keep going toward my goal of 25 missions. Occasionally my progress toward that goal was interrupted, and I expressed my frustrations about that in my letters home.

November 20, 1943

>I was under the weather most of the week with a fair case of the flu, but I'm perfectly OK now. In fact, the rest was sort of nice for a change. I was in bed for four days and confined to my quarters for three more. I never did go to the hospital, but remained here in my room. The Mess Sergeant at the Officers' Mess is one of my boys, so he more than took good care of me and sent me all my meals and all sorts of fruit juices, etc. In fact, he sent me the only real honest-to-God steak I've eaten since leaving Palm Beach. Where he got it, I don't know, and I didn't ask; but he produced the most delicious filet mignon complete with mushrooms that I have ever set my choppers into. It was a good two inches thick and as tender as butter. Boy, oh boy! I'll have to make that man a General.
>
>We have all our new crews in now and we are in the midst of a prodigious training program. As I believe I wrote you, we have doubled the size of the Group so that I have eighteen airplanes and crews. It also means a Lieutenant Colonel's position for me. That promotion will happen in the next few months, according to the Colonel. He is going to bring all his Squadron Commanders up to that grade as rapidly as possible. It won't be hard to take! However, I won't be eligible until after the first of the year, and it will probably take some time after that to go through.

> These new crews are filled with trepidation as to what the future holds for them. Evidently the stories that got to the boys in the States about fighting in this theater are pretty gruesome. They all seem to expect the worst. We, of course, all laugh at them and try to make them see that it isn't as bad as it's cracked up to be. I certainly hope they get a few easy ones at the start to bolster their morale.
>
> The base is certainly jam packed now. We had to erect new buildings to accommodate them all. It is strange to see so many new faces. It makes the few remaining members of the original Group — there are only twelve of us — feel like strangers on a strange base.

Only 12 of us in November 1943 remained from the original 100 men of the ten crews in the 334th Bomb Squadron that flew across the Atlantic in April, 1943, only 12 of us that hadn't been killed or captured so far in this war. Not one man in our squadron had yet achieved his 25 missions. When we looked at the numbers of crews that didn't return from our missions, it made us realize that the chances of any of us making 25 missions alive and unharmed were pretty darn small. These statistics, while awfully scary in retrospect, were something I just couldn't allow to get too near my conscious thoughts for very long.

One thing that did stay in my consciousness, though, was my old crew headed up by the pilot I had trained, Little Joe Noyes. It was on a mission to a target near Paris on September 9, 1943 that they all, in *Blondie III*, disappeared in the dark of a late evening return. I frequently reviewed the records of known prisoners of war held by the Germans and escapees returning from the occupied territories, but no mention was ever made of any members of that crew. I could only surmise that they had all been killed in either a crash or an explosion. But I still looked for their names in case they were listed on POW records.

Apparently the newspapers in America picked up enough stories about the Germans bombing England to cause my parents to ask about how we were protecting ourselves from them.

> ...You mentioned our "bombings" here and your hope that we all take to the shelters. While I imagine that they play up these German bombings in the papers at home, they really don't amount to much.

We are situated between the two most bombed towns in England, Norwich and Ipswich. The Jerries come over almost every night they can, but it is only individual aircraft and they don't do much damage. No one even bothers to move when there is an air raid alarm. The British papers refer to them as "scaredy cat" raids. All they amount to are isolated enemy fighter planes with one or two bombs tearing across the coast at high speed, dumping their bombs, and tearing for home before the British night fighters get them. They are certainly not bombings in the sense of what we're carrying out.

Being in command was not all "beer and skittles," so to speak. I found out that I occasionally had to do some things as a commander of men that I didn't enjoy doing.

November 30, 1943

As I write this I am in a damned poor mood to bolster the morale on the home front. Frankly, I feel like a dog. I just completed one of the most distasteful tasks I have yet been faced with. Namely, ousting my Squadron Adjutant who is a personal friend of mine. He is a swell fellow, but a lousy administrator, so I was forced to have him transferred out of the Group and off our station. I know that I did the proper thing so far as the good of the Squadron is concerned, but I still feel lousy about it. It is just one of those things.

Our kind of battle was so different from the kind experienced by men in the infantry, who were eye to eye with their opponents. Although, sometimes when the enemy fighters charged into us with their guns blazing, passing within a few feet of our wingtips, it seemed close to being eye to eye. But when we killed our enemies, it was more like a game than warfare on the ground would be. No blood, except our own, did we see. But battle lust became a real experience. I suspect it was a way that warriors supplant their fears.

...Yes, we did have some pretty hot shows around the middle of October, some of the best, or worst, that I have seen. But they were fun and I enjoyed them fully.
I don't know exactly what combat experience has done to me, but it certainly has brought out my sadistic instincts. I love to see those bombs hit and to see those Jerry fighters go down. It gives me the

greatest thrill I have ever experienced. The whole thing holds a certain fascination for me. I just get a great kick out of it all.

Winter weather was settling in over all of Europe by the end of November, and our ability to fly our bombing missions was strongly affected by the weather.

...For the last month things have been a lot easier for several reasons. Primarily, we have been doing a lot of blind bombing through the clouds. These clouds over the Continent are anywhere from 5,000 to 20,000 feet thick and usually full of turbulence and ice. That makes it practically impossible for the enemy fighters to get up to us in any great numbers. Fighter pilots, as a rule, are not good instrument pilots, and fighter planes are difficult to handle under most instrument conditions.

Secondly, our fighter force over here has increased tremendously and we now get fighter cover on most of our trips. Fighter cover is not foolproof, but it sure does help to break up organized attacks. They still knock down a few B-17s but not as many as in the "old days" when we went in alone and in clear weather. It is cold as the devil up there now. I was out the day before yesterday, and at 27,000 feet it was 55 degrees below zero. That is so cold that the metal on the interior of the plane sweats and the moisture forms a coating of ice all over the inside of the ship.

You probably wonder how we overcome the weather if the enemy can't. Well, due to some meteorological phenomena, the overcast is rarely more than 10,000 feet thick over the island and usually has breaks, which our fighters can climb through. No breaks, then we get no fighter support. Our bomber pilots, however, are wonderfully trained in instrument flying, as you may recall from my experiences back in the States. We can assemble the Bomber Command on top of any overcast that has yet confronted us.

Today, for example, our boys were out. It was raining when they took off, ceiling at 300 feet, and they didn't break out until they reached 11,000 feet. Yet all our aircraft made their rendezvous and carried out a very successful mission. It is absolutely amazing what these youngsters are doing over here. We fly as a matter of course in weather that back home would ground every aircraft in the country. That is the side of the picture that gets the least publicity, yet calls for the most skillful and precise flying technique on the part of our pilots.

Accumulating mission credits continued to occupy our minds, although we were now getting to the point where we weren't sure what we would do when we had credit for 25 missions and could go back to the States.

> ...As I previously wrote, Bob and I do not fly together any more, but take turns leading the Group on alternate raids with the other four Command Pilots in the outfit. Bob has three more to finish his twenty-five missions, and I have five more to go. We are seriously considering continuing on to thirty, which is the maximum allowable, but we have made no decision as yet.
>
> You mentioned that you didn't think that, as Operations Officer, Grif Mumford would fly in combat. That is the secret of our success and high morale in the 95th. All staff officers fly in their turn. The four Squadron Commanders, Group C.O., Operations Officers, Air Executive ALL take their turns in rotation. I was out on my turn the other day, November 27. It was an uneventful trip.

It was the accidents, the unnecessary losses that seemed to bother me the most. The losses in air battles were considered part of the game of war, but when we saw our comrades die because of "pilot error" or something else of our own doing, it really hurt.

December 9, 1943

> I had a terrible accident today that cost the lives of seventeen of the twenty men of my two oldest crews. We sent them off for a week's leave over at Southport near Liverpool. One of my new pilots was flying them over and about fifteen miles north of Liverpool they let down through a low overcast and ran into a little hill. It killed them all instantly. I feel particularly bad about it because I was going to fly them over personally, but at the last minute I had to ask the other boy to take the flight as I couldn't get away. I certainly thought that if he couldn't find a hole to let down through, that he would go out over the water where there is always a definite ceiling to an overcast. With the exception of the boy flying, every one in the airplane had over 19 missions to his credit.
>
> I don't feel so badly when the boys get shot down because it is part of the game. But something like this is pretty rough. It is so unnecessary. One of the boys, Captain Louis Reno, my Squadron Lead Pilot, came from Oakland. He and the other old pilot were back in the

plane's radio room when they hit. If either of them had been up front, I feel certain that no accident would have occurred.

The day after the accident in which we lost Lou Reno, it was my turn to lead the entire 13th Bomb Wing on a mission. No more indulging in sadness, it was back to work.

December 10, 1943

Hello again! Back in my quarters again after a long old day.

Got up at 2:30 a.m., had breakfast, attended the briefing, and then sat down for a couple of hours and studied the plan for the day and maps of all the countries adjacent to our route, made my necessary operational notes, and finally got out to the airplane five minutes before takeoff time.

The boys had a real initiation. The weather was so bad here at the base that we had to assemble the Group on top of the overcast. We took off in a snowstorm and finally broke out at 12,500 feet into the most beautiful sunlit scene imaginable. The top of the overcast was just like a model of the mountainous Sierra country. There were peaks and valleys and plains and rolling hills of cloud tinted with the delicate colors of early morn. All over the place, as far as the eye could see, B-17s and B-24s were emerging from the billowing mass, climbing to their assigned assembly altitudes, and joining into their respective Groups.

I know all the details and intricacies of such a rendezvous, yet it is always such a source of amazement and pride for me to witness such a performance. Those youngsters had taken off under the most adverse conditions and climbed for 12,000 feet through clouds so dense that their own wing tips weren't visible to them. Then they all came out on top and in such close order to form into Group formations with a minimum of trouble. It is a real tribute to those youngsters and to the Training Command back home. At any rate, we formed our Groups and then our Combat Wing, and fell into our proper position as per schedule. As our navigation instruments told us, we were leaving the English Coast and setting out across the North Sea, but all that was not visible to us, as it was undercast as far as we could see in every direction. We climbed on course and reached our bombing altitude about twenty minutes before we reached the German Coast. As we reached our assigned altitude, we could see the undercast break away, making the Friesian Islands and the German Coast visible through the haze. We paralleled the coast for a time and then turned to our target.

Friendly fighters were supposed to meet us at the coast. We were met at the coast by fighters, but they were not at all friendly! They were Hermann's boys! We later learned that our P-47s had been jumped over the Zuider Zee by the Jerries, and consequently were late in reaching us.

The Jerries put on quite a show for a few minutes. There were only about 150 of them, so it wasn't too bad, but our new boys were greatly impressed. The flak didn't amount to much, either.

The Jerry fighters tried with some pretty good success some brand new tactics that I had never seen before. They attacked us head on in line abreast with four to six twin engine fighters in each wave, firing rocket guns and driving right through the Group. It was effective as Hell! Their single engine boys stayed above as top cover for them and pecked away at our stragglers. I lost only two ships, but was luckier than some of the other Groups. The attack continued from the time we entered the coast until we bombed, about half an hour in all. Soon after leaving the target, our friendly fighters came up to us, and as far as we were concerned the battle was over. We flew along and watched the fighters dog fight around us.

Soon we were out over the sea, and the clouds once again formed below us. We started our let down, and by the time we reached the English Coast we were at the cloud level. We found a hole right at the coast and spiraled down. The ceiling was now at 2,000 feet so we continued home with no trouble. Just another day's work. Oh, yes, we hit the target!

Shortly thereafter as Christmastime neared at the end of 1943, we decided to return to Ballater in Scotland and give a cocktail party for all those people who had been so kind to us on our first visit to their town. So the same group of us — John Gerhart, Bill Lindley, Dave McKnight, and I — went up there again, accompanied by Bill Pratt. We had figured on procuring our Scotch whisky in Ballater, and we knew they had their own distillery there. What we didn't know was that they didn't have any bottles. At the inn, they didn't sell bottles of whisky; they only sold whisky by the drink. We searched around for a vessel to put the whisky in to get it back to the inn for our party, and what we finally found and used were four chamber pots from the inn. We washed them

thoroughly, of course, and carried the chamber pots down to the distillery to fill with whisky. Then we marched back through town carrying these chamber pots full of whisky back to the inn. At our party, we lined the chamber pots up on the mantle of the fireplace, and when we wanted a drink we just dipped our cups into the chamber pots. We really had a great party!

We stayed on for Christmas dinner. They didn't have turkey or even goose, but they served us a "porker," a large whole roasted pig, and sliced the meat right off the body at the dinner table. Potatoes with gravy completed the meal. Dinner was delicious! These folks in Ballater ate very well, much better by far than the folks in London. And we certainly had a good time participating in their Christmas celebration. When we returned to Horham, we continued our Christmas celebrations, between bombing missions, of course.

December 29, 1943

Please excuse the time between my last effort and this, but the gay life of the holiday season has occupied my time more than somewhat for the last week. To say it has been a social week would be an understatement.

Friday, Christmas Eve, the boys went hunting over France. It wasn't my turn to go, so I took a gun and went hunting in nearby beet fields. Shooting was good and I came home with two pheasants, three grouse, and a cottontail rabbit. That evening the Colonel came back from the hospital, where he'd been confined for several days with a throat ailment. About a dozen of us had a special dinner with him in the Mess and a party full of good liquid Christmas cheer in his quarters afterwards.

Christmas Day I staggered out of bed at noon just in time to eat an excellent meal at the mess. The afternoon, believe it or not, I put in behind my desk catching up on odds and ends. Then about 4:30 p.m. Grif Mumford, the Group Operations Officer, and I went down to Ipswich to a really marvelous Christmas dinner and party at the Brays', the home of a pair of sisters we had taken out on various occasions, mainly to our dances up here. We had been there to their home on several occasions, and they really have been wonderful to us. They have a lovely home, not to mention two attractive daughters.

There were sixteen at the party and we were the only Americans. One of the guests was a British Naval Lieutenant, who the previous day had been sunk for the third time. He is in a Corvette and twice has struck mines. The other time he was bombed into the water at Dunkirk. Typically British, he mentioned his experiences as though they been casual everyday routine.

At any rate, to get back to the party, we had this wonderful meal. They must have saved their rations for some time to provide the fare that graced their table. Then after dinner, we danced and played games until 4:00 AM. It was one of the nicest parties I have ever been to.

The next day was Sunday, and as there was nothing on I again slept until noon, when I was rudely awakened by Bob. He thrust a cigar in my face and proudly told me that his Majority had come through. Naturally, that called for a celebration! So that evening we rested on our elbows at the Officers' Club bar. We downed quite a few by way of rejoicing. Then a group of us repaired to the Mess for a special meal of pheasant, etc., the fruits of my Friday's labors. Needless to say, it was superb.

Then on Christmas Day, Grif and I asked the Mess Sergeant to give us some food to take down to the Brays' with us. He certainly fixed us up. The box included a carton of oranges and lemons, which were priceless over there. We had heard that they auctioned off a lemon in Ipswich for the Red Cross and it brought nine pounds and 12 shillings. You can imagine the excitement the box of oranges and lemons caused at the Brays'. Also, the box included various fruits, sugar, butter, and about ten pounds of wonderful steaks. The whole family was quite pleased, and our gift made a big hit with the Bray girls, too. It earned us a return engagement.

...Monday we had nothing on, so we flew a practice mission. It was my turn to lead, which I did. When I got down, Grif met me and said that the girls had called and had asked if we would come down to dinner again that evening. So we did. We sat down to the finest meal I have eaten since leaving your board.

It seems that families over here belong to "pig clubs". In other words, several families get together and buy a lot of pigs and have some farmer raise them. Then when they mature, they have them slaughtered and divide the bacon, hams, pork, lard, etc. In that way they are able to supplement their rations, which seem to be normally pretty short on meat. This particular evening we enjoyed a roast leg of pork that was simply delicious. We had pan roasted potatoes and the best attempt at apple pie since I have been over here. We came home early as we thought that we would be busy the next day, but as it was, they scrubbed the mission.

Bob and I, now both Majors, discussed our futures as we did our jobs.

> ...Despite the fact that he was away from Pat again, Bob had a pretty nice Christmas. He finished his tour a couple of days before the 25th and his Majority arrived on the 26th. With a little luck I should be finished in about a month. However, don't get the idea that we'll be home soon, because our best future lies over here in staff jobs or in our present positions; so here we will remain for a while at least. We are free to go home if we so desire, but old Uncle Ugh Kessler advised us to stick around. His advice is good enough for me. He looks out for his boys.

Again, interestingly enough, the idea of my writing a book about my adventures was put in front of me. Although I gave it some lip service, it would take more than 50 years to get me to actually do something about it.

> ...As for my writing a book, the thought is not original with you. As I have told you previously, the United Press correspondent with the Eighth Air Force is a former classmate of mine from Stanford and a good friend. He has asked me several times if I would write a book with him. I feel very partial to the idea, but other duties stand in my path at present. Perhaps when things quiet down a bit we can get rolling on some literary epic.

One of the more unusual and interesting things to happen to Bob and me was to be thrust into "public relations" work for the USAAF with our British allies. We were privileged to see and do things that very few Americans were allowed to see and do, and we did it under orders. Fun duty!

Major Harry M. Conley

One of our 95th Bomb Group airmen was a cartoonist who decorated the walls of our new Bomb Wing Officers' Club with caricatures of members. The caricatures included John Gerhart, the wolf, and Harry Conley, the horse, of course. On the right is Jiggs Donohue, another wolf.

The 95th Bomb Group headed for an attack on Brunswick, Germany.

Under all that smoke was the Focke Wolfe aircraft factory in Danzig after we visited and left our calling cards.

Grif Mumford, Al Brown and crew of I'll Be Around *stepping out after the first Berlin Raid.*
Life Magazine

Col. Chester Gilger, 95th Bomb Group Commander, congratulates Grif Mumford and crew after the Berlin Raid.
Eighth Air Force

General Curtis LeMay pinning the Silver Star on Lt. Col. Grif Mumford for leading the first successful American daylight bombing of Berlin.
Eighth Air Force

Lt. Col. Grif Mumford, Commander of the March 4, 1944 Berlin Raid, standing by Pilot Al Brown's B-17, I'll Be Around.
Life Magazine

Lt. Col. Grif Mumford in the cockpit.

Life Magazine

Lt. Col. Grif Mumford with Eighth Air Force Commander, General Jimmy Doolittle.

Life Magazine

Generals LeMay, Spaatz and Doolittle at the ceremonies honoring the Berlin Raiders.
Life Magazine

The 95th Group personnel assembled on the wing of a B-17. This was the centerfold in Life Magazine *March 20, 1944 issue.*
Life Magazine

January 18, 1944

As I write this I am down in London with Bob, who says to say "Hello" to you. We came down this morning, traveling in very fancy company. Lord Beaverbrook, the British Minister for Aircraft Production and Speaker of the House of Lords, was our guest at our station for a couple of days. Bob and I played host to him. So we accompanied him to the city on the early train today, and spent the day in Parliament with him. He took us through the whole place, including the House of Lords, and introduced us to Bevins, Morrison, Atlee, Lord Tydings, and all sorts of prominent British figures.

He is a fascinating person. He is widely traveled, and he actually told us more about the United States than we knew. It was a real experience to meet him. At the Houses of Parliament he took us into places the public is not allowed to visit, such as the Lords' Library, the King's Chambers, and on to the floor in the House of Lords. We really had a marvelous time. Tonight we are going out to dinner and onto someplace later.

Our Eighth Air Force had really been plastering the German aircraft and other munitions manufacturing facilities, as well as shooting down a great many German fighter planes on our missions, and it was starting to look like things were turning the corner in the war in favor of of the Allies.

…We have been quite fortunate and all our trips have been very quiet. It has just been our luck to be in the middle of the procession into the targets and, except for flak, we have not had any difficulty. It has been our luck not to see any fighters for some time. They seem to attack the front and rear Groups and leave the others alone, because they do not have enough aircraft to attack us all. It is some change from the old days of last year when we fought for our lives every minute we were over enemy territory. I can remember when if we had sixty aircraft on an operation we thought it was a large force. The other day I was out and we had 1,500 American bombers and fighters in the air. The sky was black with them as far as you could see. Really an impressive sight!

By the end of January 1944, I had 22 missions and Bob had completed his 25. Big Fitz had also completed his 25 missions and the Colonel ordered him to take a week's leave; he went to England's southern coast, which unfortunately was still pretty cold in midwinter. The poor flying weather and the rotating Command Pilot schedules were still keeping me on the ground a lot, but I still got to fly now and then, and when I did I made the most of it.

January 25, 1944

    I led two of the shows against the rocket emplacements on the French Coast. They were fun. Low level jobs and no fighters to worry about, just a little flak. Had a funny experience on one of them. My bombs hung up in the racks and I got so mad that I decided to stay there until I finally got them out. Consequently, I made FIVE runs on the target before I succeeded!

I really got into pondering where my future would lead me. So far, I certainly couldn't complain. But where would I go, and what would I do after my 25 missions? I was hooked on flying, and I was still young and foolish enough to believe that I could continue to fly in combat until we had beaten the German war machine.

    ...A staff job wouldn't be better than what I have, to my way of thinking. Of course, it would depend on what the job would be. But I prefer to stay with the 95th if possible. Also, in a staff position I wouldn't get to fly as much.
    When I go on a mission, I usually fly about 50% of the time, and that's usually on the bomb runs and then home. Up until that time, I am pretty well occupied with command duties. It is necessary to keep a constant check on the entire formation, to maintain contact with the fighter escort, and I usually work out the navigational problem as a check on my Navigator to ensure our being on the proper course. After we get to the target, I usually fly the bomb run personally, depending on the experience of the pilot with me. I nearly always fly home and leave the navigation to the Navigator. It is a hell of a responsibility and a terrific pressure to go wandering around Europe looking for a target a few hundred feet square that is usually well camouflaged. I am not listed as copilot, but as Command Pilot. However, I sit in the copilot's seat and usually we do not carry a copilot.

The real rewards for me had become the "wins" in air combat and the successful bombing missions when we hit our targets and brought our crews back home. But in the course of all that, the Army had presented me with a few tokens of appreciation. It felt good to be recognized. And I knew my parents would feel good about them, too.

> ...About those medals I sent home, I have the Purple Heart and three oak leaf clusters to the Air Medal and one oak leaf cluster coming up to the Distinguished Flying Cross (D.F.C.), seven decorations in all.

On into February, the war continued. I still had not completed 25 missions, and I was still concerned about my future in the USAAF.

> February 14, 1944
>
> Happy Valentine's Day, Mom!
>
> I have been on the ground since I last wrote. By that I mean no combat. As I told you, I now only go on Wing leads, so I have to patiently wait my turn. It comes all too seldom. Nevertheless, we have been going pretty hot and heavy. Even if I don't go on the missions, I do have to get up for the briefings and stay up most of the previous night on the planning. Especially now, because I have no Operations Officer temporarily. He has been borrowed by Eighth Air Force Headquarters to fly a secret mission to a secret destination, the lucky guy! He'll be gone about six weeks. He promised to bring me a bottle of vodka. His absence means that I have to do his work as well as my own. It's too much bother to break in someone new for such a short time.
>
> I still haven't decided what my course will be for the future. There are several things in the offing, any one of which will be a step in the right direction. As it stands there are four likely possibilities outside of staying with the Group. In any case, so long as I am with the Group I shall continue on combat. I have definitely decided that much.

Command of the 95th Bomb Group was changing. I was learning that nothing stays the same, and organizational changes were part of the experience of being in any large organization, including the Army Air Forces.

...Colonel Gerhart, my old C.O., has been made Chief of Operations over here. Well, he called Bob and me up to Headquarters the other day and asked us what we had in mind for the future. We told him, "nothing definite", except that we didn't want to go home and get stuck in some Training Command. He agreed that we would be foolish to go home without a definite assignment in view. So he told us he had called us up to offer us a choice of two jobs over here, both excellent. One, a position on the Operational Planning Board at Bomber Command, and the other, as Chief of Operations in a couple of new Combat Wings being formed. A Wing is the intermediate control between Bomb Divisions and the individual Groups. Both jobs carry the rank of Lieutenant Colonel. The other two alternatives he discussed were back in the States, one as permanent personnel at the Army Experimental Station at Orlando, Florida, where they test all sorts of new combat tactics and equipment, and the second as Route Supervisors with Air Transport Command, not necessarily in the States. The latter would be in charge of a transport route with about twenty four-engine transports under his command.

Bob and I have not made any decisions as yet. Before we can accept any of the above, we have to get released from the Group. But the fact remains that we have the proper contacts and can practically write our own tickets when the time comes. If we go home, the promotions will come more slowly, and that is a definite consideration. On the other hand, we will get to fly more in those jobs than in either of the Staff jobs offered on this side.

I think Bob is rather more anxious to go home to be with his wife and baby son and I can't blame him, but somehow my interests seem to be over here. This is where the war is being fought and I hate to leave in the middle of it.

Bob and I have been extremely fortunate in traveling this far together and keeping apace of each other in promotions, etc. We are the only two that I know of who have done so. We have also made some extremely valuable contacts in higher headquarters with ranking men. And, as I said before, we can practically write our own tickets. Colonel John Gerhart told us the other day that we were the two most promising lads of the Third Bomb Division. Take it for whatever it is worth. Neither of us has ever led an unsuccessful raid.

The immediate change for the 95th Group was replacing Colonel John Gerhart.

...Our new Colonel Gilger is an OK guy. He fell right into the 95th groove. Tonight Bob and I took six dollars from him playing cribbage.

It wasn't long before Colonel Gilger became known among the ranks as "Cheerful Chester." He was a very upbeat fellow, and I don't think his characteristic smile and optimistic outlook were unreal, although there certainly was a lot of pressure for all of us to put on a "happy face" to help keep up morale. We surely didn't need a dour commander.

One of the more rewarding experiences in the war was the excellent relations that existed between the British and the Americans. In particular, the RAF pilots were a good bunch of guys, and the respect was mutual.

...As I write this I can hear the RAF coming home from their night's outing. Just had a phone call asking how many I can put up for the night. Evidently we will have some RAF boys stop in here as they do quite often. That is the nice thing about operations over here; everyone is so cooperative. The RAF and the USAAF are just like one outfit. We are always using each other's bases and facilities as well as equipment. It is an ideal situation!

As the Allied High Command formulated its mission for the Eighth Air Force early in the war, the first priority was to disable the maintenance bases for the German U-boats, as a part of crippling that undersea force so it could not stop the shipments of men and material from America to England. By the end of 1943 this objective had been largely accomplished, although the German submarines remained a threat to Allied shipping throughout the war. The next priority, then, for the Eighth Air Force was to destroy the effectiveness of the Luftwaffe so that the Allied Forces would have air superiority over the landing sites and preferably, well inland from those sites, when we chose to invade. The invasion of Europe was set, roughly, for late spring of 1944. Thus this second priority mission to rid the skies of the Luftwaffe was, therefore, becoming more and more urgent by the beginning of 1944. But the weather was not cooperating with the Allies. The

Eighth Air Force was too often unable to carry out heavy concentrated bombing missions against the Luftwaffe. The Planning Staff reporting to General Eisenhower noted that a customary weather pattern for Europe was to have a period of clear skies, due to high-pressure areas, moving across Europe for five to ten days in the latter part of February. So they watched for signs that this weather pattern might occur this year, 1944. By mid-February it appeared to be happening, and the Commanders of the Eighth (based in Britain) and Fifteenth (based in Italy) Air Forces were instructed to conduct massive attacks on German aircraft production as soon as weather permitted.

The first good weather forecast reached the Eighth Air Force on February 20. As that occurred, between February 20th and 25th the Eighth carried out a large number of raids with thousands of aircraft participating in an attempt, as General Fred Anderson said "to kill the octopus" of the Luftwaffe. That time period became known as the "Big Week."

My personal frustration about getting through my 25 missions continued through the end of February. But for various reasons I was not able to fly on any of these Big Week raids. I had a chance to fly a fighter plane during Big Week. A friend of mine brought a brand new P-51 Mustang over to our base and let me fly it. Or rather, I was going to fly it, but in starting the engine I flooded it, and we had to wait an hour before all the excess gas drained out of the cylinders. By then, he had to leave. So there went my chance. Was my face red! I got quite a razzing from my buddies about it.

February 23, 1944

> I still can't get a ride across the way to finish up. I just fly around the countryside for amusement. Actually, I fly around to the different bases and visit with different people and tend my administrative duties. Not very exciting, is it?
> The weather has been quite cold and we have had considerable snow, but it doesn't stay on the ground very long. However, it is mean for flying because it impairs visibility and makes it nasty. It hasn't stopped us, however, and as you probably see by the papers, we are

really putting forth a maximum effort. As I see it, it looks like the prelude to the Big Show. We are attempting to knock out the Luftwaffe before the Main Event starts. If we can succeed, it will mean a savings of thousands of lives.

I see Churchill finally came out and told the British public yesterday that the war over here may not be over in 1944. I feel much the same. I look for a possible end next November. If not, then it will be another year. This is going to be a hell of a rough go when they start across the Channel. People at home have no conception of just how tough it is going to be.

Big Week[5] was aptly named. On February 20, the skies were clear of the heavy clouds we had experienced the previous few weeks and the Eighth Air Force took advantage of that good bombing weather. The First Air Division was sent off to bomb aircraft factories at Leipzig, Oschersleben and Bernburg, the Second Air Division to Magdeburg, Brunswick and Gotha, and our Third Bomb Division over the North Sea and Denmark to Tutow and Rostock. All these areas were heavily into production of Me-109s, Me-110s, Ju-88s, Ju-52s, Ju-188s, FW-190s and He-111s — until we bombed them that day! Our losses were 25 bombers and four fighters, while we confirmed 153 German fighter planes downed.

The next day, February 21, again had clear, cold weather as the high-pressure area passed over most of Germany. So the Eighth Air Force planned another "maximum effort" mission against German aircraft factories at Brunswick and Diepholz, railway yards at Lingen, and German airfields at Hannover, Achmer, and Hopten. Bad weather over Foggia prevented the Fifteenth Air Force from participating on this day. Nevertheless, the Eighth Air Force sent out some 861 bombers accompanied by 659 fighters. Heavy clouds over the aircraft factories caused less than satisfactory bomb damage, but the losses of aircraft looked better for the Americans

---

[5] For more detailed information, see *Big Week, The Classic Story of the Crucial Air Battle of WWII*, by Glenn Infield, published by Brassey's, 1974 and 1993.

with 19 bombers and 5 fighters downed, while our confirmed kills of German fighters amounted to 60.

Weather forecasts looked better for bombing over Germany the next day, February 22. The Third Bomb Division, with its Commander, General Curtis LeMay, as Mission Commander, was to bomb Germany's critical ball-bearing facilities in Schweinfurt, while the Fifteenth Air Force, taking advantage of clear skies from Foggia to Schweinfurt, would fly north to Regensburg to make another strike at the Messerschmitt aircraft complex. That morning the cloud ceiling was low as I watched Chester Gilger lead the 95th Bomb Group as it took off to assemble over a very cloudy East Anglia. Unfortunately, this was one of those times when misfortunes occurred as two bombers collided in the clouds as they ascended for assembly, causing a lot of other bombers to move off course and the resultant confusion created such hazardous flying conditions that LeMay, regretfully, recalled the Third Division. Then the B-24s of the Second Division got strung out over the Channel so badly that it, too, was recalled. That left the First Division to go it alone. Their 255 bombers hit a great many important targets, but their losses were high at 41 bombers. The Fifteenth Air Force put up a force of 183 bombers headed for Regensburg, but many of them encountered unpredicted heavy clouds and ended up bombing secondary targets. They successfully bombed the Messerschmitt factory at Obertaubling, but the cost was 14 bombers lost. The Luftwaffe lost about 50 fighters that day.

The weather reports for February 23 essentially ruled out any bombing missions over Germany from England. Despite the need to keep the pressure on the Luftwaffe, the Eighth Air Force took a much-needed rest, while the Fifteenth Air Force sent out 102 bombers from Italy and destroyed a significant portion of the ball-bearing plants in Austria.

All the pressure on our air crews and all the losses were causing severe morale issues, many of which I had to deal with. Those of us in command positions had to be extremely sensitive to the concerns of our men. We had to observe them carefully, listen to them attentively, and quickly weed out the ones whose signs of battle fatigue could cause a contagion in a crew or a barracks full of airmen. Nevertheless, we had to continue to destroy the effectiveness of the Luftwaffe in order to allow the invasion of the European Continent to proceed that coming spring.

On February 24, the weather appeared to be ideal for another trip over Germany. So the Eighth Air Force sent its First, Second and Third Divisions with a total of 505 bombers in three forces accompanied by a total of 767 escort fighters, hitting ball-bearing facilities at Schweinfurt, aircraft production facilities at Gotha, and other aircraft plants at Tutow and Kreising in Germany and Posen in Poland. Simultaneously the Fifteenth Air Force sent 114 bombers to Steyr to bomb another aircraft plant. As expected, the Luftwaffe put up a tremendous resistance. In all, we ended up with 61 bombers and 10 fighters lost — none, however, from our Third Division — but the Luftwaffe lost 145 planes. Generally, the bombing results as shown on reconnaissance photos were good.

Big Week ended with a clear weather forecast for February 25. The Eighth and Fifteenth Air Forces combined to fly over 1,300 bombers to strike at aircraft factories at Regensburg, Augsburg, Stuttgart and Furth. They were accompanied by about 1,000 escort fighters. Bombing results were generally excellent. We lost 33 bombers, while the Luftwaffe's losses were high this day.

Big Week essentially broke the back of the Luftwaffe! The Allied air forces could now go anywhere in Germany to bomb. The German production of new aircraft was virtually shut down for at least a couple of months, and their supplies of ball bearings were critically low. We had a great many losses, too, but we were now receiving from the States a large number of new airplanes and replacement crews were arriving daily. We could — and did — rebuild our forces quickly, whereas the Germans could not after we had destroyed so much of their manufacturing capability, and with their limited manpower, they had to use younger and less experienced pilots and crews. So our forces continued to grow in England in preparation for the final confrontation with Nazi Germany, while Germany's resources were being depleted.

One of the frustrations that everyone in the Eighth Air Force experienced was that we had not yet been able to carry out a daylight bombing mission on Berlin itself — the "Big B," as we called it. Between the 20th and the 25th of February, we had bombed many aircraft plants and related industrial and military targets in Germany, but we had not as yet bombed Berlin. The British had carried out some night bombing raids on Berlin, but we knew that a daylight raid by B-17s with our Norden bombsights could do much more damage to German facilities and morale than the bombs from night area bombing. "Big B" held the ominous distinction of being the most highly defended target in Germany. Nevertheless, we really wanted to drop bombs on Berlin. We felt challenged by Hermann Goering telling his Fuhrer and the German people that the Luftwaffe would never let Berlin be bombed in daylight by the Americans. We knew we could do it; we just wanted to get the opportunity. But for several days after the end of Big Week, the weather over the Continent, and Germany in particular, had not been good for bombing missions. Nevertheless, the Allied High Command had made the daylight bombing of Berlin an important objective. Successfully doing that would strengthen the morale of all the Allied Forces, and we believed it would crush the morale of the German people and help convince them to end this war they were losing.

Because of my duties as Squadron Commander, I was not able to participate in the bombing missions in late February, but when my turn came up to lead a March 3rd mission, and it was going to be Berlin, the capital and heart of the enemy, I was really looking forward to it. To put the icing on the cake, this would be my 25th mission. What a grand finale!

The weather was predicted to continue to be very cold and snowy in England, but there would be openings in the cloud cover over Germany that should allow us to prove that the Luftwaffe couldn't stop us from dropping our bombs on Berlin. It might even be "iffy" enough to keep the German fighters on the ground.

Nine Groups of the 3rd Bomb Division took off early in the morning of March 3rd in snow and freezing rain. It was definitely one of those mornings when we wondered if we were crazy to be flying. We assembled at 26,000 feet above the bad weather and headed for Germany and our target, Berlin. Then as we came over the Continent, the cloud level became higher and higher. This was not as forecast. We climbed through solid clouds the whole way and finally broke out at 28,000 feet southeast of Hamburg. We were immediately confronted with another wall of clouds that reached to about 35,000 feet. As we had planned to fly at considerably lower altitude, we had neither sufficient fuel nor oxygen to climb over that massive wall of clouds and return. The weather was being so difficult that we weren't able to fly in formation; we couldn't even see our own wingtips. So I elected to turn back from Berlin and head west for our secondary target, Emden, on the western German coast. Needless to say, my crew and I were greatly disappointed, as we had really looked forward to leading the first American daylight bombing raid on Berlin.

We were crossing open sea when the clouds opened up under us and we saw a German ship convoy down below us. There were about ten ships, as I recall, sailing in a line one behind the other. Definitely a target of opportunity! We were flying at about 18,000 feet then. We circled around to make a bomb run, and our wing bombardier immediately went for his Norden bombsight. He lined up the lead ship in the convoy and had the bomb bay doors open and bombs away quickly. Amazing! Our bombs went right into the stack of that ship and blew it up! All our formations went down that line of German ships dropping bombs and wreaking havoc with them. We sank at least two or three of them and left the others in big trouble. Having no more bombs left for Emden, we then headed home to England.

The next day, March 4, was the 95th Group's turn to lead the mission with their Operations Officer, Grif Mumford, as Command Pilot, again with Berlin as the prime target. I attended the briefing as usual; but my job this day was to stay at Headquarters and sweat it out. There were some reasons given that encouraged all of us that this could be the day we actually bomb Big B. First, the weather was predicted to be more open over the target area. Second, the mission would have a "Pathfinder"[6] aircraft, equipped with radar navigational gear to help see through the heavy clouds to stay on course and to help the lead bombardier in case the target became obscured by clouds. And third, there were to be several squadrons of P-51 fighters with long range fuel tanks to provide friendly fighter cover. We knew that if the skies were relatively clear, there would certainly be lots of fighter opposition dedicated to preventing us from bombing the German capital city. Our 13th Combat Bomb Wing was to be led by the 95th Bomb Group, divided into Flights A and B, plus the 100th and 390th Bomb Groups, about 72 airplanes in all, loaded with enough 500 pound bombs to let Hitler know we had visited his capital.

Starting at 7:00 a.m. I watched some of our planes take off and disappear into cold and snowy clouds; and I wondered whether or not today's mission would be more successful than our mission yesterday. I went back to my desk and handled correspondence and other administrative matters, all the while thinking about this day's mission and whether or not the weather would clear up enough to let our bombers get through to Big B. Then in the early afternoon I got a report that several flights had turned back and were headed for their secondary targets. That didn't sound very good. But my spirits picked up later when I heard that the 95th Group led by Grif Mumford had made their bombing run on Berlin and were headed home. Wow! We finally did it!

---

[6] The 482nd Bomb Group (Pathfinder) was activated on August 20, 1943 at Alconbury to provide leadership on combat missions over Europe by means of radar and other electronic navigational devices. For some time it was obvious that because of bad weather over Europe, especially during the winters, the Eighth Air Force needed a radar capability to bomb Germany during periods of partial or complete cloud cover. On September 26, 1943, radar equipped B-17s of the 482nd Bomb Group led a successful mission to Emden, Germany. The 482nd continued from that date on to lead Eighth Air Force missions to Europe until March 22, 1944 when a mission to Berlin was the final day mission flown by the 482nd Bomb Group. Navigators and bombardiers trained in radar by the 482nd were sent to bases throughout the 8th Air Force, and became pathfinders for future Eighth missions. The 482nd became a radar-training center, and also a radar research and development operation until the war in Europe ended. The 482nd did fly day missions in support of the D-Day Invasion.

When I got to General LeMay's office, there were a lot of news correspondents there, as well as some other Air Force brass, all very excited about our bombing Berlin. We all went to the field at Horham where the 95th Group's planes would be returning, and we watched them come in; and I counted. Yes, there had been some casualties, but the lead aircraft with Command Pilot Grif Mumford landed successfully, and General LeMay personally greeted that crew.

Then everyone went into the briefing room, where flashbulbs lit the scene as pictures were taken of General LeMay awarding a Silver Star to Grif Mumford, and the news correspondents were all crowding around him to ask questions and get the story. One of those correspondents was Andy Rooney, whom we see now on *Sixty Minutes*. Then Al Brown, the pilot of the lead ship, was awarded a Distinguished Flying Cross for his leadership, courage and determination in carrying out the mission[7]. Grif, however, as Mission Commander, was definitely the star of this show! And he really deserved it! Lots of excitement!

Lt. Bill Owen, pilot of the Pathfinder B-17, returned his aircraft to its home base at Alconbury. He and his crew were actually part of the 482nd Pathfinder Group, although Bill and his original crew started their mission tours as members of the 95th Bomb Group. They were specifically assigned to accompany the 95th Bomb Group on this mission, because the overcasts over Berlin had been such a hindrance to the Eighth Air Force's previous attempts at that target. Because of his perseverance and leadership in completing the mission and bomb drop with the 95th Bomb Group, Lt. Owen was awarded the Distinguished Flying

---

[7] For his courageous and determined leadership of the first aerial bombing mission over Berlin, Lieutenant Colonel H. Griffin Mumford was awarded the Silver Star by Major General Curtis LeMay. The pilot of the lead aircraft, 1st Lieutenant Alvin Brown, was awarded the Distinguished Flying Cross for his courageous leadership and devotion to duty. A commendation of high praise was awarded to the navigator of the lead aircraft, 1st Lieutenant Malcolm Durr, for his outstanding job of dead reckoning in directing the flight almost exactly as briefed in spite of almost impossible difficulties encountered.

Cross. As the use of radar was still considered "Top Secret", there was no publicity allowed regarding the role of the Pathfinder aircraft. The world was very well-informed about the 95th Bomb Group's success, but no one, except the mission participants, had any information about the role played by the Pathfinders.[8]

In the post mission meeting it became clear that this mission was no picnic. The Luftwaffe was out in force to keep us away from Berlin, but our friendly fighters did an excellent job of chasing them off of the bombing force. When the attacking B-17s arrived at the target area in Berlin, the crews were elated to find that P-51s were circling the city. These P-51s of the 4th and 357th Fighter Groups engaged the Luftwaffe single-engine Me-109s and FW-190s and were credited with destroying five German fighters. Chuck Yeager of the 357th Fighter Group shot down his first enemy fighter on this mission.

Apparently Grif and his crew found some openings in the clouds, but they used the Pathfinder plane with its radar to help the bombardiers line up their targets. Interestingly, the lead plane's bomb-bay doors stuck shut, so they had the Pathfinder plane act as lead bombardier and signal with flares to have all planes drop their bombs with those of the Pathfinder. Later on the lead plane's crew were able to open their bomb bay and drop their bombs on a bridge, a target of opportunity.

Only 30 B-17s, mostly from the 95th Group, went on to bomb Berlin led by Grif Mumford's plane. And the Luftwaffe turned out in force to knock them down or turn them back. Again, the good discipline in the 95th Group in staying in close formation proved to be one of the reasons they were able to defend themselves so well. The rest of the groups turned back. There was quite an

---

[8] For many detailed first-hand accounts by the aircrews who participated in this memorable mission, see *B-17s Over Berlin, Personal Stories from the 95th Bomb Group (H)*, edited by Ian L. Hawkins, published by Brassey's. Also for first hand stories by the crew of Bill Owen's Pathfinder, the first B-17 to drop bombs on Berlin, see *Bombs Away By Pathfinders of the Eighth Air Force*, by Marshall J. Thixton, George E. Moffat and John J. O'Neil, published by FNP Military Division.

interesting story about the groups that sought targets of opportunity. It didn't fully come out at the interrogation meeting, but in his book, *B-17s Over Berlin* (and its predecessor, *Courage — Honor — Victory*), the British writer, Ian Hawkins, brought it out from interviews of various crew members from the March 4th mission. Shortly after the Wing crossed over into German territory, a Morse Code message was received by all of our aircraft. It was encrypted properly for the day, and it appeared to have originated at Eighth Air Force Headquarters. Because of weather conditions, it said, the original mission was recalled and the planes were given the option of hitting their secondary targets or returning to base. Most of the pilots heeded this recall. The radioman in the lead aircraft noted some unusual things about the message and pointed them out to Grif Mumford and Al Brown. First, the signal containing this message was strong, much stronger than normal for a signal coming from England. Second, the right code words were used, but in the wrong places. Could it be that the Germans were sending this message to head us off our target? Anyway, at this point, Grif decided that they were already close enough to Berlin to make it, and the weather wasn't bad enough to abort the mission. Besides, if it did get bad, he could choose to abort the mission later. So Grif and Al decided to continue on the original mission. They tersely announced their decision by radio to the rest of the mission force, and kept on flying toward Berlin. Only 35 aircraft stayed with them; the rest turned around. After everybody returned to England, no one at Eighth Air Force knew anything about any recall message. It probably had been a German trick intended to divert us.

But because of the determination of Grif Mumford and Al Brown and the courageous crews of the 95th Bomb Group, it didn't work. And Berlin experienced the first of many daylight bombing raids by the American Eighth Air Force. This act probably had a very significant effect on helping to bring this war to a close.

Note

For the mission on March 4, 1944, the 95th Bombardment Group (H) was given its third Presidential Unit Citation, which reads as follows:

HEADQUARTERS 3D BOMBARDMENT DIVISION
Office of the Commanding General

GENERAL ORDERS
Number 923
3 November 1944

UNIT CITATION

Under the provisions of Executive Order No. 9396 (Sec. I, Bull. 22, D, 1943) and Sec. IV, Cir. 333, D, 1943, the 95th BOMBARDMENT GROUP (H) is cited for outstanding performance of duty in action in connection with the first aerial daylight attack by United States heavy bombers on Berlin, Germany, 4 March 1944.

The energies of the entire Eighth Air Force were devoted to this vital operation but only the 95th Bombardment Group and twelve aircraft from another Group got through to the primary target and bombed it.

At take-off time, the weather conditions were so bad that one entire Division was forced to cancel the mission. The 95th Group assembled in proper formation and departed the English Coast as scheduled, despite local snowstorms and generally adverse weather. Soon after the continental coast was crossed, all participating units of the Eighth Air Force except one wing either abandoned the operation or attacked other targets because of treacherous, towering cloud formations and dense, persistent contrails which made formation flying difficult. The one wing, led by the 95th Group, resolutely continued on to the objective. In the target area twenty to thirty single engine enemy aircraft pressed home vicious attacks, mostly in elements of two or three aircraft at a time. Friendly fighter support was inadequate and enemy ground positions fired heavy concentrations of anti-aircraft fire at the attackers. Nevertheless, the 95th Group maintained a tight defensive formation and released forty-two and a half tons of high explosives on the cloud covered German capital. Even after the target was bombed, enemy fighters continued to attack the formation until the rally point. The courageous crews of the 95th Group destroyed three of the hostile fighters, probably destroyed one and damaged one more. A safe withdrawal was completed, although it was necessary to fly directly through solid clouds since the exhausted oxygen supply made it impossible to rise above them. Nine bombers were damaged by enemy action, four were lost. Forty-one officers and enlisted men were missing in action and four were wounded.

By heroically electing the more hazardous of two equally acceptable and honorable courses of action, the 95th Bombardment Group clearly distinguished itself above and beyond all other units participating in this momentous operation. The extraordinary heroism, determination, and espirit de corps displayed by the officers and enlisted men of this organization in overcoming unusually difficult and hazardous conditions brought to a successful conclusion our country's first combat operation over the capital of Germany. The fortitude, bravery, and fighting spirit of the 95th Group on this historic occasion constitute a noteworthy contribution to the war effort and add notably to the cherished traditions of the Army Air Forces.

By command of Major General PARTRIDGE:
OFFICIAL: N.B. HARBOLD
                                     Brigadier General, U.S.A.
                                     Chief of Staff

CHAPTER 15

D-DAY, JUNE 6, 1944

After my abortive attempt to fly one of my friend's fighter planes when I flooded the engine trying to start it, I had many more opportunities to fly fighter planes. Of course, I wrote my parents about it.

March 12, 1944

Of late have been flying fighters, quite a bit for fun. They are easy after a complicated four engine job. Just like training planes. No instruction is necessary. We just get in and fly them. As they are single seaters, it's just you and the airplane. Believe me, they are really fast and maneuverable. I've been flying Thunderbolts, Mustangs and Lightnings. I think the greatest thrill I've received in flying was the first time I flew a fighter, a Thunderbolt. I took off, pulled the wheels up, then looked around. I was lost! In less time than it takes to tell, I was out of sight of the field and had climbed 5,000 feet! It is fun to do loops and rolls, etc., again — things you aren't supposed to do in four engine bombers. However, I have seen some B-17s do them in combat.

I'd like to do some trips across with the fighter boys, but I can't get permission to do so from Higher Headquarters. So I'll confine my fighter activities to just playing around over here.

Destiny or good fortune or whatever was good to Bob, Fitz and me in April of 1944. Bob and I were both promoted to Lieutenant Colonel. Fitz was promoted to Major, which was practically unheard of for a Bombardier. With Fitz's promotion there were only three Bombardiers who had attained the rank of Major. Bob Cozens decided to accept a position in Washington, D.C., on the Staff of General Craig, Head of the Bombardment Section of the Army Air Forces. Colonel Gerhart had recommended him for this position. But I had even more good news to share with my parents:

the Army and I had determined what my ongoing assignment would be.

April 9, 1944

> I have some news that will no doubt surprise you. Today I bid farewell to the 95th Bomb Group. As of yesterday I am Lieutenant Colonel Conley (also Lieutenant Colonel Cozens on the same set of orders) of the 93rd Combat Wing. Colonel Gerhart was given command of a new Wing, the 93rd, to be formed here in the Eighth Air Force, and he asked for me as his Chief of Staff. It is quite an advancement! My position calls for a full Colonel, and Colonel Gerhart's, a Brigadier General. But it will be some time before we are promoted to T.O. (Table of Organization) strength. At any rate, I am very happy to be a Lieutenant Colonel at present. After only twenty-one months of commissioned service, I'm not complaining!

Leaving the 95th Group included moving out of my familiar barracks and into Elveden Hall with Colonel Gerhart. He had one big room divided into three rooms, and Jiggs Donohue also left the 95th Group and moved in with us. These changes in my life were exciting. What was happening was that a new Wing, the 93rd Combat Wing, was being organized to encompass the 385th, 490th, 493rd, and much to my surprise, the 34th Bomb Group to which I was attached back in Spokane. The 34th was one that was still flying B-24s. In fact, John inherited a total of about 500 B-24s in his new Wing. We tried to work with those aircraft, but in the European Theater with our requirement for flying tight formations they just didn't do the job for us like our B-17s did. It didn't take Colonel John long to request Washington to exchange those B-24s for new B-17s; and after a while he successfully made the trade.

In the Army Air Forces, a Wing is the equivalent of an Army Division, which generally comprises about 15,000 soldiers. This was a really big job that was thrust upon me.

> ...We have quite a job of organization as we are starting from scratch. Also, Colonel Gerhart will not be relieved from his present duties for another couple of weeks. In the meantime it is my job to organize the

Wing. It will be one Hell of a job. This all represents quite an opportunity for which I am grateful. It means I won't fly operationally very often, but it will still be very interesting work.

As I have said several times, I was very lucky, riding the crest of the wave of the buildup of the U.S. Army Air Forces in Europe. I expressed in my letters my amazement about it all.

> ...It seems very strange to be called "Colonel Conley," and somewhat difficult to get used to. I have certainly progressed far beyond my fondest dreams at the time of my enlistment. Being a Senior Officer is a new experience. Tonight I ate dinner with four Generals and a couple of Colonels. It is quite an experience to hobnob with such rank. I never expected to reach this level. Of course, I knew most of the Generals when they were Colonels; now they are two-star and three-star boys. Nevertheless, it is strange to be called by my first name by the powers that be.
>
> They have really fixed me up in my new capacity. Not only do I have a swell car (a comfortable British sedan) and driver but I also have a P-51 fighter airplane so that I can get around and visit the airfields in our command.
>
> Our headquarters will be only ten miles from the base of the 95th, so I'll be able to visit them frequently. After all, that is still home to me.

April 22, 1944

> We have been terribly busy. Not flying, but all paperwork now that I am a Chief of Staff. We are about to try some new and experimental operations with B-24s instead of B-17s. It should be very interesting. When we are ready for operations, I expect to fly several missions with the B-24s just to see how our planning turns out. All this stuff is very interesting and very new to me. As you know, I'm working with my old C.O., Colonel Gerhart. He is tough and demanding, but a darn fine man to work for. We get along well.
>
> Fitz has gone home for a couple of months and will be back the first part of June. Don't be surprised if you receive a phone call from him from Michigan. I imagine that Bob will also be out your way sooner or later and that you will see him. He will be able to give you a pretty fair picture of things over here.

As far as my homecoming is concerned, with things the way they are at present and as they will be in the very near future, I won't be able to get away for at least a couple of months. I may see you in July or August if all goes well. I could have gone home now, but it would mean passing up my present job, and opportunities like this don't grow on trees.

In my new grade, I feel like a real junior member. Outside of Bob, I have yet to meet a Lieutenant Colonel with less than five years of commissioned service. Bob and I each have one year and nine months. We feel pretty lucky about it, to say the least.

I'm glad to hear that Dad wants to go on a ride in a B-17, too! He'll get a kick out of it, I know.

May 16, 1944

First of all, let me wish you a Happy Mothers' Day, as of yesterday! I had sent you a cable, but this morning I was told that it was never dispatched because of the present ban on cables from the island.

I'm so glad that Bob got home and that you were able to spend so much time with him. He can tell you a lot more about what is going on over here, things that I cannot write about.

As for the debut of our new outfit, the first Group will be ready in about a week. I will fly with them the first couple of times out; after that, I'll only fly a couple of times a month. We have put them through a really intensive training, and now time will tell. I chase them around the sky every day in my fighter, herding them into formation and observing their technique. Incidentally, I gave up my P-51 and now I will be flying a P-38. We just got it today, so I'll try it out tomorrow.

Today Col. Gerhart and I took the afternoon off and went over to Cambridge. We each bought some beautiful sporting prints for our quarters, which are really swanky. One of the boys in our outfit is an interior decorator by profession. "Swanky" is his doing. We have bed spreads, drapes, and slip covers on all the furniture in the living quarters. It makes the place so home-like. Also, we built a little bar in a corner of the living room, and borrowed a guy from one of the bomb groups to paint it. He was formerly an animator for Disney, so the results are most professional. He did an English barnyard scene with all sorts of farm animals, complete with caricature heads of all the Wing officers! Quite a place! Saturday night we had an informal party here, sort of a house-warming, and Grif came down.

It makes me feel very odd to be doing business with all these officers who have had so much more time in service than I, and to offer my recommendations to them, in view of my junior service. As Chief of Staff, I am second in command of the Wing; and all the Group Commanders and their Deputy Commanders with whom I deal are Regular Army career men with five to twenty years in the Army. I am very flattered to hold the position, and I must say that all these men treat me as one of them, as an equal. In fact, they all respect my combat experience and are only too happy to receive my suggestions and recommendations. But I feel like a fish out of water.

I am certainly getting a marvelous experience in administration. In the past six weeks I have set up three complete air bases. As these outfits come over here, their entire ground personnel have to be reassigned to meet the requirements of local conditions. It is a tremendous task and I have learned much.

This is Big Business, and like any other big business, the higher you climb, the further you get from the basic function — in this case, piloting — and the more involved you become in administration and planning. I never thought I'd become a "Brass Hat" or staff officer, but I'll be damned if I'm not one now!

Finally, the long awaited big day — D-Day! — arrived when the Allies would land in Europe and attack the Germans on land. As Chief of Staff of the 93rd Combat Bomb Wing, I was the Mission Commander of our unit of 108 B-17s on D-Day. As I recall, there were probably close to 11,000 Allied aircraft — American, British, Canadian, and Free French — all airborne and scheduled to hit their assigned first targets in the invasion area at 6:00 a.m. on June 6. What a massive array of aircraft this was! It was a sight that we'll never see again. The entire sky became so filled with airplanes that it was hard to see the sky from below. And they all hit their targets, the German defenses on the Normandy coast, at 6:00 a.m. What a concentration of aerial force and bombs!

The weather had been fierce leading up to this time. For a week the rains had been heavy and the winds were blowing terribly. The whole invasion force had been at ready alert. In the 93rd Combat Bomb Wing we had been sitting on the ground with the storm blowing all around us with our bombs loaded and our gas tanks full. Finally, the weather gurus determined that there would be a 36-hour window in the violent weather pattern plaguing us, starting late on June 5th. General Eisenhower, through his staff, gave the order to "Go!" The field order came to us at the 93rd Combat Bomb Wing Headquarters at about 5:00 p.m. on June 5. We called the crews together for briefings and started our pre-takeoff procedures. It was still raining hard and blowing a gale.

What isn't generally known to this day is that one of the primary reasons General Eisenhower and his staff selected the first week of June, 1944 for the invasion was because that was the time when General Curtis LeMay had said that the Eighth Air Force should have destroyed the effectiveness of the Luftwaffe. Aerial reconnaissance proved that to be accurate; the German Air Force had been decimated. All this information was covered in highly classified security briefings at General LeMay's Headquarters attended by John Gerhart and his senior officers, including me.

Extremely intensive planning had been done prior to D-Day to accommodate the huge number of aircraft that were to be aloft at the same time. The longer range aircraft had to take off as early as 9:00 p.m. the previous night and were directed to a holding area over the Irish Sea, there to circle until their appointed assembly time at daylight. That night we had the skies over the western coast of the British Isles filled with aircraft circling, out of the vision of the German radars, awaiting the time to cross the Channel and strike their targets. Our Wing took off at 10:00 p.m. in terrible rain and dense clouds. We circled there as a single aircraft until daylight when we could see to assemble our formations. By this time the weather was improving and we proceeded to our target areas. Each group had a specific target within the target area, the coast of Normandy. There was a detailed route in and out of the target area. It was like a series of one-way streets. Because of the extremely large numbers of aircraft going toward the target area and returning, all aircraft had to approach the target area from the northwest and return to England from the southeast. The traffic was like today's freeway traffic at commute time! Only worse!

General LeMay briefing the Wing Commanders regarding D-Day plans at the War Room at Elveden Hall. John Gerhart is in the front row, center, listening attentively.

Eighth Air Force

Mission to Norway to bomb submarine pens.

Cologne, Germany, after our bombing showing the old cathedral still standing intact among the ruins.

95th Group Bombardier, Major Wayne "Big Fitz" Fitzgerald.

Heavy flak over Germany. Scenes like this one created the expression, "flak so heavy you could walk on it."

A supply drop to the Maquis in occupied France while we passed over slowly, flaps and landing gear down, at 300 feet altitude. Note the people on the ground rushing to pick up the dropped supply canisters to load into their vehicles.

B-24s from the 34th Bomb Group, part of the 93rd Combat Wing, in formation on a mission when Harry Conley was Command Pilot.

Our B-24 wingman was hit and burning as I took this picture. Immediately thereafter, that plane exploded, rocking our B-24 and nearly bringing us down with it.

In late 1944 we ran into the first German air-to-air rockets over Danzig. They were fired at us by Me-410s. In the background you can see several B-17s out of formation and in trouble.

A protective smoke screen, put up by the Germans over Danzig in November, 1944. Using Pathfinder bombers equipped with radar, we were still able to aim through the smoke and bomb our targets accurately.

Big Fitz at home on leave in his Class A uniform. On March 30, 1946, Major Fitzgerald was awarded the Croix de Guerre Medal with Etoile Vermeil. The citation was signed by Gen. Charles de Gaulle.
Peggy Fitzgerald

Left to right, Harry Conley, John Gerhart and Ken Kimborough, who created this lovely patio at 93rd Combat Wing Headquarters.

Molly Bray with Bill Pratt and Ken Kimborough.

Molly and Peggy Bray, and three friends. Harry Conley on the left, unidentified officer, and Ken Kimborough.

Harry and Jane Ann's wedding reception at the Shoreham Hotel, Washington, D.C. in 1945. Harry is seated fifth from left directly behind Bob Cozens, who is sitting on floor. Gen. John Gerhart is second on left; Patty Cozens is sitting on floor looking at husband Bob. Jiggs is on Harry's left.

As we crossed the English Channel, we could see below us the thousands of ships, the British and American invasion vessels, pitching in the rough seas as they proceeded toward Normandy. The entire Channel was filled with ships! It looked to us as though you could step from one ship to another.

The major mission of the Eighth Air Force for the previous four months had been to destroy the German Air Force, and by D-Day that mission had been successfully achieved. The Germans had less than 700 combat-ready aircraft, and on the day of the invasion the German High Command chose not to fly them. Not a single German aircraft was seen by any of us over Normandy on D-Day![9] The only opposition the Allied Air Forces encountered was from anti-aircraft batteries, and during the course of the day most of these were eliminated by our bombs.

We of the 93rd Combat Bomb Wing flew FOUR missions that day! Our first target at 6:00 a.m. was a key bridge on the main highway into the city of Caen. Destroying this bridge immobilized the German ground forces. Our second target was a large artillery emplacement that was wreaking havoc with the British Naval Forces and their troop landing craft. Our third target was a railroad bridge that the Germans needed to get reinforcements to the invasion area. And our fourth target was a concentration of German tanks and armored vehicles. All our targets were successfully destroyed! Everybody in the Wing participated in these missions the entire day. This was all made possible by the great spirit and extraordinary efforts of our ground crews back at our home bases who labored tirelessly to keep us in the air. On our return from each mission we were met by cheers and eager hands who re-armed and refueled our planes while the Red Cross girls plied us with hot coffee and sandwiches. It was this wonderful morale and spirit of cooperation of all the troops involved that made for the success of the total war effort.

---

[9] Later on, however, there were reports of some scattered Luftwaffe activity over the Allied beachheads on D-Day, but those German pilots were clearly avoiding all possible contact with our heavily concentrated Allied air forces.

One interesting glitch in the Allied planning was that, unbeknown to our planning staff, the German Seventh Armored Division was having maneuvers in the Normandy area. All the other German defense forces were set up in anticipation that the Allied invasion, when it came, would be north of Brest. The Allied High Command knew this, and put that knowledge into our invasion plan. None of our planning conceived the possibility that the Germans would have an armored division as close to our invasion site as it turned out to be. This unfortunately caused Allied casualties among the landing forces. Although these tanks and other armored vehicles were unexpectedly nearby, as soon as we became aware of this, we ordered airborne strikes against them and wiped them out.

A week later, on June 13, Bill Lindley, Grif Mumford and I, were telling war stories, literally, as we stood at the bar of the Embassy Club, a posh watering hole for American and British airmen and British Navy types, in the Mayfair District of London. We were celebrating our good luck and longevity, having survived many missions. It was just one year previous that we three had survived the disastrous American attack on the German submarine base at Kiel. That was one of the major early air battles of the war, and all three of us came close, far too close, to losing our lives and those of our crews that day. We talked about many other missions, some with lots of danger and excitement and some with humorous incidents, culminating with D-Day, only one week earlier.

Standing next to us at the bar was a group of Royal Navy fellows recounting their wild experiences on D-Day. When they saw us, they came over and excitedly hugged us, calling us their saviors. They told us how our bombing saved them from the intense shelling they were being subjected to by the German artillery on shore. The whisky flowed! One tale led to another. One Royal Navy Lieutenant was the most exuberant of all. He loved us dearly! He had been on the bridge of a destroyer off the Normandy coast opposite the city of Caen. The artillery fire from a major German gun emplacement on shore had the range of his group and was wreaking havoc with the landing craft and support vessels of his unit. They were taking terrible casualties. His ship had been seriously damaged and another hit would put them all in the water! He could see the battery on shore and was helplessly watching the scene unfold through his binoculars. It was then about 11:00 a.m. Suddenly, a formation of American B-17 bombers flew overhead directly toward the enemy gun emplacement. WHOOM! BLAM! BLAM! BLAM! A series of flashes burst, followed by a great cloud of dust and smoke. Then silence, as the B-17s flew off into the distance. The Royal Navy crews were to live another day! After further comparing the time and place, we all realized that his savior had been none other than ourselves and our 93rd Combat Bomb Wing! This particular bombing run was the second of four missions we flew over the beachhead that day. What a coincidence to meet here like this! More drinks!

This chance meeting with the Royal Navy officers at the Embassy Club was the beginning of a special friendship between the three of us American pilots and the Royal Navy Lieutenant from the destroyer escort. We met in London several times and he visited me at our Wing Headquarters at Mendlesham in Suffolk. Unfortunately, our friendship was destined to be short-lived. In November of 1944 I received a note from his mother. He had been killed in an encounter with German U-Boats off the Frisian Islands in the North Sea.

CHAPTER 16

"JIGGS" DONOHUE, INTELLIGENCE OFFICER

In several of the earlier chapters I mentioned Jiggs Donohue, who was the Intelligence Officer of the 95th Bomb Group from its initiation and eventually the Intelligence Officer of the 93rd Combat Wing, where he roomed in Elveden Hall with Colonel John Gerhart and me. His full name was Florence Joseph Donohue, but he was known as "Jiggs" all his life. He was a native Washingtonian of Irish extraction and a Washington, D.C. attorney. He was part of Col. Alfred "Uncle Ugh" Kessler's original cadre set up to become the 95th Bomb Group.

Jiggs was a unique guy. He was in his middle 40s when Pearl Harbor was attacked and war was declared. A very sincere and patriotic man, at his age he had no need to join the armed forces, but he felt quite deeply that it was his place to go to war. At that time he had a successful law practice in Washington, D.C. Nevertheless he felt a calling and he applied for and received an appointment as a Captain in the Intelligence Service of the Army Air Forces.

When I first met Jiggs, he was the Group Intelligence Officer. Since he was a non-flying officer in a training unit, he seemed to me just another member of the group; but as time went on, I saw that he was becoming a real leader of the spirit of the Group. There wasn't a great deal for Jiggs to do while we were in training in the States, but as we moved overseas and got involved in combat missions, his role increased dramatically. Domestically, he presented the briefings to all the crews regarding their training missions, and those briefings were pretty much a formality. He was telling us about our next cross-country flight and so forth, most of which we already understood. Once we were in England, he continued to present all the briefings before each and every mission, and what Jiggs had to tell us was new and vital to us all. This was the function of the Intelligence Officer in the 95th Bomb Group.

Jiggs had been a trial lawyer, and he was an extremely articulate, dramatic and spellbinding speaker. We couldn't have had a better man to present our briefings. With his "gift of gab" he certainly kept us very attentively listening to his words. A charming guy, he was very likable. About 6 feet tall and roughly 180 pounds, he was a dapper dresser and always well-shaven. His uniform was immaculate and his shirts were always creased just so.

He was a bachelor, a graduate of Georgetown University and their law school, who, in addition to his flourishing law practice, had become politically prominent in Washington. Jiggs' law offices were situated in Henry Clay's former home and office in Washington. His best friend in civilian life was a fellow by the name of Milton Kronheim, who was the lobbyist for the National Distillers Association in Washington D.C.; and he had the liquor distribution franchise in Washington for National Distillers' bourbon whiskey. Milton was also an avid baseball fan, and every Sunday afternoon, he and the amateur team he coached played baseball. This baseball league used semi-retired professional ballplayers as coaches and trainers, as was the custom in large cities in those days, before professional ballplayers had today's big salaries and retirement plans. Milton Kronheim's team consisted largely of U.S. Senators and Representatives, and it was considered quite a plum to be on Milton's team! His son, young Milton, was an attorney and junior partner in Jiggs Donohue's law firm. When Jiggs joined the Army Air Forces, he turned over all his legal work to young Milton.

As I said, Jiggs was a bachelor, and he had a number of the most beautiful women in Washington calling and visiting him. In fact, Myrna Loy, the movie star, was one of his favorite girlfriends, and she remained a long-lasting friend before and after the war.

As the Group's Intelligence Officer, Jiggs had the responsibility to receive and digest all the Security Classified "secret" intelligence data from British Intelligence and the RAF, as well as U.S. Army Intelligence. This included information about the number and types of German aircraft ready to fly that day, their locations and their current "orders of battle." From all this information, he gave the mission briefings to the flying crews at 3:00 am to 7:00 am in the early mornings before each mission, depending on the distance to be flown. These were "secret" briefings, given to the crews just before they took off on their missions, and the data given were specific to their missions. His briefings were outstanding; they covered many important details of our planned targets, the fighters we could expect to encounter and the strength of their forces, the anti-aircraft artillery we could expect, and so on. He gave us all this information in a spellbinding presentation. It was fascinating for us flying crews, and everybody loved to attend his briefings.

I want to mention here that the quality of intelligence data we received from British Intelligence was outstanding. They apparently had operatives on the ground all over occupied Europe who fed them detailed information about German troop strength, aircraft in and out of operation, movements of forces, locations of anti-aircraft batteries mounted on railroad cars, and so on. We were genuinely greatly appreciative of this information that helped us to prepare for our missions.

Early in 1943 it became evident to Jiggs that the enlisted people and the ground personnel had no way to find out what was happening either in the immediate target areas or in the rest of the world. News was quite restricted and censored then, but Jiggs received complete news coverage from all over the world. He felt strongly that the non-flying personnel needed this information, so that they, too, could have a much better feeling of participation in this war that was taking all their efforts. So Jiggs established his own "Sunday Evening Briefings" for all the maintenance and other ground personnel. He gave a real news update covering the Group's combat areas and the rest of the whole world. It had been that the movie theater was the big attraction on the base every Sunday night, but soon the main attraction on Sunday evenings was Jiggs' briefing. It came to the point when we had to close down the movies on Sunday night because everyone was attending Jiggs' briefings. Then we moved his briefings to the movie theater. These briefings became so popular that there were people standing jammed into the theater.

Always a showman, Jiggs enjoyed his popularity, and designed a new "grand entrance." He told us that the crowds were so jammed packed in the aisles and back in the lobby that he had to go around to one of the windows and crawl through it to get to the stage to put on his show. That became routine; from then on, Jiggs always came in through the window to make his presentations. And he did make it a good show, as well as one that was extremely informative. He used maps and charts to better illustrate what was happening in the world. He was both entertaining and sophisticated, and his briefings certainly raised the morale throughout the Group. Later, when John Gerhart formed the 93rd Combat Wing and moved it, with Jiggs and me, from Horham to Mendlesham, four miles away, Jiggs would religiously get in his staff car every Sunday evening and make his way, driving with his blackout lights on, to Horham to give his Sunday Night Briefings to the guys in the 95th Bomb Group.

For his many contributions to the effectiveness of the 93rd Combat Wing and previously to the 95th Bomb Group, Jiggs was awarded the Bronze Star, which from then on he wore with well-deserved pride.

As Intelligence Officer, Jiggs was not required to fly combat missions, and he didn't volunteer to do so, except once, which I'll tell you about. He explained, "I don't trust those Germans!" Finally, though, in 1944 after John Gerhart organized the 93rd Combat Wing, and I became John's Chief of Staff and Jiggs became the Wing Intelligence Officer, he decided that he could trust Bob Cozens or me to fly him, even if he didn't trust the Germans. He had flown locally around England with both of us. So he volunteered to us, "I'd like to go on a mission with you. I trust you guys!"

Then I finally took him on a "milk run" mission, figuring that would be least scary for Jiggs. This was a mission to the coast of France to knock out German V-1 launching installations[10]; we wouldn't penetrate far into enemy territory and fighter opposition was expected to be minimal or non-existent. Nevertheless, he was so nervous, he was like a cat on a hot tin roof. I had him sitting in the seat behind me where the engineer/top turret gunner usually sat. To divert his attention from the mission itself, I told him I had a job for him to do. Our routine when we gained our flying altitude was to send up a series of color-coded flares to alert the other

---

[10] After American and British bombers had destroyed the German Navy's submarine facilities on the coast, we went further inland for our bombing missions, with the objective of wiping out the German transportation and aircraft production facilities. The Germans had, by mid-1944, built installations along the French coast to send their V-1, a self-propelled flying bomb with a preset gyroscopic navigation system, to bomb British urban centers. These missiles were fired off from concrete bunkers along the French coast. So our missions had to return to the coastline to knock out these new V-1 installations. By that time, the Luftwaffe was keeping its fighters inland to defend Germany itself from Allied bombers.

There persists a widespread belief that these V-1s devastated London, but that's not really the case. The press would come in after a V-1 had hit some buildings and take photos, which showed terrible damage, but the damage was not really widespread. Some sections of London, particularly the eastern sections of the city, had considerable damage from repeated hits, while most of the city experienced few hits or none. Of course, to those people whose families, friends and properties were destroyed, the damage was catastrophic. The Nazis' objectives were mostly psychological: to make the German population feel good about the British people having to endure some of the bombing they were experiencing, and to make the British people more willing to negotiate an end to the war more favorable to Germany than "Unconditional Surrender." Many of these V-1s were destroyed at their launch sites; many landed in the Channel; nevertheless some 6,725 approached the British coast, killing about 5,000 people, wounding about 18,000 others, and destroying about 23,000 houses. Over half of those approaching the coast were downed by anti-aircraft guns or fighters. Those V-1s could fly at speeds nearing 400 m.p.h., but our British and American fighter pilots with their fast Spitfires and P-51 Mustangs soon learned that they could fly beside one, use their wingtip to catch a wingtip of the V-1 and flip it, destabilizing its gyroscope and causing it to fall into the sea. Occasionally this maneuver could even make the V-1 turn around 180 degrees and head back toward the French coast. V-1 attacks started just after D-Day and, because their launch sites were mostly along the French coast, V-1 bombings became rare events after August 1944, when the invading Allied forces overran those launch sites.

planes in our Squadron to assemble and we'd then proceed in close formation to cross the Channel. So I gave him the flare gun and told him, "Here, Jiggs, you fire these flares and just keep 'em going until I tell you to stop, when all our aircraft are assembled." So he happily started firing flares. Well, I got involved in what I was doing and I forgot to tell him to stop. He had fired off about eight cases of flares, long after we were all assembled and had started across the Channel. I looked back and he was still firing flares! We always maintained radio silence on the way to our target, but as we returned from the target area, we were back on our radios, and one of my other crews called in and said, "Why were you sending off all those flares? Do you have somebody wounded aboard?" Flares on the return flight usually meant that there were wounded men aboard. I reassured them that was not the case this time. Well, it certainly did take Jiggs' mind off the dangers of the mission, and he ended up quite proud of himself for being "the best damned flare-firer in the Eighth Air Force"! He just relished that!

You recall I told you that his best friend in Washington, Milton Kronheim, was the Washington distributor for National Distillers. Well, all the time we were in England, about every two weeks we'd get this call from the Air Transport Command Base in Prestwick, Scotland, to go pick up a package for Major Donohue. He was sent a case of bourbon whiskey, which Jiggs generously shared with all of us. In England, we couldn't get bourbon, strictly an American product, even though we could get, through various means, ample supplies of Scotch and gin. So Jiggs' bourbon shipments from his friend in the States made a big hit with the guys!

After the war, when he returned to civilian life, he resumed his law practice in Washington, D.C. There was a big party given at the Mayflower Hotel to welcome home Jiggs Donohue, and the entire hotel was sold out for that evening! He became even more prominent there at the seat of our national government. Twice he became the appointed head of the District of Columbia's government, once as the Commissioner, and, once later, as the

Mayor of Washington, D.C. Every day he used to have his own table at the Mayflower Hotel's dining room with about ten or twelve seats. No one involved in government missed the opportunity to sit with Jiggs at his table for lunch at the Mayflower. And if they couldn't sit there, they would come over to his table to chat with him.

After he came back to his office in Henry Clay's old house, he really did it up. He hired Kenneth Kimbrough, who had also been an Intelligence Officer with us, but who was professionally an interior decorator, to redo the old Henry Clay house. No one could have been better qualified; Kenneth was, after returning from the war, the leading society decorator in Memphis, Tennessee. As a result, Jiggs' redecorated offices became a real showplace!

Jiggs became quite a political organizer back in Washington. When Estes Kefauver made his run for the President's office, Jiggs Donohue was his campaign manager. Jiggs had also been a close personal friend of Harry Truman as a Senator, before he became Vice President. In fact, Jiggs was the first person that Harry Truman called right after President Roosevelt died, saying "Jiggs, what the Hell do I do NOW?" And do you remember Vincent X. Flaherty? He was a nationally syndicated columnist who wrote an article about Jiggs in February, 1945, and I still have a copy of it. Later on Jiggs was selected to be the Prosecuting Attorney when Harry Bridges, head of the International Longshoremen's Union, came to trial in San Francisco, charged with being a Communist. Jiggs won his case, getting a conviction, but it was subsequently set aside in an appeal. Nonetheless, Jiggs gained national fame during that trial. He was a silver-tongued orator, with silver hair to go with it.

When I was assigned to the Pentagon and was working for General Curtis LeMay, it was Jiggs who arranged my wedding to Jane Ann. She was a Naval Lieutenant also in Washington at the Navy Department. As I mentioned earlier, she had been introduced to me by my former bombardier, Big Fitz, there in Washington. At that time I was extremely busy, working on training procedures for the 509th Bomb Squadron for a special mission to drop the atomic bomb, and I just didn't have time to make my own wedding arrangements. We finally arrived at a date, and it was to be at 4 p.m. on a Saturday afternoon at the Washington, D.C courthouse. Jiggs got us a judge to perform the ceremony. That morning Jiggs called and told me, "The judge has a problem with the 4:00 p.m. wedding; he just found out that his father is seriously ill and he needs to leave town right after noon to visit his father. But he can make it if we can reschedule the ceremony for this morning. Can you work that out?"

Wow! I explained that I still had not been able to find time to run a bunch of errands, including getting a ring, since the custom ring I had ordered from a jeweler in San Francisco hadn't yet arrived, but we could have the wedding at noon. So I called my friends, Johnny Gerhart, Fred Anderson, Big Fitz, Bill Pratt, and several other friends to tell them that the wedding would be at noon. Then I called Jane Ann and told her that I'd pick her up at her apartment and bring her to the newly scheduled noon wedding. Next, I departed to get a suitable ring and the champagne for the reception. Well, it seems that on Saturday morning in Washington, there weren't any jewelry stores open; after several futile tries and lots of driving around, I finally found a simple gold band at a hockshop, but it would do the job for that day! Then to get the champagne. By the time I got to the courthouse it was close to noon, and I ran inside.

The place was full of news correspondents. Apparently, that very day, in that very courthouse, Norma Beach, a notorious Washington madam, was being arraigned, and all the local news media were there to cover it. Well, I ran into the rotunda of the courthouse, pleased that I wasn't late, and Jiggs called out to me, "Where is Jane Ann?" Oh, my God, I forgot to pick her up at her apartment! So I ran out to a public telephone and called her, and asked her to call a cab to bring her downtown to the courthouse. I knew that there was no way I could get in my car and drive back to get her and still be in time for the judge. When I came back into the courthouse, I saw all the news hawks talking to Jiggs. They had been standing around looking for a story, and they saw all this

Army brass, three generals and a bunch of colonels, and they were wondering what was going on with all these USAAF big shots. Well, Jiggs, bless his heart, told them. He told them too much. So the next day, all the newspapers had our story and one even headlined "THE COLONEL FORGOT HIS BRIDE!" We received, thanks to Jiggs, more unneeded and undesired publicity than the notorious madam of Washington, D.C.

Just to close this story, Jane Ann did get a cab, she did arrive in time, we did get married, and our friends and we did finish the champagne! General Fred Anderson, my boss at the time I was training the 509th Bomb Group, generously offered to cover my job for me for an extra few days and sent me to New York for our honeymoon. And we spent 26 happily married years together and produced four wonderful daughters, Karen, Vian, Sue and Robin, before she died from cancer.

While Bob Cozens and I were still working at the Pentagon in Washington, D.C., but before Jiggs got married, he maintained his bachelor quarters at the Shoreham Hotel, then one of the foremost hotels in Washington. They were beautiful rooms and Jiggs entertained lavishly there. One time he invited Bob and Pat Cozens and Jane Ann and me to have dinner with him at his apartment there at the Shoreham. Bob and Pat had had a baby boy while Bob was overseas, and "little Robbie" was then about two years old, so they brought him along. Well, Jiggs had in his bedroom a large picture of a reclining woman, very beautiful and very nude. As we toured the apartment and went into Jiggs' bedroom, Robbie's eyes went to the picture. He smiled and said, "Oh, pretty baby, pretty baby!"

Rob grew up, of course, and when his dad retired a few years ago Rob chaired a retirement party for him. It took place in San Diego where Bob and Pat were living. I was one of the speakers and Rob introduced me. As I started to speak, I thanked Rob for his introduction, and then I told the story on him about "Oh, pretty baby." Rob blushed. Now whenever I see Rob I kid him about his wise comment at the age of two while visiting Jiggs' bachelor quarters.

Yes, Jiggs eventually got married after the war was over. Interesting, though, about our small world: he married General Ira Eaker's sister-in-law, a very nice lady named Martha. General Eaker was Commanding General of the Eighth Air Force until January 1944. The couple subsequently moved out of Jiggs' bachelor quarters at the Shoreham Hotel (no, I don't know what happened to the picture) and into a new condominium at the Watergate Apartments, where they lived until Jiggs passed away in the late 1970s.

Jiggs and I maintained our friendship, and he used to come by our home when he was in the San Francisco Bay Area. One time when he was in San Francisco with the Harry Bridges trial, he visited my family and me. He and my daughter, Robin, were chatting — she was about seven years old then, I believe — and they were discussing some of the people he knew in Washington, D.C. He asked her what he could bring her from Washington, and she said, "Well, how about an autograph from President Kennedy?" "I'll see what I can do," he replied. About ten days later, a large envelope appeared in the mail for Robin from Jiggs. When she opened it, she was ecstatic with joy! It was a photograph of President John F. Kennedy with a handwritten personal message to Robin followed by his signature. As I said previously, Jiggs always knew the right way to treat the ladies, and he made a real big hit with Robin with his gift.

CHAPTER 17

THE 93RD COMBAT WING

Once "D-Day" had occurred and our Allied Forces were on the Continent headed by the Supreme Commander, General Dwight D. Eisenhower, we in the Eighth Air Force, and particularly in the 93rd Combat Wing, were kept extremely busy. Not only were we continuing our strategic bombing of Germany, but we also were frequently called on for tactical support of Allied ground forces.

June 19, 1944

> Business is good. While I wait for some information to come in tonight, I'll try to get a few lines written. I haven't been to bed before 4:00 a.m. for the last three weeks.
> There really isn't very much to tell in the way of news. You get more than I'm allowed to write in the newspapers anyway.

As Chief of Staff, I was flying as Command Pilot on missions, often now with over 1,000 American bombers, B-24s and B-17s, alternating with Colonel John Gerhart. We seldom got away from our work, but when we did, we had fun.

> ...My social life these last weeks has consisted of a cocktail party held here at the Wing on Saturday last and a couple of trips to Lady Elveden's for dinner with Colonel Gerhart. Elizabeth, Lady Elveden, has a beautiful home on a large estate about a half hour's drive from here. Best of all, she has several polo ponies and every time we go up there we ride. You can't possibly know how wonderful it is to get on a good horse again!

Administrative work filled my non-flying time. I found there were very few details about what I was doing that I could share with my parents in letters home, and most of what I did would probably not have been very interesting to them, anyhow. But occasionally some part of my work touched on someone or something they recognized.

> ...Now that Bob is in Washington working on B-17 and B-24 modifications, I sent him a long, and unofficial, list of modifications we could use over here.

Being typical parents, my mother and father wrote back asking why I didn't come back to the States while I was still in one piece, but I wasn't ready for that yet.

> 3 July 1944
>
> I am still free to go home whenever I choose, but I can't reconcile myself to leave now. Too much is happening here to have to read about it in the papers. I guess my old curiosity is too strong. I have to see it all for myself first hand.
> Gosh, it is difficult to believe that tomorrow is the Fourth of July! Tempus fugit! Really, these last few months have gone by at a full gallop. Speaking of gallop, I still get to ride that fine polo pony about once a week. Colonel John Gerhart and I go over about once a week and ride, and then have dinner and spend the evening with them. They have a beautiful home and it makes a most enjoyable time. Lady Elveden is about 31 and a very attractive person. Her husband is the polo player. He is now in the British army in Normandy. He is a swell guy. As I wrote, they have been most hospitable and generous to us.
> Saturday evening I was sitting around in our lounge when the phone rang and it was one of the boys from the 95th. Old "Uncle Ugh" Kessler, complete with star, had dropped in for the evening and wanted to see all the old boys who were left over here. He brought numerous bottles of vodka with him, and a big time was had by all. He was only here for a couple of days, and then he went east again.

By the middle of 1944 we were beginning to see the light at the end of the tunnel as far as the war in Europe was concerned, even though the German government was continuing to force its people to support the war effort and live through our now constant bombing. I began to consider what I would be doing when the Germans finally capitulated.

17 July 1944

I'll tell you this in strictest confidence, Mom. Please don't even tell the family until I have reached a decision. I have been offered one of a VERY few Regular Army commissions allotted to the Eighth Air Force. It was proposed to me by General LeMay and Colonel Gerhart several weeks ago. Fortunately I don't have to make up my mind immediately. As yet, I haven't come to a decision, but I do feel quite complimented by the gesture.

Events of the past week in the German political scene look most encouraging. However, I am disappointed in the progress of our ground forces. True, they are fighting in most difficult terrain for mechanized offensive. Nevertheless, I can't help but feel that the end of the war over here is close at hand. It will come suddenly when it terminates. Then we will be able to move eastward and give our undivided attention to the Sons of Nippon. That will be a pleasure, I assure you. After flying in this theater with its terrifically developed flak defenses and hordes of fighters, it will be considerably easier in the Land of the Rising Sun.

Fitz got back the other day and really looks swell. He told us all about the States and, best of all, brought us a whole case of bourbon, which is a rarity in these parts. I don't know if I told you, but he got married while he was at home.

Between missions and my constant administrative work, I relaxed by flying my P-47.

27 July 1944

A week ago I went down to see Walter Newman, an old friend from home, but he and his unit had moved out a couple of days previous. I made the whole trip, 570 miles, in two hours and three minutes, including forty-five minutes on instrument flying though a rough storm. Made the trip in my Thunderbolt and never exceeded normal cruising speed. I had that ship up to maximum speed PLUS the other day, and I would hate to tell you just how fast I was going. It approached the speed of sound. Oh yes, I was headed straight down at the time.

I recall that I was a little sorry I told her about that, as I got back a very concerned letter, to which I responded in my cocky youthful manner.

> ...Oh, don't bother your pretty head about my doing anything foolish with an airplane. I've flown them too long not to respect them. If I fly them fast you can bet your bottom dollar that they are OK at that speed. Furthermore, I am not a test pilot nor anything else so romantic. I fly an airplane for all that it is worth when I fly operationally. In order to prepare myself for that, I utilize my so-called pleasure flying time to find out for myself just what any airplane will do. That is the only way to prepare to meet any emergency. Just as an example, the last time I went to see Walt, my engine in the P-47 quit right over Cambridge at a thousand feet. Instinctively, I knew what was the trouble and before I thought at all I had switched gas tanks and turned on the booster pump and the engine started again. I was out of gas in the main tank and the gas gauge failed to show it.

Even though Bob Cozens was now stateside, we kept in contact with each other frequently.

> ...Had a letter from Bob, and while he is happy to be with Pat and little Robbie, he finds it difficult to settle down to an administrative routine. That is very easy to understand after such a long time over here where things are happening. The tempo of events is so much slower in the States. It's just another reason why I don't want to come home now.

A little R&R in Ballater, Scotland, was what I needed to come down a bit from the hectic pace of my duties as Chief of Staff of the 93rd Wing.

> 8 August 1944
>
> Just returned from a wonderful vacation week and found your letter awaiting me. I took three other boys, Bill Pratt, Harry Wolf, and Ken Kimborough. First we went sailing for a couple of days just northeast of us here. Had a wonderful time. Then we returned to the base and picked up the A-20 and flew to Scotland for five days. We

left here and flew to Prestwick, and spent the day visiting friends. We left Prestwick and flew on to Aberdeen, where we left the airplane and caught a bus to our old retreat, Ballater. It took longer to make the forty mile bus trip from Aberdeen to Ballater than it did to make the whole rest of the trip.

Our friends in Ballater entertained us royally. We ate, slept, golfed, fished and generally had a wonderful time. The country is just beautiful. All the heather is in bloom and is really an inspiring sight. We have an invitation to spend Christmas with them if we are still in the area at that time. Very reluctantly we left Ballater this afternoon and arrived home this evening.

You need not worry about my being in danger by going to London; I just haven't had much spare time while I'm here. Actually, those buzz bombs aren't too bad. You can see them coming, and when they go off, they are all blast effect. No shrapnel. I have seen quite a few.

As for my current combat, I don't go very often. I was out last week to Brussels. Encountered a little flak and that was all. I flew a B-17 for a change, and it was fun. The boys were flying a new formation we worked out here in the Wing, so I flew alongside to take pictures and see how it worked. While they bombed, I circled off to the side and watched the show. I get one or two missions a month now and that is all.

Elmer Bachman was shot down the other day over France. Several chutes were seen to open, so we expect to hear from him shortly. It is too bad; he was on his thirty-third ride and leading the show. That leaves Bob and me the only two flying officers of our original squadron. Such are the fortunes of war.

Got a letter from Bob today. I hear from him about once a week. Think he is settling down to the office routine now and liking it a little better.

By the way, Grif Mumford went home a couple of weeks ago. He wrote from Lake Tahoe that he had tried to call you, but you weren't home. Said he'd try again when he returns to town.

About this time it was my turn to take a mission as Command Pilot, this time to Leipzig, one of the most heavily defended industrial cities in Germany. The Germans definitely didn't want us near it. There were literally hundreds of 88 millimeter anti-aircraft guns placed around this target, and, believe me, they were all active when we came over. We were flying B-24s on this mission, and I was with the 34th Bomb Group, one of the Bomb Groups of B-24s assigned to the 93rd Combat Wing. The 34th Bomb Group, incidentally, was the same one to which I had been initially assigned at Geiger Field before the 95th Bomb Group was established.

The barrage of flak was so heavy as we passed the IP on our bomb run that the skies, which had been clear and sunny, became as dark as dusk. Shells were exploding all around as we pressed on toward our target. On this particular mission, we were positioned in the latter part of the attack. The lead bombers ahead of us were, according to our normal procedures, dropping high explosive bombs and we in the latter Groups were armed with incendiary bombs. Our purpose was to burn the damaged factory buildings after our high explosives had opened them up. As was my usual practice when I was flying in the right hand seat as Command Pilot, I had a K-20 aerial camera in my lap to record events on our mission.

Suddenly the B-24 on our right lurched upward from a direct hit by one of those 88 millimeter shells and started belching smoke from amidships. I grabbed my camera and snapped a picture of that burning plane, probably less than 50 feet away from our right wingtip. Immediately after I took the photo that whole plane exploded in a big flash, debris flew everywhere and the concussion jolted our plane so badly that its airframe was twisted almost twenty degrees. Apparently there wasn't enough time between the hit and the explosion for any of that plane's crew to escape. We in our B-24 were so badly damaged that the twist in our airframe had put kinks in the cables to all the control surfaces, so our elevators, rudders and wing flaps were frozen in position. We couldn't use them to turn or change elevation. We completed the bomb run and flew back to England using the power controls on our four engines to maneuver our plane. We were even able to land successfully using only the engines as our controls. (As is often said by pilots, a good landing is one you can walk away from.) We walked away, and in the mission debriefing we reported that our right wingman had blown apart and no escaping crewmen were seen.

Time passed, and no word was received about any of these missing crewmen, so we assumed they had been killed in the plane's blast. They were recorded as "Missing in action and presumed dead." Some years after the war, when I was on a cattle-buying trip to Great Falls, Montana, I was hailed by a man as I was walking down the city sidewalk. I looked up, and there was the navigator of that plane that had exploded next to me over Leipzig. We were both amazed to see each other there, and greeted each other warmly. Then we went into a nearby bar and had a drink, while he told me his story.

The navigator, who was in the nose cone prior to the bomb drop, was blown out of the plane by the explosion. We were at 26,000 feet in the middle of an air battle, which many of the people of Leipzig were watching from the ground. The explosion and blast through the nose cone caused the navigator to lose consciousness, but he awoke as he was free-falling down toward the ground. He couldn't have been more than 500 feet above the ground when he came to his senses and pulled the ripcord on his parachute. As his chute opened the force from changing his speed of descent was so abrupt that his shoes came off. He swung once in the air on his chute and hit the ground. German civilians who had been watching his fall immediately captured him and then turned him over to the nearest uniformed German troops. They happened to be SS troops, who had a reputation for handling captives their own way without consideration for the rules of the Geneva Convention. They gave the navigator some severe beatings and then for the next two weeks paraded him around on exhibition, never giving him any shoes to wear. His feet became badly damaged and infected from having to walk around without any shoes. He became unable to walk at all, and then the Germans sent him back to England as part of a prisoner exchange.

He was sent back to the States, hospitalized and after the war returned to civilian life. Before the war he had been a practicing attorney in Great Falls, and that's where he returned to practice law. I could tell from the way he walked that he had not been able to recover fully from his foot wounds. But he was alive and working productively at his profession, while the rest of his crew never made it back from Leipzig that day.

Neither that story about the nearby bomber exploding nor the picture could be sent back to the States, so I continued to write what I could in my letters home.

17 August 1944

Happy Regensburg Day! Today is the first anniversary of our shuttle raid. It certainly doesn't seem a year since that memorable day. How clearly I remember every detail. The Colonel and I were discussing it today. Things certainly have changed!

I received a letter from Walter Newman, written from a hospital about 180 miles west of us. He was hit in the chest with a machine gun slug near St. Lo. Naturally, I was quite concerned when I read Walt's letter, so I immediately jumped into my P-47 and arrived at the hospital 45 minutes later. I found him sitting on the edge of his bed with his feet dangling in the air, laughing and joking with the nurse. He received a nasty wound, but thanks to excellent medical care, he is completely out of danger and well on the road to recovery. He is really a great kid, just as cheerful as he can be. He had a really rough time of it, yet he can't wait to get back in the show. Not a bit of complaint out of him.

There isn't much new that I can write about. We are very busy supporting the ground troops as well as carrying out our own strategic bombing. The "paddlefeet" seem to be doing pretty well. It looks like just a matter of weeks before this thing folds up over here. Then where? Who knows? All sorts of rumors are prevalent. However, time will tell.

At this time, two of my former commanders had some notoriety in the American press.

26 August 1944

Thanks for sending me the newspaper articles. I was especially interested in the one about Russia and "Uncle Ugh" Kessler. Incidentally, when Fitz came back from Russia a couple of weeks ago, he brought me a message from Ugh. He's a great old guy.

I also noticed that you recognized General LeMay's latest jump. He should get a third star any day now. Keep your eye on him. He will be the next Chief of the Air Forces. He is without a doubt the most brilliant officer in the Air Force today. If he does half the job with the B-29s as he did over here with the B-17s, God pity Japan!

Uncle Ugh, now Brigadier General, was in Russia as the American Air Corps Liaison Officer. Little did I know I would actually see him there in Poltava, Russia, within the next few weeks. And as for General LeMay, little did I know how his new assignment to bring the war in the Pacific to a victorious close would affect my own future in the Army Air Forces.

Working at the command levels gave me the unexpected opportunity to get to know and work with Jimmy Stewart, who as Chief of Staff of one of the other Combat Wings, was my counterpart. Although he probably could have finagled himself into a soft, protected billet, he was just like all the rest of us, exposed to death on every mission. He had risen to Lieutenant Colonel just as I had, by going on his missions doing the best job he could. He was a B-24 pilot and had commanded a B-24 squadron. One would never know, in any meeting with him, that he was anything other than a competent USAAF officer and pilot.

Ken Kimborough continued to improve the quality of life for our airmen here in England.

> ...Enclosed is a picture of our new dining room. Not bad, eh? Isn't it surprising what can be done with a Nissen hut? One of our boys, Captain Ken Kimborough, is an interior decorator from Memphis and was responsible for this job. It is the talk of the Air Force being the only room in the E.T.O. (European Theater of Operations) with wallpaper. We have French doors and a little patio that can be seen through the window in the picture. It is all very comfortable and homey, and we are very happy with it.
>
> Tonight we have a mission on, so I'll be up all night. If I can get to bed by 7 a.m., I'll get a few hours' sleep and run down to see Walt Newman in the afternoon.

An amusing, although very nearly tragic, incident occurred on one of my missions. As we were going down a bombing run, the Flight Engineer in one of our Squadron's planes had a strange thing happen to him. The Flight Engineer also had as his ancillary duty manning the Top Turret Guns in aerial combat. Anyhow, he was standing at his guns, firing away at the attacking fighters, when a big spinning piece of an 88 millimeter shell blew through the left side of his plane right behind him and tore into the backside of his pants, ripping off all of the covering for his behind, and taking that clothing through the right side of the plane and lodging itself in the plane's wing. He stood there, without a scratch on his body, and without any covering over his butt! When we returned and landed, he went to his plane's wing and pulled out that piece of shrapnel, about 18 inches long with some residual cloth attached. What an odd way for a shell to split! The long, curved piece of metal went spinning through the air, grabbing hold of his pants seat while spinning and then traveling on through the other side of the plane. I remember seeing him walk back from his plane, bare-assed, with that big piece of shrapnel tucked under his arm. That was his souvenir from the war — probably the one that had his name on it!

12 September 1944

It's about time I wrote to you, but we have been terribly busy working and celebrating this past week.

First for the celebration. We've had three big parties this week! To start, a week ago Sunday night, Colonel John, Jiggs Donohue, our Intelligence Officer, and I were invited to a party at the 95th to say goodbye to Dave McKnight, one of our original boys and Deputy Group Commander for the past year. He is going home after making 42 missions. A well deserved rest. He is a hell of a popular guy and it was a real get-together. A lot of the old fighter boys were there as well as the old 95th boys who are left over here. It was a wet old time!

Dave McKnight was certainly one of our more colorful pilots in the 95th Bomb Group. An American citizen incensed by Hitler's aggressions in Europe, he had originally joined the RCAF, the Royal Canadian Air Force, before the United States declared war on December 8, 1941. Right after that time he left the RCAF and joined the U.S. Army Air Forces, and he caught up with those of us who were the cadre for the new 95th Bomb Group at Geiger Field, Washington. Dave stayed on with the 95th Bomb Group through most of the war in Europe as a bomber pilot and later as a Squadron Commander. He had charm and dash, and was well-liked and admired by the men of the 95th.

Dave McKnight had as one of his good friends a fighter pilot named Dave Schilling of the 56th Fighter Group. In fact, he idolized and envied Dave Schilling, because Schilling was also quite a colorful guy, a real "devil may care" type of pilot — the very picture of a dashing fighter guy. McKnight envied him because his job was sporting around in high-powered fighter planes, while McKnight's job was piloting heavy bombers. But every chance he got on his off-duty time, he flew fighter planes with Dave Schilling. You may have heard of Dave Schilling, as he became a leading "Ace" fighter pilot in the war in Europe and later was killed in a tragic automobile accident in England.

One day in England when I was leading a practice mission with my 334th Bomb Squadron, Dave McKnight and Dave Schilling were having fun sporting around in a couple of P-51 fighter planes. It was one of those days over England when there were lots of clouds; in fact there was a lower level of clouds at about 1,500 feet and another higher level of clouds at about 3,500 feet, plus bunches of clouds between those layers. We were flying our B-17s through all those clouds, practicing our instrument flying when those two guys in their fighters came out of a batch of cloud right at our altitude flying upside-down. Between cloud layers as we were, we weren't able to see either the ground or the sun. Dave McKnight called to us on the radio and tried to convince us that we were the ones flying upside-down and telling us that we needed to roll over right away to right ourselves! Fortunately, we didn't fall for that trick.

Right after the Allies had liberated Paris from the Germans, these two guys wanted to go to Paris to join the celebrations, so they got into the cockpits of a couple of fighter planes and flew them to Paris, where they flew over the city and "buzzed" the Eiffel Tower. They flew wing to wing under the lower spread of the legs of the tower, several times. Crazy! They landed their fighters at Orly Field outside of Paris and did the town together. Then they went up and did another buzz or two through the Eiffel Tower. In fact, they made such a nuisance of themselves continually buzzing the Eiffel Tower that General Eisenhower personally issued a special order forbidding ALL Allied military personnel from buzzing the Eiffel Tower!

Grif Mumford, the pilot who led that first American daylight bomb raid on Berlin, recalled to me a story about Dave McKnight that Dave himself had told to Grif:

> Dave had grown up in New York City. After he was of an age when he was taking young ladies out on the town, but before he joined the RCAF, he took a gal to Jack Dempsey's nightclub restaurant in downtown New York. But before they went into the restaurant, Dave was busy trying to impress the young lady by telling her that he was a close buddy of that famous prize fighter. He knew that, at that time, the restaurant no longer belonged to Jack Dempsey, and he assumed that he could get away with his story because Dempsey wouldn't be there. Of course, the new owners had bought Dempsey's name along with the nightclub restaurant, and actually they required him to put in an appearance there every so often. Well, much to Dave's surprise as he and his date were sitting at a table in the restaurant, Jack Dempsey walked in. Then Dempsey started walking right toward their table. Dave shuddered, as he was scared to death that he and his story would be exposed as phony, and he didn't know what the heck to do, but with much bravado he waved at Jack Dempsey and called out "Hello there, Jack!" And Dempsey said, as he probably said to everyone, "Hello, Mac!" Saved!

Grif also reminded me that at Geiger Field, after Dave McKnight had been there only about a month or so, he and Bill Brown used to get up at 4:00 AM and run around the whole perimeter of the field before breakfast as a conditioning exercise. Bill Brown was a well-conditioned athlete before he joined the USAAF, but this daily run he made with Dave certainly helped him maintain his condition, which held him in good stead when he had to jump out of Harry Stirwalt's plane on the Kiel Raid into the cold water of the North Sea.

Major Dave McKnight, one of our more colorful and dashing leaders.

The "Silver Queen" brought these war weary officers to Aberdeen, Scotland on the first leg of their R&R trip. Back row standing, Ken Kimborough, Bill Lindley, Lou Reno, Harry Conley, and John Gerhart. Kneeling are Rodney Snow and Dave McKnight.

B-17s headed for Hamburg in October, 1944.

The War Room used by the 93rd Combat Wing at Elveden Hall.

An A-20, used by Harry Conley while on the 93rd Wing Staff.

General Curtis LeMay.
Eighth Air Force

Lt. Col. Robert C. Cozens.

Lt. Col. Harry M. Conley.

Grif Mumford receives a Croix de Guerre for his participation in the many supply drops that the 95th Bomb Group made to the French Maquis when France was occupied by the Germans.

The 95th Bomb Group assembled in parade formation in front of Elveden Hall, to honor the visit of distinguished French dignitaries, including General Charles de Gaulle.

When John Gerhart received his star, we had to do it up right.

A photo of the 93rd Combat Wing Staff, taken early in 1945 after Harry Conley was transferred to the Pentagon. Recognizable are General John Gerhart and Major Jiggs Donohue, seated, 4th from left and 5th from left, respectively.

Eighth Air Force

And it was Dave McKnight that met the Vicar in a pub in London, had a few drinks with him, and ended up getting us senior officers of the 95th an invitation to visit his parsonage in Aberdeen, Scotland, as a refuge from the war. Then there was the time we of the 95th raided the New Year's Eve party given by the 100th so as to free up some nurses to attend our New Year's party, and Dave McKnight was John Gerhart's "copilot" driving the command car. He was quite a guy, and always upbeat. Yes, he was a colorful and lively character, and a hellova good man to have in our cadre!

Dave always loved flying fighters, and after World War II, he finally got his wish and had a second career in the Air Force as a Wing Commander of an F-100 Fighter Group in Korea.

> ...Then two nights ago we held a private goodbye for Dave McKnight. He delayed his going home because he got a chance to go to Paris for three days, which he did. So he didn't leave for home until yesterday. This little party was just Colonel John, Dave, Jiggs Donohue and me. We sat around the fire after dinner and sipped a few and reminisced about the old boys. We stayed until the "wee sma" hours.
>
> The next Saturday and Sunday the 95th had a two-day celebration of our 200th mission. It was a little late, as they are well past that figure now, but they waited until they could get what they wanted in the way of entertainment. It was well worth waiting for. We had Glenn Miller and his band, Bing Crosby and Dinah Shore. What a party it was! The Eighth gave the Group a two day layoff and the carnival spirit reigned. Dancing all day and all night, two big turkey dinners, and plenty of liquor. All work stopped on the entire base and every man participated in the celebration.

It was the next morning after he and his band played for the 95th Bomb Group's party that Glenn Miller got aboard a single engine British transport plane headed for the Continent and was never seen again.

When I had the duty of being Mission Commander of some of our frequent and massive bombing missions, I observed some evidence that some of our newly arrived boys were becoming a bit lax in the discipline that had helped us in the past.

...I got in a couple of good raids last week. As you have probably seen in the papers, we have been beating at Germany's heart again in force. On both these raids I had the honor of leading the whole Eighth Air Force, over 1,600 aircraft, into Germany. One day it was like old times. We got in a pretty fair scrap for a few minutes with about forty fighters. With all due respect to the kids we have flying now, I wouldn't trade one of the old boys for the whole lot of them. They aren't the pilots and gunners our old kids were. We only <u>claimed</u> four fighters out of the lot, and we lost pretty heavily. Our old boys would have gotten at least a dozen <u>confirmed</u> fighters and lost less than a third of what we did. These kids think the war is over, damn it! Then the Jerries hop on them and knock 'em down before we even know there are fighters around. Boy, it makes me mad! You may think our losses are high now; 75% of them are because the kids aren't awake. I observed four gunners the other day <u>out</u> of their turrets over Germany! No wonder we lose airplanes! These youngsters expect the fighter support to play nursemaid to them!

Occasionally on our bombing missions we saw Hitler's new "secret weapon," the Me-262 jet fighter. The first time I ever saw one was from my right-hand side Command Pilot seat; a single strange looking airplane approached our formation very rapidly from about 2:00 o'clock, low at about 3,000 feet below our altitude. After he disappeared beneath us, he must have turned upward 90 degrees, because he flew right through our formation headed straight up! It was an astounding sight! But he didn't fire a shot at us. He zoomed vertically through our formation a couple more times. Then he flew around us a while before taking off to somewhere else. He seemed to be traveling almost twice as fast as any fighter I had ever seen before. Later on other missions we would see one or sometimes two of these Me-262s, and again they just seemed to be practicing their aerobatics, as they never apparently tried to shoot at us. I certainly didn't understand what they were up to. After a few such encounters we just got so we didn't worry much about them. Then about nine months later when the war in Europe had ended and I was in Washington, I saw some intelligence reports that explained why they were not shooting at us. These super-fast fighters were equipped with the same compensating gun sight used on the Me-109s and FW-190s, and it was too slow for the speed of the Me-262. The compensating gun sights on fighter aircraft — we had them on our P-47s and P-51s, too — were basically computers, similar in concept to our Norden bombsight. The pilot had to get his target in his sights and then lock it on to his compensating gun sight. But the mechanism of the gun sight couldn't adjust as fast as the angles of approach would change in such a fast-moving airplane. I now believe that the pilot of that first Me-262 was testing his gunsight, as well as having a little fun with us. He was moving so fast our gunners weren't able to shoot him, either. I am frankly quite glad that the Germans didn't solve this problem while our B-17s were flying bombing missions. Enough of us were still getting killed by the Me-109s and FW-190s, although by the latter part of 1944, the flak was more deadly than the fighters.

It was always disturbing when someone we knew, some good friend or relative, would be killed in an accident having nothing to do with enemy action. One day when I opened my mail I received some unpleasant news.

> ...Had a letter from Bob Cozens a few days ago. He lost his younger brother in a B-24 crash at Ft. Worth, Texas. He was pretty badly burned and died in the hospital. However, Bob flew down and was able to be with him a bit before he died. Bob is happier with his job now and getting to fly a bit more, so that helps. He got checked out in a B-29 and says it is pretty good.
>
> Colonel Ed Witten, who was my first C.O. when I was at Spokane, and who I took for his first combat ride when he came over here, was killed yesterday when he ran a P-47 into a hill in a rainstorm. He was a swell guy, and has been a Wing Commander over here for the past few months.

I had to be more careful now about what I told my parents about my extra-curricular flying in my fighter plane.

> ...I had a couple of hours free this afternoon and flew down to see Walt Newman. But the weather was terrible. Visibility was about a half mile. I got down there without any trouble. I circled the field at

4,000 feet and could barely make it out, so I turned around and came home without attempting to land. It is a small field and ringed with hills — definitely no place to play around in that kind of weather. So, see, Mom, I don't take chances with "these here flyin' machines". I'll stick my chin out whenever they will let me over across the Channel, but I take no chances on this side.

I always tried to end my letters home on a cheerful note.

...Speaking of the other side, I am back in B-17s again, and, boy, is it like home! For my money, that is the best airplane in the world, bar none!

Our own morale was up because, by the end of September, John and I had finally been able to convert all our bombers from B-24s to B-17s, making our tight formations easier to control and therefore much easier to defend. And in addition, we were now getting good support from our "little friends," P-51s and P-47s with wing tanks that gave them the range to cover us into Germany.

CHAPTER 18

POLTAVA

By the second half of 1944 the strength of Poland's resistance movement, known as the Home Army, stood at some 300,000. Organized in cells, it was Europe's largest and most professionally organized and efficient partisan army, making life for the occupying German forces as difficult as possible while gathering intelligence and carrying out military and industrial sabotage. As examples of their efforts, the Home Army Intelligence Service captured and sent parts of the German's deadly V-1 ramjet "Buzz Bomb" missile to London for examination, provided information on German military movements, including advance warning of the German General Staff's plan to invade Russia, and fully briefed the Royal Air Force about the exact locations of the manufacturing facilities for the V-2 liquid fuel rockets that were pounding London.

Originally commanded by General Stefan Roweki, whose code name was "Grot," who was captured early in 1943 and subsequently murdered, the Polish Home Army was under the command of General Tadeusz Komorowski whose code name was "Bor." The Home Army fought a war on many fronts, at times in open combat in brigade or division strength, sometimes acting as execution squads eliminating German officials, and at other times waging a psychological campaign against the occupiers. It was a costly resistance, however, because the Germans always took brutal reprisals.

Komorowski, or "General Bor" as he was known to us at the Eighth Air Force, was determined to drive the Germans out of his country at the earliest opportunity. He was said to have 100,000 members of the Home Army — we called them "Freedom Fighters" — in Warsaw ready to rise up when Allied forces drew near. His plan called for them to strike at German strongholds within the city when the Allies had advanced to within ten miles of its outskirts. It was reasoned that the Germans, caught between Allied columns and Polish Freedom Fighters could be defeated, perhaps even compelled to surrender.

It might have worked had not the Russian Army been assigned to carry out the Allied role. On August 1, 1944, with the Russian forces just ten miles away from Warsaw on the right bank of the Vistula River, the Home Army rose in Warsaw as planned. General Bor's Polish Home Army did, in fact, capture many key strongholds in the city within the first couple of days. The Russians, however, just stopped cold in their tracks and didn't move forward. Inside the city, virtually the entire population was involved in the street fighting as the Russians stayed put. As it became evident to both sides that the Russians were not going to intervene, the German forces were able to drive the Home Army forces back from their initial conquests. Home Army members, fighting under a savage German bombardment, used the sewers as lines of communication and escape. They started their drive with less than two weeks' supplies of food and ammunition, believing that the Russian forces would move in quickly and relieve them. After a month there was still no relief in sight and they radioed to London for help. The battle, however, would go on for over two months.

At Allied Headquarters in England it became apparent by late August 1944, that the Russians intended to let the Poles fight the Germans on their own. Relations between the Soviets and the Polish partisans were bitter; the Poles knew that the Soviets betrayed their movement whenever it suited Moscow's interests. Worse, the German-Soviet pact of 1939 had divided Poland in two. The Soviets took the eastern half (Byelorussia and the West Ukraine), the Germans incorporated Pomerania, Posnania and Silesia into the Reich, and the remainder was designated as the Polish General-Gouvernement, essentially a Nazi colony ruled from Krakow by Hitler's friend, Hans Frank. The Poles had no illusions that the Soviets were really allies at all; they were temporarily united in their desire to defeat the Germans. Based on that history

I assume that the Russian motive for refusing to help the Home Army was a desire to see the Germans and the Poles annihilate each other, after which the Soviets could absorb the country into the Soviet Union without fear of Polish resistance — which is exactly what they did.

Allied Headquarters decided we had to do something to help our Polish allies, but diplomatic efforts with the Russians had consistently produced only a *Nyet!* Finally, early in September 1944, the Eighth Air Force received permission to fly one relief mission to the Warsaw Poles. The 93rd Combat Wing was assigned to fly this first and only relief mission to drop supplies — primarily medical — to the besieged Home Army. I was designated Mission Commander of this relief mission. It was to be an exceptionally long flight, across France and Germany directly to Warsaw, a first leg of about 900 miles. We would make our drop and continue east for another 550 miles into the Soviet Union to Poltava in the Ukraine east of Kiev. The plan called for us to lay over in Poltava and depart the following day for Foggia, Italy, the base of the Fifteenth Air Force, and from there return to England with a bombing mission over France en route. As this route was substantially beyond the range of any Allied fighters, we would be without the protection of any of our "little friends." To protect us from the Luftwaffe, the Soviet Air Force would, we were told, rendezvous with us over Warsaw, and then escort us to the Poltava airfield.

There had been five prior shuttle missions into Russia, but these were bombing missions against Nazi Germany, of which two had utilized the Third Air Division of the Eighth Air Force.

On June 2, 1944, General Ira Eaker led the Fifteenth Air Force out of Italy, accompanied by P-51 fighters, on the first Russian shuttle mission, dubbed "Frantic Joe." The overall establishment of a refueling and emergency repair base in Russia was called "Operation Frantic." They bombed the Nazis' railway yards at Debrecen, and then landed at Poltava in Russia. Over the next week they made several raids out of Poltava to strike at other nearby targets before returning to their home base at Foggia. It became a big PR (public relations) event with lots of news correspondents taking photos and writing stories about the Russians, British and Americans cooperating in their Allied efforts to defeat Germany.

The second "Operation Frantic" shuttle, called "Frantic II" took off on June 21, with both the Fifteenth Air Force and the Eighth Air Force participating. The 95th Bomb Group was led by its Commander, Colonel Karl Truesdell, while the entire Eighth Air Force task force was commanded by Colonel Archie Old. This mission, and all the succeeding shuttle missions to Russia, were shrouded in secrecy from beginning to end.

On August 6, the last shuttle bombing mission sent B-17s from both the Eighth and Fifteenth Air Forces, escorted by P-51s, to bomb the Focke-Wulfe aircraft factory at Rahmel, Poland, and then continue on to land at Poltava, Russia. The following day the bombers, with their fighter escorts, targeted the oil refineries in Trzebinia, Poland. On their way back to England, via Foggia, they hit the Buzau-Ziletsia airdromes. This mission was called "Frantic V" as part of the overall Operation Frantic shuttle program, and it was the third mission in which the 93rd Combat Wing participated.

This mission that I was to lead on September 18 was very different. It was to be the first American shuttle relief mission to drop desperately needed medical supplies to the Polish Freedom Fighters in besieged Warsaw, and fly on into Russia, landing at the Operation Frantic base at Poltava. General Al Kessler, "Uncle Ugh," the original Commander of the 95th Bomb Group and now the Air Force Liaison Officer to the Russian Army, was assigned to make arrangements for our stopover in Poltava and to meet us there. Our 93rd Combat Wing was selected for this critical mission because of our previous experience in making a series of successful supply drop missions in France to the French Resistance forces.

We took off in the morning with about 150 aircraft, crossed over France and Germany without incident, and sighted Warsaw in late afternoon as the sky was beginning to darken. As we approached Warsaw at about 26,000 feet, we looked ahead in the distance and saw fighters, which we took to be our promised Soviet escort. As they drew closer they became quite unfriendly and fired right at us — they were German Me-109s and FW-190s. There was not a single Soviet fighter to be seen.

While our gunners fought back we descended toward Warsaw, dropping way down to 300 feet to make our drops. We were using our flaps and wheels to slow our air speed in order to maximize the accuracy of our drops, all the while being hammered from above by the German fighters. We dropped six-foot long canisters, full of relief supplies similar to those we had delivered to the French Resistance; its color-coded paper parachute identified the contents of each canister. Given the shifting battle lines in the city, however, we had no way to know who would actually take possession of them. After completing our drops we gave our engines full power and roared over Warsaw's eastern outskirts as we climbed back up to cruising altitude, headed for the Ukraine. All this time the German fighters kept up their attacks.

It was a running battle reminiscent of the Regensberg shuttle mission. As night came on it became increasingly difficult for us to maintain the close defensive formations we relied upon for safety and concentrated firepower because we could not see one another well enough to risk flying close together. The Me-109s and FW-190s kept on us until dark, when they were replaced by Me-110s, their twin-engine long-range night fighters.

As darkness fell we spread out our formations. The Me-110s took advantage of that to infiltrate our ranks. They appeared only as dark shapes, indistinguishable from our own aircraft. We dared not fire into the gloom, lest we destroy one of our own or perhaps one of the promised Soviet fighters. We had not given up hope of their coming to our aid. Only when a shadow suddenly emitted machine gun muzzle flashes did we know who it was. They would fire a burst and then dart away overhead. We couldn't return fire for fear of hitting our own planes. These sneak attacks went on all the way to Poltava — we lost several airplanes on the way — and continued even as we lowered our wheels to land. As far as we knew, not one Soviet fighter had come to our aid.

The Germans were determined to destroy us any way they could. As we taxied toward the parking area, the Me-110s flew back and forth across the field, strafing us. There were no antiaircraft guns firing and still no Soviet fighters. We parked the B-17s and scrambled out as the Germans machine-gunned them, inflicting grave damage to many of our B-17s before they finally broke off and flew away. Fortunately, nearly all of our crewmen escaped in good shape. The Germans, however, were not finished. They returned to their bases, loaded up with anti-personnel bombs, deadly little "butterfly" bombs, which upon hitting the ground and burying themselves in the turf become land mines, and returned in force to drop them. The airfield was soon turned into a "no man's land."

By then it was around midnight. The Russian commander of the base ordered us to evacuate and sent a convoy of American-built two-and-a-half ton trucks — given to the Soviets as part of Roosevelt's "Lend-lease" program — to take us about ten miles away overnight. I was concerned about the security of our airplanes, and asked him what we might do to protect them. He insisted that he would "take care of it," and repeated his order that we leave the airfield. Given the Russian failure to provide air cover, I was skeptical that he could, or would, do anything.

Who knew what his orders were? Perhaps the Russians had withheld their fighter escort hoping our mission would fail. We were, after all, helping the partisans the Soviets would soon betray. (After helping the Russians liberate eastern Poland, the Home Army was forcibly disarmed. Many of the Polish partisans were deported to Siberian labor camps, and many were simply murdered.) But we were deep in the USSR where the Russian Army ruled. We had no choice. We climbed into the trucks and were ferried away into the night.

When we arrived at the place where we were to stay, General Kessler was there to greet us. Our hosts were in a festive mood. They uncorked vodka bottles and started pouring, welcoming us to Mother Russia with shots of straight vodka — *Neecheva!* We raised toasts to Soviet-American friendship, such as it was. The Russians were all smiles and their supply of vodka appeared to be unlimited. For all the insistent gaiety and backslapping, however, they made it clear that we were not to leave the area of the party. I sensed that they did not want us to be anywhere near our airplanes, and that troubled me. I was after all the Mission Commander, responsible for the bombers' security, and this didn't feel right to me. By now it was closer to dawn than midnight. I commandeered a jeep from one of General Kessler's men and drove back alone to the airfield at Poltava.

I got there as the sky was beginning to lighten. The airfield had been declared off limits and was being guarded by Russian sentries. While I watched, another convoy of two-and-a-half ton trucks arrived as the coming dawn lightened the sky. Their tailgates dropped and scores of people got out. They were all dressed like peasants. Each group had one or two armed soldiers guarding them. The peasants, if that's what they were — they might have been Poles or Germans or Russian political prisoners, or something else — were lined up at gunpoint. Then, on a command from a loudspeaker, the soldiers prodded the captives to walk ahead of them. I realized in horror that they were being forced to walk en masse toward the dirt and turf airfield that the German night fighters had sown with land mines.

What happened next can only be described as an atrocity. The prisoners began to step on the mines. It sounded like a battlefield as they advanced, as every now and then one of them detonated a mine. The Russians had them march forward shoulder to shoulder until the sun rose and the entire field was cleared. When the survivors, with soldiers still behind them, had crossed the field, trucks followed onto the strip they had cleared to pick them up. Those who were wounded but still alive were not distinguished from the dead — the dead and the injured were all loaded like cordwood onto other trucks. All were ferried away, to what fate I have no idea. It was the most brutal and gruesome thing I have ever had the misfortune to see — and I was the only American to witness it. I was stunned!

In England, when the Germans had mined our airfields with these same butterfly bombs, we eliminated them by driving heavily armor-plated tanks all over the mined fields, without such needless human destruction.

Later that morning our crews were delivered back to Poltava in another truck convoy, and we set about taking inventory of the damage to our aircraft. Seventy-seven, more than half of our original number, were so badly shot up they could not take off. The bombers that were airworthy took off for Italy. We radioed to Foggia for help. Replacements were dispatched from Foggia to Poltava to pick up the crews stranded there. Our ground crews were able to repair some of the damaged bombers, which were eventually flown to Italy; others had to be written off as salvage.

Within a day or two we were back in England, after completing a bombing mission over France on the way home. I told my superiors what I had seen in the Ukraine, and I filed my mission report, but so far as I could tell no official American acknowledgement of the incident was forthcoming. We at the 93rd Combat Wing had so many other things to concern us — our own survival was a day-to-day question mark — and I suppose we simply preferred not to discuss our Polish relief mission to Poltava but to concentrate on our current missions.

The Warsaw Uprising lasted 63 days before the Germans put it down. Warsaw was in ruins. Thousands of captured Polish resistance fighters and civilians were executed or sent to German concentration camps where they died or were put to death. Warsaw was razed to the ground. After all, Hitler's grand plan called for the total eradication of the Polish people and every vestige of their culture by 1975. The defeat of the Home Army in Warsaw destroyed the political and military institutions that might have prevented the Soviet takeover of Poland that followed.

My memory of that awful dawn in Poltava remains vivid and disturbing to me. Perhaps because the exigencies of the war forced our high command to stomach the Soviet way of getting things done, lest relations between our governments break down at a time when that could have been disastrous, the Russians were not confronted over what happened at Poltava. During the war crimes trials, however, there were references to "the Poltava incident," but so far as I could learn at that time there were no accompanying details to reveal to what occurrence those words might have referred.

Despite considerable searching since I have found in our governmental archives, only a passing mention of this Polish relief shuttle mission[11] and no mention at all about these killings. The politics of that time and place were complex. The Ukrainian Insurgent Army, or UPA, a powerful militia that wanted independence from the Soviet Union, harbored bitter hatred toward the Poles because of the Second Polish Republic, a military dictatorship that arose in 1926 and had attempted to take over the Ukraine by force. The Poles, sadly, had treated the Ukrainians much the same way the Russians treated the Poles in Warsaw. As the Second World War progressed, the Ukrainians' bitterness led to atrocities against Poles. Therefore, it's possible, I suppose, that the soldiers I took for Russian Army troops were in fact members of the Ukrainian force, which was at the time fighting alongside the Soviet Army in essentially identical uniforms, just as our various National Guard units from around the USA often mix with regular forces in time of war, as they did in the Persian Gulf in 1991. I don't know for sure, but I am quite positive that the slaughter at the Poltava airfield has never been verified by anyone else.

Nevertheless, the Russian army's utter disregard of the value of human life exemplified in their use of peasants, political prisoners, penal battalions and even their own soldiers to clear minefields as I had observed that early morning in Poltava has been

---

[11] Bernard C. Nalty, *Wing Shield, Wing Sword, A History of the United States Air Force, 1907-1950*, Volume I, page 306, contains the following comment:
"When Soviet officials refused to cooperate in efforts to drop supplies to noncommunist Polish resistance forces in Warsaw — the Eighth Air Force received permission for just one such mission using the Ukrainian airfields — the shuttle campaign came to an end."

documented in several post-war publications[12]. It was part of a general policy of exterminating all potential opposition to the totalitarian Soviet regime anywhere within the control of Russia[13].

Only recently as I was preparing to write this book I found that one of the pilots in my 334th Bomb Squadron, Glenn B. Infield, had done quite a bit of research into official U.S. Army records about "Operation Frantic."[14] Although there was a void in the official records about my relief mission, he revealed that the first shuttle to Russia, "Frantic Joe" although accompanied much of the

---

[12] Dept. of the Army Pamphlet No. 20-230, *Russian Combat Methods in World War II*, 1950, in which it is said:

"The most common Russian form of combat was the use of mass. Human mass and mass of material were generally used.... The Russian disdain for life — always present but infinitely heightened by communism — favored this practice... In the winter of 1941, the Russians cleared a German mine field south of Leningrad by chasing over it tightly closed columns of unarmed Russian soldiers shoulder to shoulder. Within a few minutes, they became victims of the mines and defensive fire... During the fighting southeast of Krememchug in September, 1943, the Russians at nighttime used to drive ahead of their armed soldiers large numbers of civilians whom they had gathered up, so that the German infantry might expend its scant supply of ammunition."

[13] Nikolai Tolstoy, *Stalin's Secret War*, 1981. In Chapter XV, Tolstoy says:

"Above all, Stalin was essentially an insecure tyrant... Stalin had always trembled at the vision of revolution in the cities. Events in 1944-5 had done nothing to diminish that fear. The nationalist Home Army had risen in Warsaw and fought for two months against the best units the Wehrmacht and SS could throw against them. A sinister-seeming pointer to subsidiary danger was the presence in the skies over Warsaw of American bombers dropping arms to the Poles, despite Soviet disapproval."

[14] For more in-depth information about "Operation Frantic" and reasons for the conclusion that Stalin was using that operation in a scheme of deception and duplicity, see *The Poltava Affair, A Russian Warning: An American Tragedy*, by Glenn B. Infield, published by Brassey's, 1973. Infield further said:

"Stalin's secret postwar plans took precedence over any "Operation Frantic" mission or any pretence of United States-Soviet collaboration. The political implications of the Warsaw tragedy and Stalin's actions during the fateful months of August and September 1944 in regard to "Operation Frantic" revealed to those who carefully analyzed the events what the United States should expect in its relations with the Soviet Union *after* World War II ended."

way by American fighters, did not see any Russian fighter aircraft in the air to oppose the Luftwaffe. General Eaker, the Mission Commander, found that although he was treated well personally as befit a high ranking Allied military officer, his operational requests were constantly and consistently bogged down in "red tape" and bureaucracy, and often the most reasonable requests, by our standards, were refused out of hand. The apparent lack of defenses by the Russians for his grounded aircraft was of great concern to General Eaker. Therefore, the mission left as soon as the weather permitted on June 5, 1944.

"Frantic II," the second shuttle to Russia, was, however, a disaster. Again, there were absolutely no Red Air Force fighters protecting our B-17s either in the air or on the ground. Despite the protests of a very worried Mission Commander, Colonel Archie Old, the defending night fighters that Russia had promised to use to protect the Poltava base and the 73 American bombers parked on it never appeared, and the Germans bombed and strafed them for almost two hours. The result was 47 B-17s destroyed and 19 damaged and unflyable but possibly repairable. In addition, some 200,000 gallons of aviation fuel, supplied by America for use in American aircraft, and numerous other supplies and equipment were destroyed by the Luftwaffe, who had free rein to bomb and strafe at will.

On the ground, the Americans had to take to the slit trenches. General Walsh, General Kessler and Colonel Old were in the trenches together when Kessler said, "Those damn bombers have been flying around overhead for more than an hour! Where the hell is the Red Air Force?" All they could do was to stay in their slit trenches and watch their valuable task force bombers burn and explode. Stalin, before this mission, had personally promised our Ambassador Averill Harriman that Russia would defend that air base while American aircraft were on it. That promise was completely unfulfilled. General Kessler, our "Uncle Ugh," said to Colonel Gray of the American task force, "In two hours, Stalin could have ordered Yaks from a dozen air bases in the area — if he had wanted to do so."

Directives issued by General Partridge and General Spaatz repeatedly stated that "the crews participating in the Frantic mission must not discuss with anyone — repeat, anyone — details of the attack by enemy planes to our aircraft or installations in Russia." All our men were further told to "say nothing critical of the Russians which might endanger our present relations with them."

The American bomber force that flew the "Frantic V" shuttle to Russia on August 6 also reported that the Red Air Force was nowhere to be seen.[15]

It truly puzzles me now that I am aware of all those problems on the three previous missions to Russia by the Third Air Division that I was never briefed about those earlier missions and what happened on them. I'm not sure what I could have done differently, considering the restrictions placed on me, but at least I would not have been surprised by the lack of fighter cover by the Red Air Force. I certainly would have attempted to persuade General Kessler to let me get my bomber force moved to another airfield. Even that, however, would have required permission from the Russian authorities, which now I think would have been denied. Why was I not told such important information? It's hard to say now, but the suppression of any negative information about the Russians, ordered by President Roosevelt himself and adhered to by the Eighth Air Force senior staff, may just have caused that information to disappear. I'm pretty certain now that my operations report from that mission "disappeared."

Glenn Infield, in his book, *The Poltava Affair*, postulates that we were all trapped in the high level politics between Stalin on the one hand and Roosevelt and Churchill on the other, and that Stalin wanted our missions to fail to prevent anyone from believing that

---

[15] Al Keeler, a B-17 copilot on the "Frantic V" mission (and author of *VIP Pilot*, 1999), told me as I was writing this chapter, that when his crew landed at Poltava on August 6, he and his crew were appalled at the extensive wreckage of American planes on the ground there that had not as yet been cleaned up from the June 21 "attacks" by the Luftwaffe. He said that General Spaatz had exclaimed that this had been "the worst disaster to befall the United States since Pearl Harbor!"

Russia had needed any help in beating Germany and to ensure that he had a free hand to take over all of Poland when the war was concluded. It is even reasonable to believe, he said, that Stalin arranged to have the Luftwaffe find out about the presence of unprotected American bombers at Poltava as a way to make "Operation Frantic" become a failure so that all the unwelcome Americans would go home.

The Americans finally did leave, in June 1945, just after the end of the war in Europe. It was not without continual difficulties with the Russian authorities, however. At this time, I was working under General Curt LeMay at the Pentagon, so I was unaware of the goings on with the aftermath of the problems experienced by the American military operation at Poltava.

But since then, I read in Glenn Infield's book an interesting anecdote about my old boss, Uncle Ugh. Late in 1944 when General Kessler was still our top Army Air Forces officer at Poltava, the Russian officials were becoming more and more uncooperative and rude to the Americans there. Stalin, I'm sure, encouraged this because he wanted the unwelcome Americans to leave, but he didn't want it to appear that Russia was forcing them out; he wanted to continue to use all the leverage he could to get as much "lend-lease" equipment and supplies from America as possible. But as part of Stalin's program to get the Americans out of Russia, he encouraged his Red Army officers to make life at Poltava as miserable as possible for the Americans. For instance, a Soviet colonel decided to remove all the butter from the American mess despite the fact that the butter was provided by Lend-Lease. So one night a young second lieutenant from Texas took a rope that he had with him from his ranch near El Paso, and lassoed the Red Army colonel, tying him, startled and angry, to a flagpole outdoors in the freezing cold. He then warned the colonel that unless there was butter in the American mess the following day, he would hang him by the neck before the week was over. When the colonel, half frozen, was freed a few hours later, he immediately protested the action to Kessler. Uncle Ugh just shrugged and said, "I like butter, too. Besides, that Texan has already hung ten cattle rustlers. He's too tough for me." The colonel, having seen a few American movies, believed Kessler and the butter was restored the next day.

Why did Roosevelt and our American leaders tolerate these actions by Russia? I can only surmise, as did Glenn Infield, that he over-optimistically believed that he could draw Stalin into being a "friendly" ally with whom we and the British could work together in the post-war world. As we now know, Stalin and the Russians who replaced him were not interested in any sharing of control in the post-war world. They wanted to dominate all of Poland, Eastern Germany and all the other lands on their western border with Communist puppet governments, which they could control completely.

Several years ago, during the celebration of the 50th anniversary of the war's end, the Russian Federation, through its Ambassador in Washington, awarded its "Commemorative Medal" to surviving members of the American military cadre stationed at Poltava, in honor of their service in Russia during "the Great Patriotic War."

What, then, did I really witness at Poltava? It remains in my mind a mysterious and horrific historical footnote to that great epic of destruction and death that was World War II.

CHAPTER 19

GENERAL de GAULLE'S KISS

After France surrendered to the invading Germans in 1940 and the infamous "Vichy French" government was installed, the French Resistance was organized. The men and women in the Resistance were brave and daring partisans who provided invaluable, often life-saving, support for the Allied forces throughout the war. Even today, more than a half-century after the liberation of Paris, to wear a Resistance member's pin on one's lapel is to wear a distinct and unique badge of honor. There were many French patriots, however, who did not live to see the day when their courage could be publicly honored. During the Occupation, to be known to the Germans as a Resistance member was a death warrant.

The Vichy Government was about as peculiar a regime as France, and indeed the world, has ever known. Right wing and authoritarian, it succeeded the Third Republic in unoccupied French territory after Germany overran France in June of 1940. The Nazi *Blitzkrieg* and France's collapse left its people stunned. Meeting in the resort town of Vichy, the French National Assembly, no less dazed than ordinary citizens, granted Premier Henri Philippe Petain full emergency powers to form a government and write a new constitution for its governance. Their deal was a pact with the devil, however, for Germany pressured the Vichy government into complicity in their anti-Semitic policies and repression of other French citizens.

I first became really aware of the French Resistance when my crew and I were transporting our B-17 from America to England in April, 1943 and we stopped in Dakar, Senegal. Only two weeks before we landed there, the French Resistance forces had wrested control of Senegal from the Vichy French. Throwing off the yoke of the occupying Germans and their collaborators, the Vichy French, the Resistance proclaimed themselves the "Free French."

That name was adopted by the French forces under General Charles de Gaulle, who commanded them in exile from his London headquarters.

The Free French disavowed the validity of the surrender agreement signed by the Vichy Government. While I was flying missions out of England, the French Resistance forces in southern France, calling themselves the "Maquis," formed the French underground, an insurgent arm of the Free French. They were France's staunchest and bravest loyalists, mounting a genuine guerrilla war against German occupation forces whose policies of repression were astonishingly brutal. Despite this, the underground was active throughout France, especially in the southeast, much of which is mountainous, heavily wooded and uncultivated. This rough terrain enabled them to strike and then disappear into the wild countryside without getting caught by the Germans. They would set underground booby traps for German soldiers. They would wreck convoys and do anything to damage and disrupt the German occupation forces. Using ingenious and devious means, from word of mouth passed from one patriot to another to clandestine coded radio messages, they kept in constant communication with General de Gaulle's headquarters in London.

There was deadly bitterness between the Free French, the Maquis, and the Vichy French. The former felt that the Vichy French had sold out the country to the Germans. The Vichy French, trying to put a gloss on dishonor, insisted that they were acting in the interest of France under the circumstances by preventing the Germans from looting and destroying their country. The Maquis rejected the Vichy rationale for surrender and collaboration. At best, they said it had been bad judgement; at worst, it was treason. When the Nazis continued the rape of France after the Vichy French had surrendered, the Vichy argument became, at least in the opinion of the Maquis, indefensible.

The Maquis were not just talk. Besides taking the sword to the Germans, they gave us life-saving assistance when our boys were downed in occupied France. We were instructed that, if any of us were forced down, to use the maps and compasses in our "escape kits" to determine our location and how best to contact the French Resistance. Printed in detail on silk scarves, these maps enabled our downed fliers to find the people who could put them on the "underground railway" back home, usually first to Paris and then through various devious routes to the Spanish border. From there we could get across the Pyrenees Mountains and contact the British Consulate in neutral, albeit Fascist, Spain. The British Consulate would then arrange for us to be shipped back to England.

Every crewman on the mission had his own escape kit, which contained a substantial amount of French currency for buying food, shelter and transportation. Once we had made contact with the Maquis, we were to turn the money over to them as a help to finance their operations. Perhaps most importantly, these escape kits also contained passport-style photos of ourselves in civilian clothes to make us look like French civilians, which the underground could use to provide us fake ID's. Some crew members carried their passport-type photos separate from the escape kits. Once on the ground, however, we were never to carry a .45 pistol or any other firearm, as that could get us shot on the spot.

Combat, however, had a way of disrupting the best of plans and preparation, as the behind-the-scenes odyssey of one of my crews demonstrated. They were newcomers to the European Theater, having just arrived. We normally received our replacements on the train that arrived at nearby Diss at 11:00 PM each night. Ordinarily I'd place those just arrived in open spots on existing crews, thereby introducing them to air combat in Europe under the tutelage of seasoned combat veterans. But one night we received ten new replacements, one complete crew, and at that time I had a whole airplane to fill, so I assigned them all to that bomber.

Later that night we were alerted for a mission the next morning to Strasbourg, France. The newcomers were duly briefed on the procedure for escaping from France if they were forced down, and off we went. Their first mission that morning didn't go well. During the usual German fighter attacks they lost an engine. That in itself was not necessarily fatal to a B-17 — these planes had already demonstrated their astounding durability — but you had to experience it to understand it. Apparently unaware that their B-17 could get them home on three engines — my own *Blondie II* had flown us back from Germany across the North Sea on only one engine — the new pilot and copilot decided to throw in the towel. But, rather than jumping out in their parachutes, they chose to land the airplane using their three good engines. They found an open field, and they did successfully land the airplane without any injuries. They all got out, and then, following proper procedure, they blew up the airplane.

They hadn't been in the ETO for more than a few hours, but here they were on the ground in France. They pulled out the maps in their escape kits, oriented themselves and walked to the nearest town and found its railway station. It turned out they had landed in occupied France, and not one of them spoke French. So they, all ten of them, bought train tickets with their French currency. They were all in their flight suits, which looked a little like workmen's overalls, and they boarded the train, acting like they didn't know each other, and picked out seats away from each other. The conductor came along and took their tickets. No one questioned them or even said a word to them. The train crossed from occupied France to Vichy France without anyone causing them a problem. They went clear across France all the way to the southern border, where they got off the train. Following their instructions they trekked across the Pyrenees Mountains into Spain, where they were picked up by the Spanish border patrol. The Spaniards turned them over to the British Consul, who provided them clothes and transportation back to England. They were back to our base in Horham in only four days!

Their good luck, which was utterly astonishing, was not over. Our policy was that once a man had been downed in German-held territory and escaped, he was to be sent home. The reasoning was that if he were to return to combat and be captured again, he might be forced to divulge information about how he had escaped. That information could fatally compromise some of our Maquis allies and make it more difficult for others to make it back to base. So we always sent escapees home to the old USA. After only five days in the war, those fortunate ten men were sent home to America with only one mission, albeit a most memorable one, under their belts.

As the war went on, tales of unlikely escapes accumulated. We had one fellow in Belgium, who had been blown out of his exploding aircraft. He parachuted down, unhurt, and landed in the countryside alone, completely separated from his fellow crew members. Like most Americans in that era, he never expected to find himself in Europe and spoke only English. He wandered, furtively, around in Belgium, hiding out for three or four days. Finally he stopped in at a bar for a drink. It could have been his last. While he was in the bar, a whole bunch of German soldiers came into the bar, laughing and joking. They even bought him a drink. He never said a word; he just made motions and smiled. I guess the Germans thought he was a Belgian who didn't speak German. Then the German soldiers went on their way. Eventually that day, he was picked up by, fortunately, a member of the Belgian Resistance. The Resistance hid him for a while, until they could drop him into the underground pipeline to Spain.

It was amazing how many of our boys, both British and American airmen, were wandering around German occupied territory until they contacted the French underground and got themselves back to England. But for every tale of luck, some of them amusing in spite of the circumstances, there was a terrible price to pay for detection, as one of our Squadron Commanders learned.

Cliff Cole was also shot down over Belgium. He found his way to a village where friendly folks took him in and hid him; they turned out to be a Resistance family. Soon another American air crewman, an exceptionally tall, lanky fellow, showed up and was secreted in the house next door. When that Belgian family discreetly tried to find civilian clothes that would fit that very tall American, their inquiries attracted the attention of the local Gestapo, who raided their home. The American was taken prisoner and all the members of that household were taken out in the street and publicly shot for harboring an American airman. The family harboring Cliff watched quietly in horror. But Cliff was still kept in their house for several more weeks until arrangements could be made for him to get into the underground railway toward home. That Belgian family's courage was typical for the people in the Resistance, and Cliff owed his life to them. We were profoundly grateful to them!

Allied gratitude took tangible forms. Between late 1943 and through 1944, the 95th Bomb Group made about 20 missions over occupied France to give them aid. The flights were conceived by the Free French, who coordinated with the Maquis. The 95th's job was to drop supplies and arms to the Resistance at specific rendezvous points that were given to us in coded messages from Free French headquarters. I led at least a dozen of these support missions in France for the French Resistance, some with as few as two airplanes and some with as many as 16. And every one of these drops was successful!

The missions had to be precisely planned and coordinated, for we had to arrive on time and at the right place. As the date for the drop neared, the Maquis would light bonfires in the drop area, arranged in a certain pattern discernible only from the air so that British night bombers could identify them. The British would mark the coordinates on their maps, and using those charts we designed a combined bombing and relief mission that would fly over those coordinates. In our regular complement of bombers we would add on a few extra planes loaded with the requested supplies for the Maquis. These requests had come to us through Free French headquarters in London. These supplies, typically firearms, ammunition, medical supplies, and tools, were contained in metal canisters that measured about six feet in length and two feet in diameter, which fit perfectly into our bomb bays.

For these special missions, our B-17s would fly to France as usual at about 24,000 to 28,000 feet on the way to the target area. As we neared the drop point, we would drop "chaff," tiny pieces of aluminum foil, that would create a metallic blizzard with an image resembling snow on the German radar screens, which effectively blinded them and obscured the images of our planes, thus neutralizing those radar defenses. Following the release of chaff, we of the support drop mission could "disappear in the snow" and rapidly descend to about 300 feet in altitude to make our drop undetected. Meanwhile the main formation of aircraft flew on to their targets. Everything was precisely timed. The Maquis again lit their marker fires to guide us and to confirm to us that the drop was still on. We had British Mosquito fighter-bombers that would race on ahead of us to check that all the marker fires were in their proper places, lest they conceal an ambush. We would fly over the clearings identified by fires with our flaps and landing gear down to slow the airplane, permitting us to drop the canisters with considerable accuracy. Each canister had a paper parachute, color-coded to tell the Maquis what it contained. After we dropped these cans, we saw the Maquis down below running around, gathering up these cans and getting them put away out of sight or loading them into trucks and vans. The Maquis had a real talent for hiding those supplies quickly and eliminating all traces of our supply drop. When we had completed the drop, we'd wave *au revoir* to the Maquis down below us, retract our wheels and flaps, throttle up our engines and climb back to 25,000 feet or so to join up with the stream of bombers coming back from their bombing mission. Regrouped, we'd all fly back to England together.

The planning and coordination of the Free French and the Maquis was impeccable. Much of their information was transmitted over the BBC using pre-arranged verbal codes. An innocuous report that "the trout are biting in Scotland, where the weather has been excellent" could very well mean something very different to a Resistance group huddled around a radio in France. The Germans apparently failed to detect these communications, or at least to fathom their real meaning. Good planning in London combined with the Maquis' daring, the Allied air forces' experience and resources, and some very good luck made every one of our relief missions successful. The Maquis were always where they were supposed to be, and the Germans were always somewhere else. Maquis' security was so airtight that not once were any of these supply airplanes attacked by German fighters.

At the end of 1944, General Charles de Gaulle and his entourage of aides and security men traveled north from London to General LeMay's headquarters at Elveden Hall. The occasion was a large and formal fête to honor Colonel John Gerhart and me for making these risky supply drops to the Maquis.

We were impressed by General de Gaulle, who was a daring leader and a good soldier. He ran a tight organization — his security system was extremely good — and most importantly he was a charismatic leader, something the French desperately needed in those years when the country was truly traumatized by the German invasion and occupation. De Gaulle's leadership had built his Free French organization into an efficient and loyal force that was wreaking havoc on the Germans in France. His personality, which included a unique ability to symbolize a country that remained undaunted and defiant despite its defeat and betrayal, had won him devotion of the French people.

It was de Gaulle's decision to award John and me the Croix de Guerre with Palms. What stands out in my memory is General de Gaulle's stature. He was a very tall man — despite my own 6'2" in height, he had to bend over to kiss me! I had not expected to be kissed, certainly not by this living legend, and certainly not twice. But, he did, emphatically, on both cheeks! That was certainly a NEW experience! Not an experience that one has twice in one's life. It was another example of my extraordinary good fortune in the midst of the vast misfortune and tragedy that claimed so many others.

There were others who were awarded the Croix de Guerre by the French for their participation on those supply drops to the Maquis, and these included Grif Mumford and Fitz Fitzgerald. Yes, the General kissed them, too.

We ended our supply drops to the Maquis after the Allied armies broke out of Normandy late in 1944 and commenced their drive towards Paris. As we advanced, the partisans rose in force against the Germans, who were in any case already on the defensive. Simultaneously, the Free French forces under General LeClere fought through Burgundy and recovered Alsace. As the

Allied forces rolled east toward the City of Light, the French celebrated the recovery of every mile of their stolen country. Once the Allies had advanced through there, the French countryside was cleared of Germans, and the French had their country back.

General de Gaulle's kisses seemed an ironic counterpoint to me in retrospect, when after the war I tried to locate an official account of these supply missions. Researching the Eighth Air Force archives, however, I discovered that the campaign to supply the Resistance was hardly mentioned, relegated instead to near-obscurity by the cryptic understatements of military secrecy. In an historical footnote, they are referred to enigmatically only as "special missions." Indeed they were.

CHAPTER 20

ENDING THE WAR AT THE PENTAGON
or
FROM COLONEL TO COWBOY

The urge to get home for a visit was building up with me. Yet my new job with the 93rd was demanding and challenging — and, to my thinking, very important — so I had to keep postponing my plans to go home on leave.

8 October 1944

If conditions permit, I hope to leave here and fly home around the first of December. That way, I'll be home over the holidays, then back here in January.

It looks as though the war will continue indefinitely over here. By all rights, the Germans are beaten and should give up; but under the surrender terms given them they will probably fight from house to house. If so, it will take years to finish the job.

Last night we had a big pheasant dinner. The season is open now and Colonel John and I went over to Elizabeth Elveden's shooting the other day. We had wonderful luck and got eight each. Then after we had hunted, we went riding. It was really quite a day! The war seemed very distant. I must say that our British friends have taken very good care of us.

16 October 1944

I still hope that conditions will be such that I can be with you all for the holidays. If I can only get a good Operations Officer for the Wing, I'll be set. At present I am Chief of Staff and Operations Officer, a dual capacity. If I were to leave, it would leave Colonel John all alone and it is too much for any one person to handle. It is very difficult to find someone with the proper qualifications to handle the job. I hope we can find someone soon. As it is, Colonel John and I alternate nights, which means that every other night we work until 4 or 5 AM, sleep until noon, and then go at it again. If one of us goes away for a couple of days, the other has to work every night. We have plenty of assistants, but we two are the only ones who can make command decisions on planning operations. But despite it all, I am the picture of health and enjoying myself thoroughly.

25 October 1944

The boss has been ill for almost a week with intestinal flu. Consequently, I have been really busy trying to plan missions at night and run the administration by day. It makes for a busy life. Haven't done any operational flying for some time. The General has restricted all Wing Commanders and Chiefs of Staff to only flying Division leads. We only fly about once a month now, damn it! My next turn will be in about three weeks.

If everything goes as planned, I'll be home for a couple of weeks sometime in December. It is very difficult to plan ahead, but unless something unforeseen arises, I'll be able to go. Don't count on it, but it will be nice if it can be arranged.

I have hopes of getting to Paris next week for a couple of days. It is practically impossible for any of us to get clearance to go over to the Continent. Actually, it is easier to get back to the States than to get across the Channel. If I go, I'll fly in the P-47. It will certainly seem strange to land on some of those airdromes we bombed so regularly a while back.

3 November 1944

The Colonel was laid up for a week, but he's OK now.

Today I was in London for the day to do a few errands. It was a miserable, cold, rainy day. Winter is here. On the road we passed about fifteen truckloads of Germans on their way to prison camps. They were really a rough looking lot.

Tomorrow night we are having a super dinner party here for three Generals, including "Uncle Ugh" Kessler. He has recently returned to these parts to take over his old command, one of the Wings. Guess I'll hear all the dope from the east.

Heard a rumor via the grapevine that Colonel John and I are to be awarded the Croix de Guerre by the French for our part in the early stages of events over here. However, nothing official has come through as yet.

November 11, 1944

    Still don't know any thing definite about going home. There is a lot of reorganization going on over here and it all depends on what happens over the next couple of weeks whether or not I can leave at this time. At any rate, I'll have to wait until my Operations Officer gets back.

One very interesting trip occurred, a trip to France without any German fighters or flak. In fact we could even land safely without being shot at. What a pleasure! For this special flight, we had boards placed across the bomb bays so we could load the plane when we got to France with barrels and bottles of France's major export, champagne for the Holidays!

    ...Had a wonderful day Thursday. The Colonel and I took a B-17 and flew over to Reims, France, for the day. We left here at daybreak and didn't return until after dinner. We flew the whole trip below 1,000 feet and circled all our former targets on the Continent. We had a wonderful time in general. At Reims we loaded the airplane with champagne. Boy, we bought it by the gallon! All the good French champagne comes from there. We went straight to Mum's, Peiper Heidieck, Monopale, and a couple of others, and got several cases of each. We had a big two and a half ton truck full when we finished. Now we have quite a stock for our bar. Had a wonderful time trying to use my limited French.

    None of the towns in Northern France have been damaged to speak of, but every air field, railroad yard, bridge, etc., is smashed to bits. Actually, we never realized how good our bombing really was. We did a great deal more damage than the photos indicated, especially to air fields where installations were hidden in woods and didn't show in the pictures. Also, the fighters really took their toll of German transport. The woods are all lined with strafed vehicles of every description.

    The story of the French underground and resistance movement is one of the great stories of the war. I could write a book about it, but I won't attempt to tell any here. I would take too long. But I will say that they were positively amazing in their deeds.

    Just as you say, General LeMay is making things hum out in the Pacific. He is the guy who can do it, as I told you long ago. We could certainly use him back here now.

19 November 1944

    There isn't anything new around here, but rumors are plentiful. We are about to undergo a reorganization and nobody knows what job they will have next week. We are hoping to get some definitive word in the next day or so. As you can readily understand, I cannot possibly leave until we know just what the future holds. So my visit may very well get delayed. Anyway, I'll probably be home before NEXT Christmas!

There was something about bombing Berlin, Hitler's capital, that we really enjoyed doing, although the Luftwaffe — what was left of it — still vigorously defended it. But when we had finished a Berlin raid and the reconnaissance photos showed that we had hit our targets there, we felt especially good about it.

29 November 1944

    We had quite a gay and exciting weekend. Saturday evening we had a little party here at the Mess. Just before the party was a pretty dramatic moment for me. I had been out all day — nine hours — leading the Air Force on a very successful mission against the most heavily defended target in Germany. It was probably the most successful job I have done to date. I received such a roaring welcome when I returned from all the boys that I was just a little embarrassed.

    We are planning a very super celebration for sometime in the very near future. Colonel John is about to get his star. It is up to the Senate now, so it should come through any day. What a day that will be!

    Things are looking up on my visit home. I hate to be the little boy who called "Wolf" but it looks now as though everything will be in order for me to leave in about three or four weeks. I'll fly both ways so that I'll not waste any time in travel.

    I have a new play toy and tomorrow I am going to try it out. The Force is going back to my target of Saturday and again I'm going along. Only instead of a B-17, I am going to fly a British "Mosquito". We got the ship to try a certain thing and as it is my baby I'll give it a whirl tomorrow. I'll whiz ahead of the Force by myself with a couple of P51's for fighter support. It ought to be fun.

14 December 1944

We have been quite busy as the papers have no doubt reported, but tonight a real English fog has descended so we don't have to work for a change. This really puts the San Francisco variety to shame.

Was in London over the weekend and saw an excellent musical review. While there I had lunch with friends at the Senior Officers' Club, a very swanky "joint." It's a beautiful old home on Park Lane that has been converted into a very exclusive club for Colonels and Generals of the Army and Captains and Admirals of the Navy. I don't eat there often — too much rank for me!

Had an interesting coincidence occur the other day. The American cast of *Blythe Spirit* — the same one that played in San Francisco — is touring the bases over here. Last Thursday they played here. After the performance they came down to our Mess for a drink. I'll be damned if the girl who plays the doctor's wife, Darleen Lange, doesn't live in San Mateo and was my classmate at Stanford! I haven't seen her for years. We had a big old time talking over old times and friends we hadn't seen in ages. Then Saturday she came down to London and we really did the town. More fun than I've had in a coon's age.

The Colonel who was to replace me while I visit you arrived today and immediately went to the hospital. He'll be OK in a couple of days, though, and then I'll start to show him the ropes. If everything goes as planned, I expect to leave around the middle of January and should be home within three or four days of whenever I leave here.

I hope you all have a wonderful Christmas. Take a big drink of eggnog for me, and I'll do the same for each of you over here. We are planning a terrific Christmas Eve party here. We have all sorts of champagne, whiskey and the like that has been stored away, so I hope we don't have to work that day.

At the end of 1944, I was getting pretty darn anxious to get a Christmas leave and visit my parents and friends in San Francisco, but my plans for taking leave were being constantly thwarted. Ordinarily on missions of the 93rd Combat Wing, which most of our missions were these days, John Gerhart and I would alternate as the Lead Command Pilot. Then John had a bout of pneumonia that put him out of flying service for almost two months, and with him out, I was the only one who could fly as Command Pilot. So

I had to keep postponing my leave plans. Well, as Christmas neared, John was recovering and was finally back on duty with flying status. John and I shared an office at Wing Headquarters, and in the afternoon on December 22, we were sitting across from each other in the office, and he asked me, "Harry, what would you like to do for Christmas? I'd like to do something for you. Would you like to go to Paris for Christmas — or would you rather go home?" "Well", I said, "I don't have to think much about that. I'd like to go home!" "How long would it take for you to get ready?" he asked. "About 15 minutes!" I replied.

"Well, OK," he said, "but you won't have to do it on leave. I'll just put you on TDY (Temporary Duty)." With that he sailed an envelope across the desk to me, and told me that he would fly me up to the Prestwick, Scotland, Air Transport Command station so that he could use his newly attained "Buck General's" rank, if necessary, to get me a seat on a plane to New York. He obviously knew what I wanted to do, because the envelope contained a reservation for me at the Waldorf Astoria Hotel in New York, plus paid airline tickets from New York to San Francisco and a return flight to Washington, D.C. All that was his Christmas present to me! What a great boss! Of course, we knew I could easily get Government transportation back to England from Washington. Well, he got me to Prestwick, all right, but there were some high-powered Government civilians who had lots of clout who wanted all the seats on the ATC's plane to New York. But with General John's support, I was able to get on it, and was the only uniformed military man on the flight.

At that time, the bad weather over the Atlantic Ocean had severely cut down the number of Government flights across the Atlantic to the States. There were no commercial flights over the Atlantic during the war. ATC had absorbed all the commercial airline personnel and planes for their flights, so they became Army personnel and planes. We were loaded into a Government DC-4, a four engine transport plane, with a former American Airlines pilot and crew. The weather was still pretty rough. Still, I was able to sit back in my chair and snooze a little. Rough flying weather was not a new experience for me.

As we approached Reykjavik, Iceland from the east, I was awakened by the flight steward, who said the pilot wished to see me, and would I please come up to his cabin. I agreed and went to see him, and when I entered I saw the copilot bent over his seat in apparent severe pain. The pilot was pleased to see me, and asked me if I might be willing to give him a hand. His copilot was having an appendicitis attack, and he was unable to assist him. And to make matters worse the automatic pilot was not working, so he had to hand fly the plane all the way. Would I be so kind as to give him a spell at the controls? Of course, I said I would, and helped move the copilot to the engineer's seat. Then I sat down in the copilot's seat and took over the controls. All this time the heavy weather was buffeting the plane and bouncing us around like crazy. Between the two of us, the pilot and I got the plane safely to Reykjavik, where we immediately got an ambulance to come get the copilot and take him to the base hospital. After refueling and having a mechanic check the automatic pilot and deciding its problems were beyond Reykjavik's abilities to solve, the pilot asked me to continue on, helping to hand fly the rest of the way to Gander, Newfoundland and then on to New York. So I got to New York, but I had to work to do it! I was pretty darn tired when my taxi pulled up at the Waldorf Astoria Hotel. I got a good sleep, and I caught my United Airlines flight the next day to San Francisco. That flight was uneventful, fortunately. Oh, yes, except for one thing. San Francisco Airport was fogged in and we were diverted about 40 miles southeast to Livermore Airfield to land. My parents, having learned of the change in landing plans from the airline, met me in Livermore. It was a joyous reunion, indeed, on Christmas Eve!

I had a very pleasant three weeks in San Francisco, ostensibly on TDY at Fourth Air Force Headquarters in downtown San Francisco, and actually having a grand vacation at home. As I reentered the civilian world in the States, I became aware of some of the sacrifices that people at home were having to make. All meat, fish and poultry, all dairy products and some other food items were strictly rationed. Gasoline for civilian use was severely limited. The War Rations Board issued packets of gas ration coupons to most people who applied for them. Almost everyone received an "A" sticker for his windshield with one packet of ten coupons for one month's gasoline, each coupon allowing him to purchase four gallons of gasoline. With some special and worthy needs, a person was given a "B" sticker and two packs of ten coupons allowing him to buy twenty gallons of gas each month. Those with very exceptional needs were allowed a "C" sticker and given coupons for forty gallons of gas each month.

I decided that, if I was going to get around at all while I was in San Francisco on TDY I was going to need some gas coupons, so I went to the local office of the War Rations Board. In uniform — those of us in the military always wore our uniforms during the War — I waited in line and watched a pompous little man officiously, but sparingly, issue packets of gas coupons to the many applicants. As my turn came, I sat down at the ration official's desk and asked for coupons for forty gallons of gasoline, which I thought would come close to handling my automobile transportation needs during my stay here. The little man responded loudly and sanctimoniously, "Heavens NO! Don't you know there's a war on!" What followed was a reaction that exemplified my emotional state at the time, although I have to admit I'm certainly not proud of it. I stood up, reached over and grabbed that man's shirt front, pulled him up so that his face was about six inches from mine, and told him, "You're damn right I know there's a war on! I have just spent the last two years being shot at by Germans in air combat over Europe, and this is my first and only time home. I want those gas coupons NOW!" I left with the coupons. As I went out the door, the remaining roomful of applicants cheered me.

The rest of my time in California was really quite pleasant and restful. It included visiting the families of many of my friends who were gone, serving in the military. At the end of my stay, I checked back out at Fourth Air Force Headquarters and took my commercial flight back to Washington, D.C. Upon landing there I took a cab and went to the Pentagon to get lined up for a flight back to England on an Air Transport Command plane.

As I was walking the halls of the Pentagon, whom did I chance to see but my old commanding officer, General Curtis LeMay! He asked me into his office. "What are you doing here, Conley?" he said. "Well, sir, I was going to ask you the same thing", I responded, and then I told him how I happened to be there looking for a flight back to England. He then told me how he had been promoted and reassigned to be Commanding General of the Twentieth Air Force, headquartered at Guam; and he needed some competent veterans to help him there in Washington. He then announced, "Harry, you're not going back to England. You're staying here. I'll fix it with John, and I'll have all your clothes packed up and sent here!" So that, in a nutshell, is how I ended up spending the rest of my Air Force career in Washington, D.C.

With my last combat mission flown in December 1944, I had completed a great many combat missions without being shot down or seriously wounded. Exactly how many? I really don't know, as I stopped counting after completing my 25th bombing mission. But I was told by one administrative officer that I had a record of 89 missions completed. Whatever the number, I guess that was enough, because in Washington, D.C., I certainly wouldn't get any more air combat missions.

Actually the way it turned out, Curtis LeMay sent for and got most of the key men he had worked with when he was C.O. of the Third Air Division at Elveden Hall. John Gerhart came back to Washington with us in less than two months because it was becoming clear that the war in Europe was drawing to a close, and General LeMay's job was to bring an end to the war in the Pacific. He had picked Fred Anderson to be his Deputy in Washington; he was a two-star General by then, and Chief of the Air Force's Training Command. General Bob Travis, for whom Travis Air Force Base was named, was there. So was General Sam Anderson, another one of Curtis LeMay's handpicked chargers. General Rosie O'Donnell was there, too, as LeMay's superior officer through most of World War II and then later in Korean War as well. He was quite a guy, an outspoken advocate of the Air Force. These were a fabulously interesting and dynamic group of men. They were the nucleus of the Air Force high command for the next twenty years. And I felt honored to be asked to be a part of such a team.

When I reported to the Pentagon, I reported to Lieutenant General Fred Anderson, and I was his Deputy. General Anderson was responsible for building up our B-29 bomber forces to enhance our capabilities in the PTO (Pacific Theater of Operations). We worked together to strengthen and expand our B-29 units. The B-29 was a more advanced airplane than the B-17. It was larger and carried a much greater bomb load and more fuel for a much longer range of operation. In Europe, our airfields were generally not long enough nor strong enough for the larger and heavier B-29s, but in the Pacific we were able to build on coral and sand atolls the longer and stronger runways required by the B-29s. These new planes had more advanced electronic control systems, and were in general the next major advance in aircraft technology after the B-17. In the Pacific Theater, General Wolfe, Commander of the Twentieth Air Force, had introduced the B-29s, but his men weren't getting the operating hours out of them that the high command of the Air Forces thought they should; they were having many mechanical problems, maintenance problems and lots of other problems that were preventing them from getting flying hours over their targets. So it was a natural decision to place General LeMay in charge of the Twentieth Air Force. His record of success in keeping his B-17s flying and bombing effectively made him the best bet the Air Forces could make to get the same kind of results out of their B-29s.

When I met General LeMay in the Pentagon, he told me he wanted me to do the same things we were doing in Europe, and make those airplanes flyable. That's what we did. We started building a cadre of experienced men from Europe, since that war was winding down and experienced people were becoming available. My mission was to organize and expand the training facilities related to the B-29s. We converted training centers all over the U.S. from working with the older bombers to working with B-29s.

My next major job was to develop bombing operations procedures for B-29 missions, using my experience from the B-17 bombing procedures we developed in the ETO, the European Theater of Operations, and to see that those procedures were in fact being implemented in the field. This job required me to fly around the country to all the bomber bases to see that the most effective procedures were being used, and to get the feedback from those actually flying the B-29s about their ideas for improved procedures.

Along with all this, we had the special assignment to train the 509th Bomb Group, which we had sequestered out of public view in Wendover, Utah. It was pretty much out in the desert in western Utah near Nevada. These fellows were getting special training in preparation for handling and dropping the atomic bomb, which at that time was a very closely guarded secret, as it had not yet been used in the war with Japan. In fact, none of these men in the 509th Group knew of the existence of such a device as an "atomic bomb" until their training at Wendover was finished and they were relocated to Guam. But they trained to deliver a "special secret explosive device."

On May 8, 1945, the war in Europe ended with the formal surrender of Germany, ending the European phase of World War II. At that point we quickly concentrated all our efforts on bringing the war in the Pacific to a successful conclusion. As history records, a B-29 from our 509th Bomb Group dropped an atomic bomb on Hiroshima on August 6. Then on August 9 they dropped another one on Nagasaki. The following day, Japan opened peace negotiations, and their surrender was agreed to on August 14. On September 2, the formal surrender documents were signed aboard the U.S.S. Missouri, finally ending the war in the Pacific and World War II. As you can see, our 509th Bomb Group and the B-29s of Curtis LeMay's Twentieth Air Force really did have a major impact on bringing the war in the Pacific to a successful conclusion.

Going back a step in time, it should be remembered that the heavy bombardment of Germany by our Eighth Air Force had brought the Nazi Government to its knees so that it could no longer defend itself against the Allied land forces, and that had a major impact in ending the war in Europe. In the Pacific, the two atomic bombs did the job much more quickly and saved millions of lives in the process.

During 1945 we had numerous people coming through Washington, whom we in Fred Anderson's offices hosted and toured around Washington. Many of them wanted to know what Curtis LeMay was up to in the PTO, the Pacific Theater of Operations. We danced around that one, being especially careful never, absolutely never, to allude to the atomic bomb, until long after the war was over. General LeMay was in Guam, and he only came once or twice to Washington while I was there.

In September 1945 I was able to fly a B-17 out to San Francisco on one of my visits to B-29 bases, and I landed it at Mills Field, the predecessor to San Francisco International Airport. By pre-arrangement, my parents met me there, for this was to be the fulfillment of my promise to take them for a ride in a B-17. We took off from Mills Field, circled the Bay Area, and then went south along the California Coast at 1,500 to 3,500 feet so they could really see places like Monterey Bay, Carmel, San Luis Obispo, Santa Barbara and on down to Los Angeles. There we turned eastward and returned back along the Sierra Nevada Mountains to San Francisco. Mom was in "seventh heaven" and Dad was excited about it, too. Actually, I had my parents for only a few more years, so I was very glad I took the time to give them their promised flight.

As one of my extracurricular activities at the Pentagon, I sat on a committee organizing the "Interim Air Force" which really meant the process of downsizing the Air Force to peacetime strength. The conclusion of the committee's recommendation centered on discharging the men who were in the "Army of the United States," and allowing the men who were in the "United States Army," the regular army men, to either stay in at much reduced rank or

Harry and Jane Ann's four daughters on one horse at their Portola Valley home, about 1960.

Harry and Marcy at their wedding in 1985.

Harry riding "Bunny", his favorite cattle-working mare, in 1997.

Harry Conley, cattleman and horseman, in 1997.

Four veterans of the 95th Bomb Group at a get-together in July, 1999. Left to right, Grif Mumford, Harry Conley, Bob Cozens, and Dick Stewart. Dick was a waist gunner on George Brumbaugh's B-17, Belligerent Beauty. *Dick, an artist, also created many "nose art" paintings during the war.*

Harry Conley and Bob Cozens in 1999.

Harry Conley, Bob Cozens, Dick Stewart, Grif Mumford, and Stu Whittelsey.

Grif Mumford, August 2001.

A B-17 arrives at San Jose Airport.

B-17 visits San Jose, May 2001.

"The Office" where the pilot and copilot do their jobs flying the B-17.

Harry Conley and a visiting B-17.

transfer to the Army Reserve. As for me, even though I had joined up just a few hours before war was declared and therefore had joined the U.S. Army, my promotions were to temporary wartime ranks. Since it had been decided that ranks in the future peacetime Air Force were to be based primarily on time in service, if I wanted to stay in, I would do so at the rank of First Lieutenant. As a temporary Lieutenant Colonel, that wasn't very appealing to me. I liked the Air Force — I really did. And politically I was in the right place. But the administrative nature of my most recent work was less exciting than combat, and even less exciting than the livestock business that I had been in before the war.

Early in 1946 I received an envelope in the mail containing my promotion orders to the rank of full Colonel. It turned out to be a real non-event. No trumpets or fanfare, no congratulatory party, no cigars were thrust at me. As I recall, the extent of my celebration was to go out and buy some silver eagles for my uniform. A couple of months before receiving those promotion orders, I had celebrated my 29th birthday, and I probably should have been more excited about it; but the facts that the war was over and my career in the Army Air Forces was winding down probably dampened my enthusiasm for celebration.

Mr. Moffatt had really wanted me to come back to his cattle business, and I, of course, seriously considered it. I really enjoyed the livestock business. Working with a good horse outdoors with cattle has always appealed to me. But I certainly didn't want to stop flying. Bill Moffatt, however, who was always pretty tight with a buck, didn't want to pay me nearly what I thought I could get elsewhere. Well, I was given an attractive offer to get back into the livestock business from a man named Joe Kaufmann who also wanted me to be his private pilot. And the offer represented substantially more money than Mr. Moffatt's proposal. Joe had worked in the Moffatt company and had known me and my work there before the war. I decided, in early 1946, to go work with Joe Kaufmann in his livestock business.

Had I known what was really going to happen with the Air Force, I'm sure I would have given much more favorable thought to staying in. As it worked out, no one had to take cuts in rank, because with the Berlin Air Lift followed by the Cold War, the Air Force was kept at substantial strength. The fellows I knew and worked with went into very high ranking and prominent positions, and I would have been in a good position to follow along with them.

However, I really have no regrets. The Army Air Forces provided me an exciting and rewarding experience. And I have sincerely enjoyed being in the livestock business since then.

(Editor's Note: Although we have not been able to confirm in written form that Lt. Colonel Harry M. Conley was promoted to Colonel, all other indications substantiate that this promotion was conferred and thus we are listing Harry M. Conley as Colonel prior to his separation from service.)

CHAPTER 21

REFLECTIONS ON THE WAR

One of the reasons I have wanted to write some of my experiences of the air war in Europe during World War II is that this was a truly unique war, and much of what it was like will never be known unless it is written down by those of us who went through it. The United States has experienced wars — even the Revolutionary War — both before and after World War II, when we were not united among ourselves about our objectives. World War II was the one and only war where this country was clearly united, where we all stopped what we were doing at the time, and turned and marched in the same direction. We all had a strong resolve to stop the tyranny and bestiality, not to let it come to America's shores, and to preserve our highly valued freedoms. The nation pitched in wholeheartedly. The men went and joined the armed forces. The women filled in for them at home, in the war factories and even in the military, where they nursed the sick and wounded, greeted them with smiles and coffee when they came back from the fighting and administered their logistical support. Even the Boy and Girl Scouts joined in Civilian Defense efforts, along with those too old for military service.[16]

The actual war itself was also unique in the way it was carried out. Weapons and tactics were used that never had existed before, and which have now been made obsolete by further advances in military and communications technology. There had never been before, nor will there ever be again, a series of battles consisting of thousands of aircraft as occurred in Europe during 1944-45. No one today can even imagine the skies filled with the vast numbers of

---

[16] Tom Brokaw, in *The Greatest Generation*, quoted Senator Daniel Inouye, a Medal of Honor recipient, as saying: "The one time the nation got together was World War II. We stood as one. We spoke as one. We clenched our fists as one."

airplanes we had on our bombing missions into Germany in 1944.[17] On many of our missions then, a person standing on the ground could look up and see hundreds of planes flying overhead, headed for their targets, for two and a half hours! That is something that is inconceivable today, almost 60 years later, as we enter the 21st century.

Nor is it likely that anyone will ever see again the vast armada assembled during the Battle of the Bulge in 1944, when the Allied Armies towed thousands of gliders, filled with infantrymen, with DC-3 and C-47 twin-engine transport planes over Belgium and Holland. Every glider was towed and cut loose near the battle area, where it landed and disembarked its load of ground troops. Even the glider pilot became a ground soldier once he had landed his glider. The skies were filled with our gliders winging in the forces that finally broke down the Germans' ground defenses. It was an improbable sight, as definitive of this age as were medieval wars between massed lancers and bowmen; it was a scene that would overwhelm anyone who could see it today. But it was a part of that war that may be erased from the nation's memory if it isn't told.

America's participation in the defense of England and the defeat of Nazi Germany was something else that ought not to be forgotten. All these aircraft, as well as tanks and other armaments, were from the States. The outpouring of war material from the United States was not only a phenomenal industrial achievement, but a cultural landmark as well, with the nation unified to an extent

---

[17] A news report in the San Francisco Chronicle, sometime in January, 1944, stated: General Eaker said "that in the last two raids by the Eighth Air Force, approximately 1,500 planes were used — more than half of them four-engined bombers." Underscoring the growth of the force the General compared this number with 53 Flying Fortresses which raided Wilhelmshaven almost a year ago, January 27, 1943.

Eaker ...added that "men of the Eighth Air Force never have been turned away from their targets by enemy action."

Major General Frederick Anderson, chief of the Eighth Air Force Bomber Command, earlier in an official report said "it was not until mid-March of 1943 that the unit could get as many as 100 heavy bombers into the air on a single day, whereas now they are able to send up more than 700 in short order against a number of targets."

never seen before, and probably never to be experienced again. All the petroleum fuels came from America then, too, for the Middle East's oil reserves were mostly still under the ground and undeveloped. What there was couldn't be easily transported to Germany. Without oil fields of their own, the Germans had to import most of their fuel from Romanian oil fields. Then we stopped that flow of petroleum with our long-range aerial bombardment. The Germans had some oil coming from parts of Russia that they had captured, until in 1944 when the Russian armies recaptured those oil fields and cut off petroleum supplies from that source. By 1945 Hitler's warlords were literally running out of fuel, unable to dispatch their planes or tanks because of lack of fuel for them. As the war in Europe ground to an end, the Germans were seen using horses — the few of them that hadn't been slaughtered for food — to pull their vehicles and carry their supplies from place to place. Meanwhile America had transformed itself from an economy mired in the Depression to an industrial powerhouse, such as the world had never seen, let alone imagined possible.

While inspecting an American supply train captured during the Allied push toward Germany, Wehrmacht Field Marshall Gerd von Runstedt was privately dismayed by the treasury of home-spun amenities filling the boxcars: woolen sweaters, mittens, stockings, and scarves, fruitcakes, cookie tins, chocolate brownies, candy bars, dried fruit, mail and Christmas cards. At that moment, he wrote later, he realized that Germany was doomed to defeat, believing that any nation was unbeatable whose people, in their unity of support for their armies, were able to deliver so much, so far, with each item individually addressed.

The Allied war effort, supplied mainly by the United States, simply overwhelmed the German war machine, the only force that has ever truly threatened the survival of the United States. The Germans had the first operational jet fighters and they were well on their way toward producing atomic bombs, as well as long-range rockets to deliver them across the Atlantic. I am concerned that history books will not be there to record and give due credit to the

Americans who produced and shipped all that material to give the British and the Russians the strength to prevail over the Germans, in addition to supplying American military forces all over the world.

At the time America entered into World War II, the Germans were masters of the seas and the skies. Their U-boats controlled the seas and the Luftwaffe controlled the skies over Europe. Because American arms and fuel had to come across the Atlantic Ocean, German control of the seas had to be overcome. That was why our first priority for daylight bombing targets was the German submarine bases. We had to destroy the effectiveness of the German submarine fleet so we could get our ships across to England with all the supplies and men to build up the force it would take to invade the Continent of Europe.

The planning for the Allied war effort was brilliant, as was the execution of its strategies. In Casablanca in early 1943, Roosevelt, Churchill and Stalin, with their war staffs, came up with the basic plan to conquer Nazi Germany.[18] For us in the Eighth Air Force, it meant that our efforts were to be directed, first, to destroying the German U-boat fleet in the Atlantic, so that American supplies and men could be transported safely to England. We would do this by destroying the submarine facility at Kiel and other key submarine bases all along the European coast from above Oslo, Norway, to the south of France.

Our second priority was to destroy the effectiveness of the Luftwaffe in order to gain air superiority over Europe. There could be no invasion of Europe across the English Channel unless the Allies had air superiority over the landing area, and preferably, well inland. We accomplished this, primarily, by destroying the aircraft

---

[18] Winston Churchill, in his book, *Closing the Ring*, discusses these priorities issued in the Casablanca Directive to the British and American Bomber Commands in England on February 4, 1943. He said: "Your primary object will be the progressive destruction of the German military, industrial, and economic system, and the undermining of the morale of the German people to a point where their capacity for armed resistance is fatally weakened."

manufacturing facilities and the ancillary supporting functions, such as oil depots and refineries and ball bearing factories.[19] The Luftwaffe pilots swarmed up from European bases and mounted a determined defense, but the Eighth Air Force took a heavy toll of German aircraft, shooting them down by the hundreds with the consolidated firepower of our close formations of B-17s as they came to attack us. We truly fulfilled our mission to meet and defeat the Luftwaffe on the ground and in the air. Between 1939, when Hitler's Germany kicked off the Second World War by invading Poland, and its surrender in 1945, its factories produced over 119,000 military aircraft. In that same period, the United States produced nearly 300,000. The fact that on D-Day the Germans had only about 700 flyable aircraft, and that they chose not to fly them that day verifies that we had achieved air superiority over Europe by then.

Our third priority was to cripple the German transportation system, and we did this by bombing and destroying their railroad yards, bridges and trains. Our fourth and ultimate priority was to bomb any and all war industry targets. We in the Eighth Air Force accomplished these objectives, albeit with a bitter price in aviators and airplanes, but we did it in time for the invasion to take place as scheduled on June 6, 1944. Had we failed to achieve these objectives, the war would probably have lasted longer and could even have ended differently. The Allied war plan was brilliantly conceived and methodically executed, but I wonder if the significance of that achievement is appreciated today.[20]

---

[19] Ian L. Hawkins, in *B-17s Over Berlin*, said that after the war, German General Adolf Galland, the Commander of the Luftwaffe fighter forces, wrote in his memoirs: "The bombers grounded our fighters by destroying our oil industry."

[20] Also in *Closing the Ring*, Winston Churchill gave this overview of the effectiveness of the U.S. Eighth Air Force in bringing about an Allied victory: "In the spring of 1944, the Allied strategic bombers were required for 'Overlord' and the weight of attack on Germany itself was inevitably reduced. *But by now we were masters in the air.* The bitterness of the struggle had thrown a greater strain on the Luftwaffe than it was able to bear. By being forced to concentrate on building fighters, it had lost all

Credit also needs to be given to the technological advances that American engineering ingenuity brought to the war that gave us an "edge" against the German enemy. First, the Norden Bombsight gave us the ability to aim our bombs with pinpoint accuracy, making our bombing missions much more effective than the older area bombing methods. Delivering a heavy tonnage of bombs was important, but even more, it was important to deliver that tonnage where it would do the most to help win the war.

Second, but no less in importance, was the engineering skill and innovation at Boeing that developed the B-17 bomber. The original prototype was flown in 1935; the improvements made in successive models greatly enhanced its capabilities. That plane was so advanced that aircraft today still utilize many of the B-17's design features. Germany had nothing anywhere remotely equivalent to it in capability. The B-17's defensive capabilities and rugged construction, together with the Norden Bombsight, gave us the ability to attack the enemy by day. Coupled with the night raids on Europe by the RAF, there was never any respite from Allied bombings.

A third technological advantage we had was the "compensating gunsight" used on our fighters. Like the Norden Bombsight, the compensating gunsight was essentially a computer, allowing the fighter pilot to sight in his target, lock it in, and then the gunsight would use the plane's flight data to adjust the aim of the machine gun bullets. This feature made our fighters much more frequently the victors against enemy aircraft. The German fighters were equipped with compensating gunsights, too, but they weren't as good as ours.

The importance of maintaining our technologic edge by keeping up our investments in advanced military technology must not be forgotten by us in extended periods of relative peace.

---

power of strategic counter-attack by bombing back at us. Unbalanced and exhausted, it was henceforth unable to defend either itself or Germany from our grievous blows. *For our air superiority, which by the end of 1944 was to become air supremacy, full tribute must be paid to the United States Eighth Air Force."*

During the war, even after our bombers started hitting military targets on the coast of France, Hermann Goering told the German people that the Luftwaffe would stop any and all Allied aircraft from violating German air space. Then as the American Eighth Air Force commenced to bomb German targets and even Berlin by day, while the RAF bombed them at night, the morale of the German people was reported to us as plummeting. No wonder, they were never out of earshot of the sounds of our airplanes as we carried out our "around the clock" bombing missions. No less demoralized were some ranking members of the German General Staff, who attempted more than once to remove Hitler from leadership, hoping thereafter to sue the Allies for something other than unconditional surrender. But they weren't able to bring it about. The German populace, although thoroughly disheartened, demoralized and quite ready to end this terrible war, had given up their freedoms and control along the way to Hitler in his rise to power, and they, too, couldn't do anything effectively to end the war. So it went on, with so much more death and destruction, until Hitler finally committed suicide in a Berlin bunker as the bombs exploded around him. Let this be a lesson to all of us not to take our freedoms for granted, and not to let our freedoms go without looking ahead to what would be sacrificed and what that could lead to!

I was a very lucky man, lucky to survive the fighters, the flak and the accidents that took a considerable toll from our early flight training to the war's end. I was one of three survivors of the original 100 men in the ten crews that comprised the 334th Bomb Squadron that went to England in 1943. The other two who completed their 25 missions without being killed, captured or seriously wounded were my friends, pilot Bob "Coz" Cozens and bombardier Wayne "Big Fitz" Fitzgerald. But I was quite lucky in another sense. I was in the Army Air Corps at the very beginning of the war; I was on the crest of the wave, so to speak. I got in on the early B-17 training and mission planning, and I got a chance to meet, know, and work with an extraordinary group of wonderful and highly competent men, like John Gerhart, Curtis LeMay, Fred Anderson, and fellow officers like Grif Mumford, Bob Cozens, Bill

Pratt, Jiggs Donohue, Dave McKnight, and many others, many of whom rose in responsibilities and high rank in the Army Air Forces and later in the U.S. Air Force. For me it was a great experience working with them in the planning and execution of our activities, our missions and our procedures.

Another thing that I've never heard discussed when people talk about the air war over Europe is the amazing teamwork that developed among the flying crews. Every flying crew member was a volunteer; there were no draftees or conscripts in our air crews. These men were there because they decided that was where they wanted to be. They had the will and the discipline to do the job when it was needed, no matter how overwhelming the enemy forces seemed to be. To be apprehensive in life and death encounters is only human, but we couldn't afford to have a crew member who hated doing what he had to do or feared flying on combat missions; if anyone felt that way, he would be released to a ground job. A lot of culling had been done before anyone was put into an airplane as a member of the crew. When I went to flying training, only the top 20% made it through and graduated. So we ended up with excellent, competent and devoted people in our flying crews in which everyone supported everyone else with determined teamwork and discipline. That extraordinary sense of group responsibility, expressed as teamwork, was the key to our ability to carry out our missions the way we did.

Nevertheless, the value of selectivity and training became more evident as the war progressed. Pressed to supply pilots and crews, the Army became less selective in flight training by graduating up to 50% of each class rather than the 20% who emerged from my training program. Training became compacted and the crews had less flying hours before they went into combat. As a result, their performance capability was not as high, and we lost more crews and planes due to poor judgment and poor flying. For instance, by 1944 we began to witness many more instances of pilots not realizing, because of their relative inexperience, the capabilities of our B-17s to keep on flying with considerable battle damage; they would put their damaged planes on automatic pilot and order everyone to bail out, sometimes over the freezing waters of the Channel, and their B-17 would keep on flying over England until its fuel ran out. The results often were lost crews and plane crashes. The loss of men and airplanes was a tragic waste.

However, regardless of all that, our winning spirit of teamwork prevailed, and it extended to the ground crews as well, who worked day and night keeping our planes operating as dependably and safely as possible, giving us the best possible chance to get to our targets and back home. Our ultimate victory in the air over Europe could not have come about without the *esprit de corps* and the quality of teamwork we achieved.

Memories, as you know, are selective, and in my reflections on that time, now over a half-century past, I recall many instances that despite the underlying realities and injustices of war seem suffused with humor and sometimes a heartwarming humanity. I have not dwelt on the terrible losses we suffered, nor the sadness they left in our hearts. An appreciation of the good times and the camaraderie engendered by war help to overcome the grief of our wartime losses. Had we not kept up our spirits with a sense of humor, my comrades and I might not be talking about these strange, terrifying and fascinating times.

BIBLIOGRAPHY

B-17s Over Berlin, Personal Stories from the 95th Bomb Group (H), by Ian L. Hawkins. Brassey's, London

A Wing and A Prayer, by Harry Crosby, Harper Collins, New York

Bombs Away by Pathfinders of the Eighth Air Force, by Marshall Thixton, George Moffat and John O'Neil. FNP Military Division, Trumbull, Connecticut

The Mighty Eighth, A History of the U.S. 8th Army Air Force, by Roger Freeman. MacDonald, London

Mighty Eighth War Diary, by Roger Freeman

Heavy Bombers of the Mighty Eighth, by Paul M. Andrews

Operational Record of the 95th Bomb Group (H), by Paul M. Andrews

The Bomber War, The Allied Air Offensive Against Nazi Germany, by Robin Neillands. The Overlook Press, Woodstock and New York

Memorials of the 95th Bomb Group (H), Eighth Air Force, World War II, by Maynard D. Stewart and H. Griffin Mumford. 95th Bomb Group (H) Memorials Foundation

Contrails, The 95th Bombardment Group (H), The 95th Group Photographic Section

B-17 in Action, by Larry Davis and Don Greer. Squadron/Signal Publications

The Munster Raid: Before and After, by Ian L. Hawkins. FNP Military Division, Trumbull, Connecticut

No End Save Victory, Perspectives on World War II, Essays by Stephen Ambrose, Caleb Carr, John Keegan, William Manchester, and Others. G.P. Putnam's Sons, New York

Amelia Earhart, The Mystery Solved, by Elgen M. Long and Marie K. Long. Touchstone/Simon & Schuster, New York

Closing the Ring, by Winston S. Churchill. Houghton Mifflin Company, Boston

The Greatest Generation, by Tom Brokaw

The Poltava Affair, A Russian Warning; An American Tragedy, by Glenn B. Infield

VIP Pilot, by Al Keeler

Stalin's Secret War, by Nikolai Tolstoy

Wing Shield, Wing Sword, A History of the United States Air Force, 1907-1950, by Bernard C. Nalty

Russian Combat Methods, in World War II, Department of the Army Pamphlet No. 20-230

Big Week, The Classic Story of the Crucial Air Battle of World War II, by Glenn B. Infield

Come Fly With Me, Experiences of an Airman in World War II, by Lloyd O. Krueger. ToExcel, San Jose, New York

Luck of the Draw, by Frank D. Murphy. FNP Military Division, Trumbull, Connecticut

Periodicals:

Air Power History, Summer, 1989, Air Battle at Kiel, by Robert H. Saltsman, Jr.

East Anglican Daily Times, July 26, 1987, Guinness heir makes home on vast estate.

San Francisco Chronicle, 1943-45, Various articles.

San Francisco Examiner, 1944-45, Various articles.

Life Magazine, 1944, Photographs

INDEX

Abbeville Kids, 81
Accident
   Great Falls, Montana, 52
Accidents during non-combat
   flying, 211
Aeronautical engineering, 6
Afrika Korps, 28, 43
Air combat in Europe
   more fierce in latter 1943, 116
Air crews
   morale problems, Feb. 1944, 224
Air Force, 250, 254
Air vs ground combat, 209
Airplane models, 3
Alconbury, 75, 78, 84, 163, 228-229
   bomb explosion during loading, 95th lost 19 men & 15 B-17s, 163
   95th BG flew first 7 missions from, 84
Allied airmen
   when shot down, told not to carry firearms, 287
Altitude, best for bombers leaving England for Europe, 164
   German 88 mm guns accurate below 20,000 ft., 164
Antwerp
   (1st mission to), 80-81
   (2nd mission to),
   1st 95th BG crew lost, 81
Army Air Corps, 2, 11-17, 56, 72, 315
Army Air Forces, 13
Arnold, Gen. Hap
   visits 95th BG, 132
AT-6s, 24
Atherton, 8

B-17
   advantages, 314
   Boeing-built flew best, 166
   bomb-bay doors
      crew members urinating on doors caused freezing at high altitude, 173
   gross plane weight important, 166
   individual planes flew differently, 166
   navigator's duties, 63
   spent gun cartridges damaged other planes, 174
   procedure changed, 174
B-17E Boeing Flying Fortress
   ability to sustain damage, 35
   guns, 35
B-17F, 49
B-17G, 109
   new gun turret under nose, 109
B-17 vs. B-24
   performance at high altitude, ability to take punishment favored B-17, 165
B-24, 28
   flight characteristics with bomb load, 33
Bacha, Elias, 87, 98
Ballater (Scotland)
   H. Conley plays golf with locals, 131
   perfect R&R, 130
Bataan Peninsula
   36,000 U.S. POWs, 28
Beaverbrook, Lord, 179-182, 217
Berlin, 36, 43, 92, 117, 172, 180, 226-232, 266, 298, 307, 313, 315

Goering boasted U.S. couldn't
bomb Berlin, 226
strong defenses, 226
Berlin, first mission (Mar. 3, 1944)
bad weather prevented
completion, 226
Berlin mission (Mar. 4, 1944)
awards, Al Brown received DFC,
229
Grif Mumford received Silver
Star, 229
Bill Owen (Pathfinder pilot)
received DFC, 229
95th BG received 3rd
Presidential Unit
Citation, 232
482nd BG Pathfinder B-17 flew
with 95th BG, 228
P-51s engaged German fighters,
230
30 B-17s of 13th Combat Wing
bomb Berlin, 228
Big Week, 1944, 117, 222-223,
225-226
8th and 15th Air Forces attack
German aircraft, 222
Luftwaffe hurt, 225
Blondie (B-17)
flown by H. Conley crew, 88
Blondie II (B-17), 109, 113, 288
flown by H. Conley crew, 109,
113, 288
lost after Kiel mission, 109
Blondie III 109, 113, 148, 208
B-17 of "Little Joe" Noyes crew,
109
crew shot down & lost, 133
Bombardier
job during mission, 175

Bombs
5,000 lbs minimum mission
bomb load, 169
on missions were fused to
detonate on contact, 167
Book by Harry Conley, 216
Bovingdon
modification center for U.S.
aircraft to England, 166
British Air-Sea rescue
effective operation, 113
Brown, Al, 229, 231
Brown, Bill, 105
Brown, Willard, 96

Californios, 5, 158-162
expert horsemen, 158
Cambridge (England), 83
Chaff
aluminum foil dropped to
confuse German radar,
290
Christmas, 1942, 53
Christmas, 1943
at Ballater, 213
at Ballater, Scotch whisky in
chamber pots, 213
at Bray home, 214
at Horham, 214
Cochrane, Bill, 87, 113
Cole, Cliff, 289
shot down over Holland, arrives
in London, 145
Commendations
three received by 95th for
missions, 90
Commissions as Second Lieutenants
and awarded wings, 26

Conley, Harry M., 62, 106, 108, 127, 154, 236-237, 303
   awarded DFC for Regensburg mission, 127
   early years, 1
   flew 89 missions in Europe, 303
   gas coupon incident, 302
   goes to U.S. for Christmas 1944, 300
   had role in downsizing USAAF at war's end, 306
   helps fly DC-4 to U.S., 301
   joins 93rd Combat Wing as Chief of Staff, 236
   left USAAF and returned to livestock business, 307
   meets C. LeMay at Pentagon and gets new job, 303
   nickname "Moo", 76
   promotion to
      full colonel, 307
      Lt. Colonel, 235
      Major, 134
      to CO of 334th Bomb Squadron, 109-110
   took parents for a ride in B-17, 306
   trained 509th Composite Group for atomic bomb drop, 305
   worked on B-29 training, 304
   wrote letters to families of men in his squadron who were killed, 151
Conley, Marcy, 12
Cordell, Dick, 26
Cowboying, 4
Cozens, Robert "Bob"
   completed 25 missions, 217
   leaves 95th BG for Washington, DC, 235
   lost younger brother in B-24 crash, 269
   married Patty, 26
   met Harry Conley in Advanced Training, 25
   promotion to
      Lt. Colonel, 235
      Major, 215
      to C.O. of 335th Bomb Squadron, 133
Crowe, Errol, 20

D-Day (June 6, 1944), 235, 239-242, 249, 255
   bombers took off starting 9 PM on D-Day eve, circled until daylight, 240
   93rd Combat Wing flew 4 missions and 4 targets destroyed, 241
   weather bad, 239
Dakar, 71
   MP incident, 72
Danzig mission (Oct. 9, 1943) bombed at low level, 134
Day of Infamy, 11
De Gaulle, Charles, 286
   awarded J. Gerhart and H. Conley Croix de Guerre with Palms, 292
DeWolf, Earl T. "Basey", 59, 90, 104
   bombardier on Bob Cozens crew, 175
   Germans exchanged as an incorrigible POW, 177
   issued ID badges, 56
   shot down on Munster mission (Oct. 10, 1943) his 25th mission and became POW, 137

Donohue, Florence Joseph "Jiggs,"
  after WW II ended, was head of DC government twice, 250-251
  arranged details of H. Conley's and Jane Ann's wedding, 251
  awarded Bronze star, 248
  flew mission to French coast, 249
  got Pres. Kennedy photo and autograph for Robin Conley, 254
  married Gen. Eaker's sister-in-law, Martha, 254
  95th Intelligence Officer, 245
  Sunday Evening Briefings for ground personnel, 247
  volunteered for military service, 245
  was friend of Harry Truman, 251
  Washington attorney before WW II, 245
Doolittle, Gen. Jimmy, 127, 182-183
Dunhill pipe
  H. Conley got for his dad in London, 112

Eaker, Ira, 254, 273
  led 15th Air Force on first Russian shuttle mission, 273
  was concerned about lack of defense for U.S. aircraft at Poltava, 281
Earl of Iveagh (Samuel Guinness), 155-156, 162
  friendly to H. Conley, J. Gerhart, and G. Mumford, 156
  interest in horses and polo, 157
  killed in Dec. 1944 at Battle of Bulge, 162
Eighth Air Force
  air crews in latter 1944 not as good as earlier crews, 268
  heavy losses in 1943, 88
  priorities
    destroy Luftwaffe, 221
    disable U-boat bases, 221
Emden mission, 80
Emergency landings
  Dodge City, Kansas 61-62
  Missoula, Montana, 43
Escape kit
  Allied airmen carried on missions, 286

Fighter escort
  increased on late 1943 missions, 210
Fitzgerald, Wayne T. "Big Fitz"
  bombardier on H. Conley's crew, 178
  completed 25 mission tour, 184
  Gen. Jim Doolittle incident, 183
  Inspector General incident, 184
  introduces H. Conley to his future wife, Jane Ann, 185
  is one of three of 334th BS to finish tour, 185
  Lord Beaverbrook incident, 181
  married in U.S. in 1944, 257
  party at Horham, "Big Fitz" and nurse incident, 179
  promotion to Major, 235
Flight training
  advanced, 15
  basic, 15
  primary, 15

Flying, 3, 89
  bad weather, 38-41
  cross-country, 23
  in close formations, 77
  on instruments, 23
Forrest, Nathan Bedford III, 89
  B-17 formation replaced LeMay formation, 89
.45 caliber Colt pistol, 16
Framlingham, 87-88, 93, 103-104
  second base for 95th, 84
Free French, 71, 239, 285-286, 290-292
  and Maquis had codes transmitted over BBC radio, 291
  under Charles DeGaulle, 286
French Resistance, 167, 274-275, 285-287, 290
  Maquis formed underground, 286
Fur suits, 33
Furlough prior to overseas, 65

Gable, Clark, 77
Galileo High, 4
Galland, Adolf
  Commander of Luftwaffe fighters in Europe, 119
  planned German attacks on Munster mission (Oct. 10, 1943), 138
Geiger Field, 26
  four-engine flight training, 26
Gerhart, John, forms 93rd Combat Wing, 236
  later other promotions, 201
  2nd CO of 95th Bomb Group, 199
German, 88 mm flak guns, 80

German military, 10
  bombing England, 208
  conquered Poles on 63rd day of fighting, 278
Gilger, Chester, 3rd 95th CO, 221, 224
Godek, Sgt. Louis A., 152
Goering, Hermann, 226, 315
Gonzales, Francisco, 111
Great Depression, 3

H. Moffatt Company, 7
Hamilton Field, 11
High Wycombe
  UK 8th Headquarters, 168

IFF
  information — friend or foe, 70
Imes, "Doc", 149-151
Italian POWs happy to be with Americans, 124

Japan, 10
Johnson, Dewey, 140, 142

Kearney, Nebraska, 64
  staging area, 65
Kessler, Alfred A. Jr.
  formed 95th BG, 195
  head of 13th Bomb Wing, 196
  other promotions, 196
Kiel mission (June 13, 1943), 104, 108-109, 173, 187, 189, 195
  Gen. Forrest flew mission as observer, was killed, 92
  German fighters attack, 94
  "Abbeville Kids," 94
  Goering's "Flying Circus," 100
  Grif Mumford Command Pilot 95th Comp. Grp., 91

H. Conley, awarded DFC, 108
   B-17 crash-lands in England, 102
   B-17 heavily damaged, 98
   crew flies to England on one engine, 101
   "little girl" at crash scene calls Harry in 1993, 106
   lead group flew beyond IP, 95
   Me-410s bomb B-17s, 94
   100 mph tailwind dispersed formation, 93
   22 of 59 B-17s were lost, 104
Kimborough, Kenneth, 251
   interior decorator, made Horham livable, 196

LaJoie, Arthur, 87, 98-99
LeMay, Curtis
   command standards, 202-203
   formation for B-17s (combat box), 88
   moves to Elveden Hall post-mission critiques, 155
   obtained officers from 8th to assist in 20th Air Force, 303
   P-47 incident with H. Conley, 201-202
   plane ride to Liverpool with H. Conley and W. Pratt, 191
   promotion to Brig. General, 156
Letters, from H. Conley to his mother, 12
Lindley, Bill, 92, 140
Link trainer, 29-30
Living with sorrow when friends were shot down, 133
Lockheed "Hudson," 17
London, Picadilly Circus, 76

Longest bombing raid by B-17s, H. Conley leads to Norway, 115
Luftwaffe pilots
   early WW II were good, later WW II were inexperienced, 172

MacNeil, J.L., 87
Maquis, 286-288, 290-292
   helped Allied airmen get back to England, 286
Marrakech, Morocco, 67, 73
Maximum effort mission, 90
McArthur, Tom, 87
McKnight, Dave, 129-130, 149-150, 184, 198, 213, 264-267, 316
   became fighter pilot/leader in Korea, 267
   became Sqd. CO 95th BG, 265
   joined RCAF before Pearl Harbor, 264
   joined USAAF & 95th BG, 264
   meets vicar of Anglican Church, receives invitation to Scotland, 129
   with friend Dave Schilling buzzed Eiffel Tower, 265
Me-262 German jet fighter buzzed B-17s, 268
Medford, Howard, 87
Meintz, Harry, 138
   received award for Munster raid, 138
Menjou, Adolph and entertainers visit 95th BG, 131
Minter Field, 11

INDEX

Mission formations
  assembly-flares fired to signal assembly, 170
  assembly more dangerous than flak or Luftwaffe, 168
  best defense against Luftwaffe was a tight formation, 172
  in mid-1944 were 1,000-2,000 planes on missions, 168
  needed precise timing, 169
  used homing beacons called bunchers to assemble, 168
Missoula, Montana, 43
Moffatt, Bill, 8
Morrison Field, Fla., 65
Mumford, Grif, command pilot on first Berlin mission, 229
  CO of 95th 412th BS, 92
  Head of 95th Group Operations, 92
  original member, 95th BG, 91
Munster, 129, 135-136, 139-141, 143, 145, 176
  Cathedral in old city, 135
Munster mission (Oct. 10, 1943)
  aiming point center of old city, 135
  awards, British DFC to Dewey Johnson and John Gerhart, 140
  DFC to H. Conley, 140
  Silver Star to Bill Lindley and John Gerhart, 140
  briefing by Jiggs Donohue, 135
  gave reasons for mission, 136
  German fighters waited for P-47 escort to return to England, 136
  H. Conley wounded by air-to-air rocket, received Purple Heart, 139
  hundreds of German fighters attacked B-17s, 137
  Luftwaffe lost many fighters, 140

95th BG received Presidential Unit Citation, 140
95th bombs hit old city center, 140
100th BG lost 12 B-17s, 139
one of great air battles of WW II, 138
some pilots objected to bombing civilian targets, 136
story of Harry Meintz and "Big Fitz," 138
25 B-17s lost by 13th Combat Wing, 138

Natal, Brazil
  B-17s serviced, 68
  U-boat shot cannon, 68
New Years Eve, 1942, 56
Night mission
  arrived back on base at midnight after bombing in daylight, 132
Night flying, 36
  England in WW II, 145
93rd Combat Wing, 161, 191, 199, 236, 245, 248, 273-274, 278, 299
  B-24s were replaced by B-17s, 236
  flew strategic and tactical missions, 255

Leipzig mission, 260
   after end WW II, H. Conley meets only survivor of B-24 that exploded from flak, 261
shuttle mission to Russia
   H. Conley led B-17s to aid Poles, 273
   German fighters attacked B-17s, 275
   over half B-17s not flyable, 278
   Russian fighters did not help, 275
   Russian military commits atrocities, 277
95th Bomb Group, 109
   awarded Presidential Unit Citation for Regensburg mission, Aug. 17, 1943, 126
   celebration of first year, 146
   CO, Feb. 1944, Col. Chester Gilger, 221
   crew on 1st mission shot down, gets back to Horham in 4 days, 288
   doubling number of crews in late 1943, 147
   flew 20 missions to aid Maquis, 290
95th Bomb Group, 334th Bomb Squadron
   H. Conley as CO, extra duties keep morale up, mail censor, 110
   of 21 crews lost from 334th Squadron, 16 accounted for, 148
Norden Bombsight, 46, 98, 101, 138, 227, 269, 314

Noyes, Joe "Little Joe", 72, 87, 105, 113, 148
   crew shot down & lost, 133

Overseas trip
   $1,500 cash for each Conley crewman, 66
Oxygen masks, 33

Pan American Airways, 6
Patton, George, 204-205
   H. Conley delivered gasoline to Patton's tanks, 204
   strategy for ending war, 205
Pearl Harbor, 1, 9-11
   one year later, 43
Pilot training, 11, 36
Poland's Home Army
   effective in aiding Allies, 271
   led by T. Komorowski, 271
   plan was Poles would attack Germans when Allies close to Warsaw, 271
   Russians got close to Warsaw and reneged, 272
   300,000 members latter 1944, 271
Pratt, William C. "Bill," 187-188, 190-193, 213, 252, 258, 316
   became, Chief Navigator USAAF and Col., 193
   pilot and General, 193
   Sqd. Chief Navigator, 190
   1st mission tough, 188
   flew 25 mission tour, 190
   joined 93rd Bomb Wing as Chief Navigator, 191
   93rd Bomb Wing, 204
   2nd mission, had fear problem, 189

stayed in USAAF after WW II, 193
Presidio, 1-3
Provost, Ray, 87, 97
Puppy, wire-haired terrier acquired by H. Conley, 146

RAF Mosquito
   H. Conley outran Me-109 in Mozzie, 171
   fast fighter/bomber used for Mission Command, 170
RAF returning from night missions posed hazards for USAAF taking off, 172
Rapid City, 49
   cold weather, 49
Red Cross, 86
   clubmobiles, 86
Regensburg and Schweinfurt missions (Aug. 17, 1943)
   Luftwaffe lost many planes, 125
   60 B-17s lost, 125
Regensburg mission (Aug. 17, 1943)
   after bomb drop, B-17s flew south to Algeria, 121
   Allied forces left Algeria prior to Aug. 17, no servicing B-17s, 123
   attacks by German fighters lasted over 2 1/2 hrs, 120
   B-17s had no friendly fighter cover over Europe, 119
   B-17s left Algeria, bombed France & back to England, 125
   bombing accurate, 122
   Col. LeMay mission leader, 121
   Italian anti-aircraft did not shoot at USAAF, 121

refueling B-17s in Algeria took 3 weeks, 124
tail gunner survives being thrown out of B-17, 122
Reno, Louis, 211-212
Roaring Twenties, 3
Rodeo, Western
   H. Conley and S. Guinness held in Norwich, mid-1944, 161
   60 USAAF airmen participated, 162
Rommel, Erwin, 28, 43, 123
Rongstad, Kenneth B., 150-153
   crew crash on takeoff at Horham, Nov. 19, 1943, all killed, 150
   destroys nearby farmhouse, 151
   crew member, Sgt. Louis Godek writes letter, 152
Roosevelt, Franklin, 10
Royal Air Force, 28, 103, 106, 155, 271
Rushmore, Mount, 55
Russian atrocity
   H. Conley witnessed victims forced to walk on land mines, 277
Ryan PT-19, 17

Salt Lake City, 26
Schilling, Dave, 265
Schweinfurt mission (Oct. 14, 1943), 140-141
   Bob Cozens and squadron led 3rd Air Div., 140
   caused heavy damage to ball bearing factories, 141
   flak at target fierce, 140
   German fighters out in force, 140

60 bombers were lost by Eighth
    Bomber Command, 141
Second Air Force, 26, 28, 32, 41
  football team, 32
  H. Conley was instructor pilot, 32
Sequoia Field, 16
Sevastopol,
  lost to Wehrmacht, 28
SOPs (standard operating
    procedures) for combat, 163
  loading of fused bombs was
    changed, 164
St. Omer mission (May 13, 1943), 78
  briefing, 78
  first 95th combat mission, 78
Stanford University, 1, 5
  H. Conley spilled salad dressing
    on former President
    Hoover, 6
  H. Conley worked his way
    through four year degree, 5
Stearman trainer, 17
Stewart, Jimmy
  wing chief of staff, 263
Stimson, Secretary of War
  visits 95th BG, 116
Stirwalt, Harry
  shot down on Kiel mission, only
    one survivor (POW), Bill
    Brown, 96-97
Stockton Field, 24
Submarine pens
  bombed sea locks to disable, 81
  pens protected by concrete roofs, 81

34th Bomb Group, 28
TIME magazine, 6

Tour of 25 missions
  Bob Cozens and "Big Fitz"
    completed by end Jan.
    1944, 217
Training
  bombing, 29
  German and Italian aviation
    tactics, 51
  gunnery, 29

U-boat bases, 28
U.S. Post Office, 4
USAAF airmen shot down, returned
    to England via
    underground, 114
USAAF fighter's compensating
    gunsight
  better than German version, 314

Vaqueros, 5
Vichy French government, 285
Vultee BT-13
  difficult to fly, 19
  learned cross-country and
    formation flying skills, 19
  Lycoming rotary engine, 19

Washing out cadet training, 13
Weather problem in England,
    1943-1944 winter, 147
Wilder, Al
  CO of 95th 334th Bomb
    Squadron, 41
  recruits H. Conley & R. Cozens, 41
  shot down on Kiel mission, 96-97